SIMSOC

SIMULATED SOCIETY

SECOND EDITION

---

participant's manual

with selected readings

---

by **WILLIAM A. GAMSON**

the free press, new york
collier-macmillan limited, london

To my favorite game players, Jenny and Josh

Copyright © 1972, 1969 by William A. Gamson
Previous version Copyright 1966 by William A. Gamson
Printed in the United States of America

Library of Congress Catalog Card Number: 69–17780
Collier-Macmillan Canada Ltd., Toronto, Ontario

printing number
2 3 4 5 6 7 8 9 10

BE
3-30-82

Contents

Selected Readings

Forms

Form A Choice Sheet. To specify your preference for a basic group.

Form B Assignment Sheet. For the coordinator to indicate the basic group you are head of (if any), your travel or subsistence agency (if any), and your home region.

Form C Moving Sheet. For moving from your original home region to another home region of your choice.

Form D Private Transportation Certificate. For purchasing private travel privileges.

Form E Permanent Subsistence Certificate. For purchasing subsistence for the duration of the society.

Form F Transfer of Certificates or Agencies. For switching ownership of agencies or of Forms D or E from one member to another.

Form G Job Schedule. For hiring and firing members of basic groups, including removing the head of the group.

Form H Industry Manufacturing Form. For purchasing anagrams from the coordinator and for filing completed words for credit.

Form I Withdrawal of Assets Form. For the withdrawal of BASIN and INNOVIN assets by the head of these groups.

Form J JUDCO Decision Form. For issuing official judgments resolving any ambiguities in the rules of SIMSOC.

Form K Minority Group Member Action Sheet. For removing Minority Group Members from their jobs and ownership of agencies.

Form L Creating a SIMFORCE. For creating a SIMFORCE.

Form M SIMFORCE Action Form. For arresting individuals, releasing those arrested earlier, and removing police forces.

Form N Assessment Sheet. For individuals to assess how well they are achieving their personal goals, group goals, political party performance, and overall societal performance.

The Forms section (tear-out sheets) starts on page 133.

Preface

SIMSOC has been developed to make social science more vivid to students at the college level. It focuses on what is perhaps the most central problem for a student of society: the establishment and maintenance of social order. When students seize a university building, when police use indiscriminate violence against citizens, or when generals seize power and liquidate political opponents, we begin to recognize that the existence of order and legitimacy is always problematic and not something to be taken for granted.

It is a considerable achievement for a society when National Guardsmen carry out the instructions of their governor on one day and, without hesitation, carry out the opposite instructions of their president on the next day. Similarly, few of us think twice when a presidential candidate who has failed to be elected by a very narrow margin calmly accepts defeat and quietly retires.

SIMSOC attempts to create a situation in which the student must actively question the nature of the social order and examine the processes of social conflict and social control. As an inevitable by-product, participants find themselves dealing with a host of issues, including interpersonal trust, leadership, "deviant" behavior, social protest, and power relations. SIMSOC is intended to be used in conjunction with conventional classroom discussion and readings. A selection of such readings is included in this manual. The manual also includes suggestions for study questions based on participation in SIMSOC. The current edition represents a newly revised version of the game.

The use of games as a teaching or training device has a long history in many fields. Recently, social scientists have developed games focused on social processes for use in teaching students about the society in which they live. Like all of these games, SIMSOC does not attempt to imitate a real society in every respect, but characteristics are included which we hope will highlight certain issues and problems. One can participate in SIMSOC at many levels. As in real life, what one learns will depend on what one puts into it.

William A. Gamson

To Play SIMSOC

Each participant should have a copy of this *Participant's Manual*, which includes the necessary materials. The instructor should also obtain a copy of SIMSOC: *Instructor's Manual*, which contains all materials required by the instructor, provides complete directions on how to set-up and run SIMSOC, and suggests how to handle a variety of situations that might arise. One copy of the *Instructor's Manual* will be needed by the instructor for each SIMSOC of up to 60 participants. The *Instructor's Manual* may be obtained by instructors who write, using their letterhead, to:

THE FREE PRESS
A Division of The Macmillan Company
Faculty Service Desk
866 Third Avenue, New York 10022

Note: SIMSOC is pronounced *sim*-sock.

Introduction

You will shortly be participating as a citizen in a simulated society.[1] If the society is to be a valuable learning experience, we will need your cooperation. Cooperation in this context means taking your objectives in the society seriously. We have tried to create a situation in which each of you has goals that depend on other people in the society for their achievement. Some of your goals will be held in common with other people, and some will bring you into conflict with others. Inevitably, some of you will do better than others in achieving your goals but, unlike some games, there are no clear winners or losers.

You represent only some of the citizens of your society. Other citizens are present only in imaginary form—that is, certain rules of the game are based on assumptions about the reactions of these imaginary citizens. Nevertheless, this is basically your society to do with as you like.

Coordinator's Role

The coordinator's role is kept to an absolute minimum once the society is in process. He (or she) will maintain the bank, receive forms, and carry out other tasks specified in the manual to make the game operate. If questions about the rules arise, he will guide you to the appropriate section of the manual and will help you locate appropriate forms but *he will not interpret ambiguous rules nor will he advise you how to deal with situations that arise in the game.* The coordinator will do everything he can to avoid becoming enmeshed as a participant in your society once it has begun.

Nature of the Rules

The rules in the manual are intended to represent certain "natural" forces in the real world rather than man-made laws. To ignore them by cheating simply renders the game pointless and meaningless. The coordinator should not be put in the position of having to monitor your observance of the rules but should be able to depend on your cooperation to achieve the larger purpose of learning. The rules of the manual, as you will see, allow great leeway for you to add your own agreements and rules. The agreements that you make among yourselves are your own responsibility—they represent man-made laws rather than "natural" forces. If a player ignores or refuses to comply with a rule that your society makes, you must face the issue of how to deal with this behavior. All players have a responsibility to observe the rules in the manual to make the game operative but they have no such responsibility toward the rules that you may establish to govern yourselves.

In spite of efforts to anticipate various contingencies, ambiguous situations will inevitably arise. The coordinator will not interpret such ambiguities but will refer the question to a group in the society for interpretation.

---

[1] If you are unfamiliar with game simulations, you may wish to read the articles by Abt (pp. 37–39) and Raser (pp. 40–44) in this manual before reading the rules of SIMSOC.

He will concern himself only with those aspects of the ambiguous situation that affect his specific tasks as coordinator.

Summary of Rules

The rules that follow are detailed but not as complicated as they first appear; you will discover this once SIMSOC is in process. A short summary of the rules is included here to give you a general sense of the nature of the society and the options available to you. It also includes page references so that you can easily look up exact details as it becomes necessary later. A careful reading of this summary is a helpful way to begin but you should read the complete rules rapidly. Once you begin to play and attempt to achieve your goals, you will need to read carefully various specific sections of the complete rules.

Simbucks.

Simbucks are the basic currency in SIMSOC. Initially, they are held in a bank run by the game coordinator (see p. 4).

Region.

All members of the society live in one of four regions (see p. 5).

Moving.

A player may move to another region by paying a moving fee to the bank (see p. 5).

Travel.

A person cannot travel between regions unless he has either a travel ticket or a Private Transportation Certificate. Travel tickets may be obtained from a limited number of players who have travel agencies and receive a supply of travel tickets each session. A Private Transportation Certificate may be purchased from the bank (see pp. 5-6).

Subsistence.

Every member of the society must, for every session at which he is present, provide for his subsistence. He can do this by means of either a subsistence ticket or a Permanent Subsistence Certificate. Subsistence tickets can be obtained from a limited number of players who have subsistence agencies and receive a supply of subsistence tickets each session. A Permanent Subsistence Certificate may be purchased from the bank.

If a person fails to provide subsistence for a session, he loses his job and other privileges. If he fails to provide subsistence in two consecutive sessions, he is considered dead and cannot participate in the society in any way (see pp. 6-7).

Luxury living (optional).

The coordinator will announce whether this option is in effect. It provides for the purchase of certain personal privileges that will increase a person's comfort and style of life in SIMSOC (see p. 7).

Basic groups.

There are seven basic groups in SIMSOC for which you can work. Only the head of these groups will be designated by the coordinator at the beginning. The rest of the players must find jobs. The head of each group receives the group's income to dispense.

The groups include two industries (BASIN and INNOVIN), two political parties (POP and SOP), an employee interest group (EMPIN), a mass media group (MASMED), and a rule-interpreting group (JUDCO). You should read the description of these groups before beginning play because you will be asked to designate a choice, and, if you are not picked as head of a group, you will be faced with the need for employment (see pp. 7–20).

Absenteeism.

Certain National Indicators (described below) are lowered when members are absent, regardless of the reason (see p. 20).

Unemployment.

Certain National Indicators are lowered if there are members of the society without jobs (see p. 20).

Death.

Certain National Indicators are lowered if members die (see p. 21).

Minority Group (optional).

The coordinator will announce whether this option is in effect. It provides for the designation of some members of the society as Minority Group Members. These people may be removed from their job and may lose any subsistence and travel agencies they own by action of any two non-Minority Group Members at any time (see p. 21).

Personal goals.

Members are asked to commit themselves to the pursuit of a personal goal such as acquiring power, becoming the center of attention, enjoying the most luxurious style of life available, enjoying personal security, or a personal goal of their own designation. These goals should be sought in addition to any that are sought for groups to which one belongs or for the society as a whole (see pp. 21–22).

National Indicators.

Numerical values for four National Indicators are calculated at the end of each session. The indicators are Food and Energy Supply, Standard of Living, Social Cohesion, and Public Commitment. These National Indicators may be raised by investing Simbucks in either of two broad public programs—Research and Conservation or Welfare Services. The National Indicators decline by a certain percentage each session and can be lowered further by various actions and events in the society. If the National Indicators decline below certain points, the income available to the basic groups in the society declines. If the National Indicators rise above a certain point, the income available to the basic groups in the society increases. If any National Indicator goes below zero, the society collapses and the game is over (see pp. 23–25).

Government.

There is no requirement that the society establish a government or formal rules regulating a government (see p. 25).

SIMFORCE.

Actual physical force is prohibited in SIMSOC but the equivalent of such physical force is provided. Any individual or group may create a SIMFORCE with the power to arrest others and protect specified others from arrest. A person who is arrested is restricted to his region and may not travel, may not hold any job or official position in the society, may not engage in any official transactions with the coordinator, and will have all Simbucks, subsistence tickets, and travel tickets confiscated. All confiscated materials will be turned over to the head of the SIMFORCE. A person is dead if his arrest is renewed for two consecutive sessions.

More than one SIMFORCE can be created, and it is also possible to remove an existing SIMFORCE. Arrests lower certain of the National Indicators (see pp. 26–28).

Special events (optional).

The coordinator may announce the occurrence of certain outside events affecting the society but you will not know in advance when the events will occur or what their nature will be (see p. 29).

The object of the game.

To achieve the personal goal you have set for yourself, to help the basic group to which you belong to achieve its goals, and to see to it that the society as a whole is a "success"—however you may wish to define this. If you try to achieve these objectives, the larger objective of learning will be achieved (see p. 29).

Simbucks

Simbucks are the basic currency in SIMSOC. They are signified in these instructions by $. You can use them to buy things you will need to achieve your goals in the society. For example, they will help you to travel or buy subsistence. You can also invest them in various ways or you may save them up in any given session for later use. As you read the following instructions, you will discover the many ways in which you can spend your Simbucks. All Simbucks not owned by an individual or group in the society are the property of the bank kept by the coordinator. The bank does not make loans or extend credit.

Each participant is assumed to have a secure place where he keeps his Simbucks and other possessions. Therefore, it is against the rules to take another player's Simbucks or other possessions even if they are left around in a careless fashion. The same rule applies to the Simbucks and tickets that are held by the coordinator or bank. The only way in which a player may take the possessions of another against his will is by SIMFORCE action as described below.

PRIVATE LIFE

Region

All members of the society live in one of four regions, designated Red, Yellow, Blue, and Green. At the beginning of each session, you must go to your home region.

Moving

Any player may move to another region by filing the Moving Sheet (Form C) and paying a moving fee of $10 to the bank. The move becomes effective at the beginning of the session following the filing of this form. In other words, if the player wishes to go to his new region immediately, he must provide his transportation as described below.

Moving to a new region is subject to the following restrictions. First, no more than one-third of the total participants (including absentees) may live in any one region. Second, a player may be refused admission to a region by the *unanimous* consent of the inhabitants who are present (that is, excluding visitors or absentees).

Travel

You may travel between regions in two ways:

1) *Public transportation.* A person who possesses a travel ticket may use it to travel between regions. A travel ticket is good for one trip where a trip is defined as leaving and returning to the home region with no more than one stop in each other region. A trip is over when the traveler returns to his home region. It is your responsibility to give the coordinator or an assistant your travel ticket at the beginning of each trip. Travel tickets can be obtained from people who possess travel agencies (see discussion below).

2) *Private transportation.* Any individual may purchase a Private Transportation Certificate from the bank at a cost of $25 (Form D). Those who possess such a certificate may make as many trips as they like. In other words, a Private Transportation Certificate allows you to travel freely for the rest of the session and for all future sessions of the society. Only the individual who bought a Private Transportation Certificate may use it. He may, however, transfer his certificate to another individual but to do so he must file Form F and pay a transfer fee of $3 to the bank.

No one may travel unless he has either a travel ticket or a Private Transportation Certificate. A certain number of players will be designated as owners of travel agencies at the beginning of the game. These agency heads will receive five travel tickets in each session which they can use, hoard, dispense, save, or sell in any fashion they see fit. Unused travel tickets may be carried over to future sessions. A travel agency with its annual supply of five travel tickets may be sold or transferred (Form F) but a transfer charge of $3 must be paid to the bank. If the owner of a travel agency is absent, his supply of tickets for that session is lost to the society.

Restrictions on Travel

Travel is subject to the following restrictions: First, no more than half of the total participants present at a session may occupy any region at any one time. A traveling member may not enter a region in which there are already 50% of the members of the society present. This restriction also applies to any other areas even if they are not official regions (for example, an "uninhabited region" used as a meeting place). Second, any player, even with valid transportation, may be refused admission to a region by the unanimous consent of the inhabitants who are present (excluding visitors or absentees). He may *not* be refused admission if one or more of the inhabitants is willing to have the traveler enter.

Subsistence

Every member of the society must, for every session at which he is present (even if present only for part of the session), provide for his subsistence. He can do this by presenting the coordinator with a subsistence ticket at any time before the end of the session; he can also purchase a Permanent Subsistence Certificate which covers his subsistence for the present session and all future sessions of the society (see details below).

A certain number of players will be designated as owners of subsistence agencies at the beginning of the game. These agency heads will receive five subsistence tickets in each session, which they can use, hoard, dispense, save, or sell in any fashion they see fit. Unused subsistence tickets may be carried over to future sessions. A subsistence agency, with its annual supply of five tickets, may be sold or transferred (Form F) but a transfer charge of $3 must be paid to the bank. If the owner of a subsistence agency is absent, his supply of tickets for that session is lost to the society.

Any individual may purchase a Permanent Subsistence Certificate from the bank at any time during a session at a cost of $25 (Form E). If he wishes to change his home region, he may do so at the time of purchase and avoid the $10 moving charge. The move becomes effective at the beginning of the next session—that is, if he wishes to move immediately, he must provide for his transportation. His move is subject to the usual restrictions on moving. He may transfer his Permanent Subsistence Certificate to another player (Form F) but a transfer charge of $3 must be paid to the bank. Furthermore, a Permanent Subsistence Certificate can be used to provide for only one individual per session.

Subsistence Failure

If a person fails to provide subsistence for a session, he suffers the following consequences:

1) As of the end of that session, he is unemployed; if he is head of a basic group, he will be removed from his position and a new head will be chosen in the manner specified in the rules.

2) As of the end of the session, he cannot engage in any official transaction with the coordinator (that is, he cannot turn in any forms) except for those relating to subsistence.

These restrictions remain in effect until he provides a subsistence ticket or buys a Permanent Subsistence Certificate. During the period in which he is without subsistence, he is free to talk to others and to travel if he has the means of transportation. Even though he is officially unemployed, he may participate in activities unofficially and may continue to hold an agency and any Simbucks which he has saved from previous sessions. Once he obtains subsistence, it is up to him to find a new job or regain his old one; he does not automatically assume his old position.

Repeated Subsistence Failure

If a subsistence failure occurs in two consecutive sessions, the member is considered dead and henceforth cannot participate in the society in any way. He will then be asked by the coordinator to observe the society and assist the coordinator.

Luxury Living (Optional)

The game coordinator will announce if this option is in effect. It allows players to purchase certain personal privileges that will increase their comfort and style of life in SIMSOC. The cost of these privileges and their precise nature will be designated by the coordinator if the option is used. Only players who have subsistence for a session will be eligible for luxury living.

Basic Groups

Before the society begins, you will be asked to express first, second, and third preferences among the seven groups described below. These choices will be used only in selecting the head of each group, not the other group members. Among those who list a first choice for a particular group, one person will be assigned as head of that group. If there are no first choices for a group, then second and third choices will be used.

Those persons not assigned as heads of the seven groups must then seek employment in one or more of the groups. In seeking employment:

1) You do not have to join the group you originally chose on Form A, but can join any group that will hire you.

2) You can work for more than one group. This also applies to the heads, who may hold positions in other groups.

When SIMSOC begins one of the first tasks will be for the seven groups to organize. The head of each group must put together an organization to accomplish that group's tasks, while other persons need to find a job so that they have enough Simbucks for subsistence and other needs. This organizational phase is accomplished when a Job Schedule (Form G) has been turned in to the coordinator for all seven groups. Remember, except for the head, no one is considered officially employed by a group until this form has been filed.

In the descriptions of the groups, various suggestions are indicated. These suggestions should not be taken as directions about what you are expected to do. They are meant only to give you some idea of what people have done in the past. If you have other ideas, by all means follow them and ignore the suggestions made here. These suggestions are intended only to get you started in your thinking.

Three different figures are given below for the basic income of each group: Size Level One, Size Level Two, and Size Level Three. The appropriate figure for all groups is determined by the total number of participants in your society. It will be announced by the coordinator prior to beginning the game and will not change. You will find it helpful to cross out the figures that do not apply to your society.

BASIN
Basic Industry

Overall objective.
To expand its assets and income as much as possible.

BASIN manufactures words from anagrams—combinations of letters in jumbled order. Its assets can be increased in the following ways.

In each session, BASIN may purchase from the bank any number up to five anagrams. They need not all be purchased at the same time, and additional anagrams up to the limit of five may be purchased anytime during the session. All purchases must be authorized by the head of BASIN, using Form H.

The cost of each anagram depends on the size level of the society and is given in Table 1. In a Size Level Two society, for example, each anagram costs $60. An anagram is solved by using its letters to complete a five-letter word found in any standard dictionary (proper names excluded). Completed words are turned into the coordinator using Form H; payment or credit for them is not received until the end of the session. For each completed word, BASIN assets in the bank will be increased as indicated in Table 1. To count, a completed word must be turned in during the same session in which the anagram was purchased. Essentially, BASIN will receive 50% more for a completed word than it paid for the original anagram.

The anagrams that BASIN buys will vary in difficulty but BASIN has one chance in five of buying *an anagram that has no solution.* In other words, out of every five anagrams purchased, on the average one will be a lost investment. This does not necessarily mean that, in any given session, you will be able to solve exactly four out of five anagrams. It might turn out that in some sessions you will be lucky enough to buy five solvable anagrams, and, in other sessions, that are less lucky, only two or three will be solvable. It does mean that over many sessions, about 80% of the anagrams that you will buy will be solvable. The coordinator sells anagrams in a predetermined, random order over which he has no control.

The head of BASIN can withdraw part or all of its assets from the bank whenever he wishes by simply filling out Form I and giving it to the coordinator.

BASIN can buy anagrams by using its assets in the bank and the income from these assets (10% each session). In the beginning of the society, however, BASIN assets and income are not high enough to purchase five anagrams. Therefore, if BASIN wishes to buy the greatest possible number of anagrams, it will need to raise additional Simbucks from other individuals and groups in the society. It may do this by promising others some return on their money, by arguments about how this will help the society, or by offering other inducements or persuasive reasons for people to lend their money to BASIN.

Effects on National Indicators.
The buying of anagrams and the manufacture of words by BASIN affects two of the National Indicators (these are described more fully later).

The Standard of Living is raised for each completed word since the economy is growing, but the Food and Energy Supply is lowered for each anagram that is purchased on the assumption that this investment depletes existing resource supplies. In other words, buying anagrams entails short-term costs for the society but at the same time produces long-term growth in the economy.

Suggested jobs in BASIN.

Chief Money Raiser: A person with responsibility for getting the funds needed to buy anagrams.

Work Coordinator: A person with chief responsibility for the production of completed words from anagrams.

Public Relations Director: A person with responsibility for maintaining a favorable climate for investment in BASIN

Regional Representatives.

Table 1. Summary of BASIN Assets, Income, Investment Costs, and Returns

	Starting Assets in Bank	Income in First Session	Cost per Anagram	Payment for Completed Word
Size Level One	$100	$10	$40	$60
Size Level Two	150	15	60	90
Size Level Three	200	20	80	120

Probability of buying an unsolvable anagram = 0.2 (that is, 20%).

INNOVIN
Innovative Industry

Overall objective.

Like BASIN, *the objective of this group is to expand its assets and income as much as possible.*

INNOVIN also manufactures words from anagrams under the same procedures as BASIN. The costs of each anagram are the same as for BASIN and are given in Table 2. INNOVIN, however, has a much higher probability of buying an unsolvable anagram and receives a much higher return for each completed word. Essentially, INNOVIN will receive triple what it paid for an anagram for each completed word (see Table 2).

The *solvable* anagrams that INNOVIN buys will have the same average level of difficulty as the *solvable* BASIN anagrams, but INNOVIN will have three chances in five of buying *an anagram that has no solution.* In other words, out of every five anagrams purchased, three will be a lost investment. This does not necessarily mean that, in any given session, you will be able to solve exactly two out of five anagrams. It might turn out that in some sessions you will be lucky enough to buy three or four or even five solvable anagrams; or, less fortunately, only one or none will be solvable. It does mean that, over many sessions, about 40% of the anagrams that you buy will be solvable. The coordinator sells anagrams in a predetermined, random order over which he has no control.

The head of INNOVIN can withdraw part of all of its assets from the bank whenever he wishes by simply filling out Form I and giving it to the coordinator.

INNOVIN, like BASIN, has insufficient income and assets at the beginning to buy five anagrams and will need to raise outside money if it wishes to buy this many.

Effects on National Indicators.

The buying of anagrams and the manufacture of words by INNOVIN affects three of the National Indicators (as described more fully later). The Standard of Living is raised for each completed word, but Social Cohesion and Public Commitment are both lowered for each anagram purchased on the assumption that INNOVIN's speculative business ventures stimulate a certain amount of strain and conflict in the society. As with BASIN, INNOVIN's investments entail short-term costs for the society but produce long-term economic growth.

Suggested jobs in INNOVIN.

Chief Fund Raiser: A person with responsibility for getting the funds needed to buy anagrams.

Work Coordinator: A person with chief responsibility for the production of completed words from anagrams.

Public Relations Director: A person with responsibility for maintaining a favorable climate for investment in INNOVIN.

Regional Representatives.

Table 2. Summary of INNOVIN Assets, Income, Investment Costs, and Returns

	Starting Assets in Bank	Income in First Session	Cost per Anagram	Payment for Completed Word
Size Level One	$100	$10	$40	$120
Size Level Two	150	15	60	180
Size Level Three	200	20	80	240

Probability of buying an unsolvable anagram = 0.6 (that is, 60%).

POP
Party of the People

Overall objective.

To determine the major public policies followed by the society and to develop programs and mobilize supporters for this purpose. To be more influential than its rival.

When the society begins, POP is a political party that has neither a program, philosophy, or ideology. It is up to the members of POP to develop these things as they see fit. The content may vary greatly depending on the circumstances in a given society and the beliefs of the citizens. POP may be given information by the coordinator at regular intervals on how well it is regarded by citizens of the society, especially relative to its rival party.

Suggested jobs in POP.

Program Chairman: A person with responsibility for developing a party philosophy and program.

Membership Chairman: A person with responsibility for mobilizing mass support for the party program.

Chief Fund Raiser: A person with responsibility for obtaining the funds that the party needs in carrying out its program. These funds may be needed to cover such expenses as magazine advertising, National Broadcasting System use, travel expenses, investment in Public Programs, and other expenses that may arise.

Regional Representatives.

Basic income per session.

Size Level One:	$40
Size Level Two:	$60
Size Level Three:	$80

SOP
Society Party

Overall objective.
    Same as instructions for POP.

Suggested jobs for SOP.
    Same as suggestions for POP.

Basic income per session.

Size Level One:	$40
Size Level Two:	$60
Size Level Three:	$80

EMPIN
Employee Interests

Overall objective.

To see to it that the members of SIMSOC who are not heads of basic groups have adequate subsistence and a fair share of the wealth of the society.

EMPIN may wish to organize the members of society who work for the various basic groups in some manner. They may wish to develop various services for this constituency. They may wish to propose programs for the society as a whole that would meet their objectives. They may want to work closely with one or more other groups. They may wish to establish a membership organization with dues. They may want to carry out various educational programs.

Suggested jobs in EMPIN.

Chief Organizer: A person with responsibility for lining up members and supporters.

Program Chairman: A person with responsibility for developing programs which will protect and further the interests of the members.

Education and Public Relations Chairman: A person with responsibility for developing a favorable climate for organizing and program support.

Regional Representatives.

Basic income per session.

Size Level One:	$40
Size Level Two:	$60
Size Level Three:	$80

MASMED
Mass Media

Overall objective.
To keep the society informed about important events.

This can be done through two media:

1) *National Broadcasting System.* This can be used for rapid, short communications. The coordinator or an assistant will travel from region to region to read any written message signed by the head of MASMED. There is a cost of $3 for each message sent. MASMED can bypass this fee, if it wishes, by delivering its own messages but its messenger must have a travel ticket or Permanent Transportation Certificate to distribute the messages. (Where available, broadcasting may be provided through an intercom system. If technically feasible, proceedings in one region may be broadcast to other regions at a cost of $10 per session.)

2) *News Magazine* (where facilities are available). This can be used for long-term developments and trends, editorials, analyses, and records. It may be prepared during sessions or between sessions for distribution at the beginning of the following session. MASMED must pay $5 to the bank for each page of copy that is published and distributed. There is no additional charge for multiple copies of the same page and the coordinator will distribute copies as MASMED desires, at no additional cost.

MASMED may wish to pass on its costs by charging broadcast sponsors and magazine subscribers and/or by selling broadcast time and space to advertisers. Or they may simply absorb the costs themselves if they wish. MASMED should regard itself as the record keeper and official historian of the society. Its members, therefore, will need to keep informed about various group activities. After the session is completed and the coordinator has had an opportunity to calculate changes in the National Indicators, he will inform the head of MASMED of the current value of these indicators and of the rates of absenteeism, unemployment, arrests, and death. This information can be used by the head of MASMED in any way desired. The coordinator will, however, turn over official forms that are filed by any individual or group only with the permission of those filing the forms.

The head of MASMED may also receive statistical summaries of the Assessment Sheet (Form N) if these become available.

Suggested jobs in MASMED.
Broadcasting Chief: A person with responsibility for running the National Broadcasting System.

Advertising and Business Manager: A person with overall responsibility for financial transactions.

Chief of Political Desk: A person with overall responsibility for reporting on political activities in the society.

Chief of Economic Desk: A person with overall responsibility for reporting on investments and economic activities in the society.

Chief of Cultural Desk: A person with overall responsibility for reporting on cultural developments and trends in the society.

Chief of Organization Desk: A person with overall responsibility for reporting on the activities of existing organizations in the society and the creation of any new organizations that may arise.

Regional Representatives.

Basic income per session.

Level One	$40
Level Two	$60
Level Three	$80

JUDCO
Judicial Council

Overall objective.

To clarify and interpret the rules as honestly and conscientiously as they can.

JUDCO members may be called on to decide issues such as the following: (a) whether the action or prospective action of some member or group of members violates the basic rules of the game, or (b) whether an agreement among members of the society violates any basic rule of the game. JUDCO may act when some action or agreement is challenged. JUDCO is the final arbiter on the meaning and interpretation of all rules, and the coordinator may refer questions to JUDCO for clarification.

JUDCO members should try to interpret ambiguous situations in good faith rather than using their ingenuity to ignore the basic rules. The coordinator will accept JUDCO's judgment even though it might differ from his own interpretation, but arbitrary and capricious interpretations can render SIM-SOC meaningless. If JUDCO, by its interpretations, removes the "natural constraints" which the rules are intended to simulate, the dilemmas which the game poses will disappear—and the challenge of the game and its value as a learning device will disappear at the same time.

1) To be valid, JUDCO decisions must be signed by a simple majority of its members. These decisions must be filed on Form J and properly signed.

2) JUDCO must have at least two other members besides its head, but it may have more than this as long as the total membership is an odd number.

Suggested jobs in JUDCO.

Appeals Judge: A person with responsibility to review cases where there is dissatisfaction with the initial decision.

Regional Judges (circuit courts).

Basic income per session.

Size Level One:	$20
Size Level Two:	$30
Size Level Three:	$40

The Group Head

Powers of the Head of a Group

The head of a group may hire and fire other persons on any terms he wishes and for any reasons. The group's basic income is at his disposal for this purpose. He hires by filling out a Job Schedule (Form G). He fires by filling out a revised Job Schedule omitting the person. No individual will be considered employed without his own consent; an individual may quit any job by simply informing the coordinator of his decision. Agreements on salary and working conditions are internal matters between the head and his employees and need not be reported to the coordinator.

Removing the Head of a Group

Voluntary removal.

The head of a group may resign at any time and simply appoint a successor of his choice. He does this by filing a revised Job Schedule (Form G) listing the new head. If there are other changes in employment at the same time, the revised form should include the signatures of both the old and new head.

Involuntary removal.

The head of a group is automatically removed from office if (a) he fails to provide subsistence, (b) is arrested, or (c) is absent. He may also be removed from office by the unanimous consent of all employees of the group who are present (not including the head of the group who is being removed, of course). There is one qualification to this rule: the head cannot be removed by unanimous consent unless there are at least two official employees present.

Replacing the Head of a Group

In the case of voluntary removal, the old head can simply designate a successor. In the case of involuntary removal, we must distinguish three cases:

1) There are no other employees or all are absent. In this case, the coordinator will pick a new head at random.
2) There is only one other employee present at the session. This employee automatically becomes the new head.
3) There are two or more employees present. They must agree unanimously on a new head. In the event that they cannot come to a unanimous agreement, the group will remain without a head for that session and its income will be lost. At the end of the session, the coordinator will pick a new head for the following session at random.

The Job Schedule (Form G) is the form to use for all transactions regarding the removal and replacement of the head of a group.

At this point, take out your Choice Sheet (Form A) and indicate on it your choice of a basic group. Put only your name on the Assignment Sheet (Form B) and pass this in also. This will be filled out by the coordinator and returned to you at the beginning of the first session.

Absenteeism

For every member of the society absent from any session, regardless of reason, Standard of Living and Public Commitment are each reduced by two units. Absentees are not required to supply subsistence for sessions which they miss. Hence, they do not suffer the consequences of subsistence failure for the following session.

If the head of a basic group is absent he is automatically removed from office, and a new head will be designated in the manner provided in the rules. Employees of the group other than the head continue to hold their position while absent unless they are removed by the head. A member is not considered absent if he is present for any part of a session.

For any session in which there are five or more absentees (but less than ten), one subsistence agency chosen at random will not receive its allotment of subsistence tickets. For any session in which there are ten or more absentees, two subsistence agencies chosen at random will not receive their allotment of subsistence tickets.

Unemployment

Unemployment may result from two causes other than arrest (see the discussion of the SIMFORCE):

1) *Inability to find a job.* An individual may find that none of the basic groups will employ him.

2) *Loss of job through failure to obtain subsistence.* An individual may not have been able to obtain a subsistence ticket and thus be forced to leave his job.

For each unemployed person during a given session, Standard of Living and Social Cohesion will each be lowered by three units and Public Commitment will be lowered by two units. (This does not include unemployment due to arrest, the effects of which are already included.)

Death

A member may die from failing to obtain subsistence in two consecutive sessions or from having his arrest renewed for two consecutive sessions (that is, having had his arrest renewed once, the next renewal is equivalent to execution). A member who dies henceforth cannot participate in the society in any way; he will be asked to observe and assist the coordinator. Each death, regardless of cause, lowers Standard of Living, Social Cohesion, and Public Commitment by five units.

Minority Group (Optional)

The coordinator may include the following optional feature. Of the members of the society 20% will be designated by the instructor as Minority Group Members when the society begins. They will be asked to wear some clear insignia or armband so that everyone can clearly identify them as a Minority Group Member.

Minority Group Members will operate under the following special restrictions: Any two non-Minority Group Members of the society may at any time, and without cost, have any Minority Group Member fired from his job and removed as head of a basic group and owner of a subsistence or travel agency. This is done by filing Form K with the instructor.

If the Minority Group Member is a head of a basic group, a new head will be designated in the manner indicated in the rules. The coordinator will assign the vacated travel or subsistence agency of a Minority Group Member to some member of the society picked at random.

The Minority Group Member who is the recipient of such action will retain any subsistence tickets, travel tickets, or Simbucks in his possession at the time, including Permanent Travel or Subsistence Certificates. If he controls a SIMFORCE, this is not affected by Form K. Furthermore, he may reacquire any former positions in the next session if he is able to do so. But he may not hold any position with a basic group or hold any agency during the remainder of the session in which the Form K has been filed against him. Furthermore, a new Form K may be filed against him in subsequent sessions.

Personal Goals

The society will be more interesting and realistic if, in addition to various group goals, individuals are simultaneously pursuing one or more private or personal goals. A personal goal emphasizes something for you as an individual (for example, being powerful) rather than a goal for the society (for example, making SIMSOC an ideal society). SIMSOC will be most realistic when participants are trying to achieve both kinds of goals *at the same time.*

A short list of personal goals is given below. You should choose one or more to pursue from the beginning but you may wish to change your personal goals once the society is in progress. Your choice need *not* reflect the goal you think is most important in real life. You need not communicate this goal to others but you should mark your choice at the beginning as a reminder to yourself that this is one of your objectives in the game.

1) *Power.* I will try to influence what happens in the society as much as possible.

2) *Center of attention.* I will try to be a central figure in the life of the society, salient to as many people as possible.

3) *Style of life.* I will try to enjoy the highest standard of living available, including any amenities or luxuries that are available.

4) *Security.* I will try to lead a life in which I will not be threatened by lack of subsistence, by loss of job, arrest, or any other misfortune.

5) *Other.* Specify your own personal goal but be sure it is something for you as an individual rather than something for a group or for the society as a whole.

Some information may be available from the Assessment Sheet which will help you to evaluate your success in achieving personal goals.

National Indicators

Numerical values for four National Indicators are calculated by the coordinator at the end of each session as one means of measuring the general effectiveness and "health" of the society as a whole. Each indicator pertains to a different aspect of the society, as follows:

1) *Food and Energy Supply* (FES). This represents how well the society is adapting to its physical environment. Is it developing its natural resources to meet the needs of its population? (The word "population" and "citizens" in this discussion of National Indicators does not refer only to the members of this class but to others as well who are represented here abstractly through the National Indicators.) Is it replenishing the resources that it consumes? A higher score means an abundant Food and Energy Supply.

2) *Standard of Living* (SL). This represents the consumption level of the society. How well are the citizens of the society living at the present time? A higher score means a higher Standard of Living.

3) *Social Cohesion* (SC). This represents how well different groups of citizens are integrated. Are some groups isolated and left-out? Are there destructive conflicts between subgroups? The higher the score on Social Cohesion, the less the presence of destructive intergroup conflict.

4) *Public Commitment* (PC). This represents the degree of commitment by citizens of the society to its social structure and values. Are there large numbers of alienated citizens who feel estranged from the society and do not participate in it in a constructive way? The higher the score on Public Commitment, the less the degree of alienation among the citizens.

Public Programs

These National Indicators may be raised by investing money in either of two broad Public Programs. The money is invested by giving it to the bank with the instruction that it be used for a specific Public Program. This money is "used up" in the Public Programs—that is, once invested it cannot later be withdrawn from the bank.

The programs are:

1) Research and Conservation.

The purpose of this program is to promote scientific research and activity in such areas as (a) developing and conserving the natural environment so as to increase the Food and Energy Supply, and (b) utilizing available manpower resources more effectively so as to raise the overall Standard of Living.

2) Welfare Services.

This program creates and expands a variety of Welfare Services for the citizens of the society, and copes with discontent, poverty, social unrest, and so forth. Investments in this program help to raise the Standard of Living as well as Social Cohesion and Public Commitment.

Any individual or group can invest any amount of money in either or both of these programs. The specific effects of these investments on the four National Indicators of Food and Energy Supply, Standard of Living, Social Cohesion, and Public Commitment are discussed below. The effects take place at the end of each session.

Any individual or group may decide to aid the society by advising its members on investment policies, work organization, or other matters which may indirectly affect any of the National Indicators and contribute to the overall vitality and effectiveness of the society.

Change in the National Indicators

Each National Indicator begins at 100 for the first session but thereafter automatically declines by 10% between sessions unless it is further affected by the actions of the society members. Simbucks invested in Public Programs raise the National Indicators; however, these programs have "administrative costs" and a Simbuck invested in them does not bring an equivalent rise in the National Indicators. Instead, only a percentage of the total investment in Public Programs is reflected directly in a change in National Indicators. Thus, $100 invested in Public Programs does not raise the National Indicators by 100 units, but only by a percentage of the amount invested. More specifically, indicators can be changed in the following ways:

1) Food and Energy Supply (FES).
   (a) Raised by 40% of the value of all new money invested in the Research and Conservation Program.
   (b) Lowered by two units for each anagram bought by BASIN.

2) Standard of Living (SL).
   (a) Raised by 10% of the value of all new investments in either the Research and Conservation or Welfare Services Program.
   (b) Raised by one unit for each word completed by either BASIN or INNOVIN.
   (c) Lowered by two units for each absentee.
   (d) Lowered by three units for each unemployed person.
   (e) Lowered by five units for each death.

3) Social Cohesion (SC).
   (a) Raised by 20% of the value of all new investments in Welfare Services.
   (b) Lowered by one unit for each anagram bought by INNOVIN.
   (c) Lowered by three units for each person arrested.
   (d) Lowered by three units for each unemployed person.
   (e) Lowered by five units for each death.

4) Public Commitment (PC).
   (a) Raised by 20% of the value of all new investments in Welfare Services.
   (b) Lowered by one unit for each anagram bought by INNOVIN.
   (c) Lowered by two units for each absentee.

(d) Lowered by three units for each person arrested.

(e) Lowered by two units for each unemployed person.

(f) Lowered by five units for each death.

Table 3 summarizes these effects of investment and other actions.

Table 3. Effects of Investment and Other Actions on National Indicators

	FES	SL	SC	PC
Research and Conservation	+ 40%*	+ 10%	0	0
Welfare Services	0	+ 10%	+ 20%	+ 20%
BASIN	−2 units	+ 1 unit	0	0
INNOVIN	0	+1	−1	−1
Absentees	0	−2	0	−2
Arrested	0	0	−3	−3
Unemployed	0	−3	−3	−2
Dead	0	−5	−5	−5

*This means that if, for example, $10 were invested in Research and Conservation, FES would rise by 40% of this or by four units. Similarly, SL would go up by one unit while SC and PC would not be affected.

Consequences of Different Values of the National Indicators

The amount of income distributed to the heads of the basic groups at the beginning of each session is affected by the state of the National Indicators in the following fashion:

1) Every group will receive 20% more than its basic income for any session in which all of the National Indicators are above 125 at the beginning of the session.

2) Every group will receive 10% less than its basic income for any session in which any National Indicator is below 90, 20% less for any session in which any National Indicator is below 80, 30% less for any session in which any National Indicator is below 70, and so forth down to 90% less for any session in which any of the National Indicators is below 10. This applies to the *income* of BASIN and INNOVIN as well, although their assets in the bank are not affected. **The society ends if *any* National Indicator falls below zero.**

Government

There is no requirement that the society establish a government, and it may wish to operate without one. If any member or members wish, however, to form a government, they may do so at any time. If a government is created, its supporters may organize and conduct it in any manner they choose. There are no formal rules regulating such a government.

SIMFORCE

For better or worse, physical force or the threat of physical force plays a role in the life of real societies. It may take various forms—police arresting citizens, secret terrorist organizations threatening citizens, guerrilla forces attacking government officials, or even two armies fighting against each other as in a civil war. Actual physical force is prohibited in SIMSOC—no participant can physically restrain the movement of another participant or in any other way use physical force against him. The equivalent of such physical force is, however, provided in the game.

Initiating a SIMFORCE

Any individual or group of individuals may create a SIMFORCE with the power to arrest others and protect specified others from arrest. A SIMFORCE is created by filling out Form L; the minimum cost is $25 (paid to the bank) but a larger amount of money will create a larger SIMFORCE. Form L requires a *decision statement* that tells the coordinator what constitutes an order of the SIMFORCE. This statement may take any form desired (for example, "an order must be signed by two-thirds majority," "an order must be signed by the head and one other member," or "an order must be signed by all members"). The only requirement is that the statement be unambiguous.

A SIMFORCE must be renewed during the *second* session following its creation or it will be considered defunct, and its orders made during that session and subsequent sessions will not be carried out. The renewal cost is $10 (paid to the bank) for a force of any size; this payment is for maintenance and does not increase its size. The SIMFORCE must also designate a head for communication purposes, but this head need not have any special powers that other members lack. The size of a SIMFORCE may be increased by giving additional money to the bank for this purpose.

A SIMFORCE has two powers: (1) *to arrest persons and* (2) *to protect persons from arrest.*

Arrest

An *arrest* is initiated by filling out Form M. (One must, of course, already have a SIMFORCE to arrest someone.) There is a cost of $10 (paid to the bank) for each person placed under arrest. The actual arrest is made by the coordinator, who will carry out the orders of any duly authorized SIMFORCE. If the coordinator cannot carry out an ordered arrest because the target is under the protection of a SIMFORCE, the $10 arrest charge will be returned. The head of the SIMFORCE attempting the arrest will be informed that the order could not be carried out.

Arrests of unprotected persons will take place as soon as the coordinator is able to carry out the order and will last for the duration of the session. The arrested citizen will be informed by the coordinator of his status and all of his materials will be confiscated (see discussion below). The coordinator will not announce the identity of the arresting SIMFORCE unless asked to do so by the head of the SIMFORCE. All confiscated materials will be turned over to the head of the SIMFORCE.

An arrested person may be released at any time by order of the arresting SIMFORCE. The disposition of confiscated materials is an internal matter between the SIMFORCE and the arrested person and is not specified by the rules. At the beginning of each session following an arrest, the coordinator will ask the SIMFORCE head whether he wishes to renew existing arrests for the session or to release those under arrest. Renewals require a payment to the bank of $10 for each arrested person for a session. The coordinator will inform those under arrest of their status for the session.

All arrested individuals are automatically released immediately if the arresting SIMFORCE is removed (see discussion below on removing a SIMFORCE).

Restrictions on the Arrested Person

A member who is under arrest:

(a) is restricted to his own region and may not travel,

(b) may not hold any official position in the society (including any position in the seven basic groups),

(c) may not engage in any official transactions with the coordinator (i.e., turn in any forms, invest Simbucks, etc.), and

(d) will have confiscated all Simbucks, subsistence tickets, and travel tickets in his possession at the time of arrest.

An arrested person does not lose his Permanent Subsistence Certificate or Private Transportation Certificate, nor does he lose his travel or subsistence agency. If he owns an agency, however, his allotment of subsistence tickets or travel tickets will be confiscated for sessions in which he is under arrest. It is assumed that his subsistence is provided while under arrest and it is not necessary for him to provide a subsistence ticket. If he is released during a session, however, he must provide subsistence for that session.

An individual whose arrest is renewed for two consecutive sessions is dead and, henceforth, cannot participate in any way. If he owns an agency it will be reassigned randomly, and he will be asked to observe and assist the coordinator.

Protection from Arrest

Any person who is under the *protection* of a SIMFORCE cannot be arrested until the protecting SIMFORCE is removed. All members of a SIMFORCE (as indicated on Form L) are automatically assumed to be protected by it; in addition, the SIMFORCE may place any other individuals under its protection by so indicating on Form L. In order to be effective, protection must be extended to a person prior to the time that the coordinator informs him of his arrest.

Fines

A SIMFORCE may wish to institute a schedule of *fines* for given actions. The coordinator, however, will *not* act as the agent of the SIMFORCE in collecting such fines. If a fine is assessed against someone and he refuses to pay, the refusal may be ignored or some action such as arrest may be carried out against the refuser. In short, the collection of fines is the responsibility of the participants and will not be assumed by the coordinator.

Removing a SIMFORCE

A SIMFORCE is automatically in effect for one full session after the one in which it was originally formed. At the beginning of the second session following its creation, the coordinator will ask the head whether he wishes to renew the force at a cost of $10. If renewed, it remains in effect for two sessions and this process is repeated. If it is not renewed, it is defunct. A SIMFORCE may also be *removed* by filling out the appropriate part of Form M and presenting the coordinator with an amount equal to or greater than the value of the SIMFORCE being removed. The coordinator cannot reveal the strength of any existing force: this must be learned or estimated by those seeking removal. If the amount given to remove a force is insufficient the coordinator will inform the removing group of this fact but he will return only half of the amount given. If the amount is sufficient, they will be informed of this. The total amount will be kept by the bank and the head of the removed force will be informed that his force is no longer in existence. Overpayments will not be returned.

To illustrate this, imagine that a SIMFORCE existed with a strength of $50. A group attempts to remove it, but posts only $40, underestimating its actual strength. They are informed that their attempted removal has failed and are returned $20. They then take this $20, add $40 more to it, and file a new removal. This time the amount is sufficient, none of the $60 is returned, but the SIMFORCE head is informed that his force is now defunct. *The group which has removed the old force may or may not decide to establish a force of its own*; this is a separate operation. A SIMFORCE cannot be strengthened after a removal form has already been presented to the coordinator.

If, in an attempted removal of a SIMFORCE, the official head is not identified accurately, those who attempted the removal will be informed that the person designated as head was incorrect and their money will be returned. A fee of $10 will be charged for this service, however. The coordinator will not reveal the name of the official head unless he is asked to do so by the official head himself.

There is no expectation that a SIMFORCE will necessarily be created. It is only a possible option, and the society may end up with none, one, or several forces depending on the decisions of its members.

Arrests affect the National Indicators in the following fashion:

For every individual who is arrested, Public Commitment and Social Cohesion are reduced by three units.

Special Events (Optional)

Sometime during SIMSOC, the coordinator may announce the occurrence of certain outside events affecting the society. You will not know in advance when the events will occur or what their nature is. They are mentioned here so that you realize that they are part of the game and not an arbitrary intervention in your society by the coordinator.

Summary

The rules are less complicated than they first appear, as you will discover once SIMSOC is in process. All the details are included here but they will not all be needed by everybody.

The basic question many people have at this initial stage is simply, "What is the object of the game?" For you as an individual participant, there are several objectives:

1) To achieve the personal goal or goals you have set for yourself.

2) To help the basic group (or groups) to which you belong to achieve its goal.

3) To see to it that the society as a whole is a "success"—however you may wish to define this.

If you conscientiously try to achieve these objectives, the larger objective of learning will be achieved. To help you to keep track of these objectives and to provide you with information on how you are doing, the coordinator will ask you to fill out and hand in an Assessment Sheet (Form N) at various times in the course of the society. These will be occasions for you to take stock of your position and plan for the future.

Some Common Questions about Playing SIMSOC

Some of the most typical questions asked by participants before playing SIMSOC are included below with answers indicated:

Question: Does each person get a certain number of Simbucks?

Answer: No. Only the heads of the basic groups receive Simbucks but they can give them to others.

Question: Does a group get its income only once or does it get a fresh supply of Simbucks at each session?

Answer: The head of a group gets a fresh supply at each session. Similarly, the owner of a travel or subsistence agency gets a fresh supply of tickets at each session.

Question: Can the members of the society decide to make travel free if no one objects?

Answer: No, because that violates the basic rules in the manual. The rules in the manual are like the laws of nature—the travel ticket represents the cost in time and manpower and energy consumption of travel from one place to another. The rules you make among yourselves are like the laws of men—they can be changed or broken—but you should all try to observe the rules in the manual or else the game will not work properly.

Question: Does one need a travel ticket to give something to the coordinator?

Answer: No. The coordinator and the bank should be regarded as part of every region. You are not considered to have left your region when you approach the coordinator for any transaction. You have traveled only when you go to some other region.

Question: Suppose a majority of the members of society agreed that some obnoxious individual should not be allowed to travel. Would the coordinator enforce this rule?

Answer: No. It would be up to you to enforce it using the means provided in the game. The coordinator will only carry out those actions specified in the manual.

Question: Are the four regions separate societies?

Answer: No. They are four parts of the same society. The National Indicators, for example, affect all of you the same way regardless of region. The region is just the place where you live.

Question: Does it make sense for us to pool our travel tickets?

Answer: It's up to you to figure out what makes sense and what does not. There is no rule prohibiting you from doing it.

Question: Will everyone be assigned to some basic group and region?

Answer: Everyone will be assigned to some region but only seven people will be assigned to groups—the seven heads. The rest of you will need to find jobs.

Question: Can you work for more than one group?

Answer: Yes.

Question: Will we be told what caused the National Indicators to change as they did?

Answer: No. The head of MASMED will be told the end result and the number of absentees, arrests, unemployed, and dead. He can do whatever he wants with the information.

Question: If BASIN solves an anagram during a session, can it use the money it gets for that to buy another anagram?

Answer: Not during that session because it does not receive credit in its bank account for solved anagrams until the end of the session. It could use the money it made to buy anagrams during the following session.

Question: Can JUDCO make laws?

Answer: Any group can make laws. The question is, who will obey them? The coordinator will not enforce the laws which the members of society choose to make, including JUDCO. He will only carry out those actions specified in the manual. If these are ambiguous, he will accept the judgment of JUDCO on how they should be interpreted. For example, suppose JUDCO made a ruling that only members of JUDCO were allowed to create a SIMFORCE. If some group ignored this and filled out the proper forms to create a SIMFORCE following the procedures described in the manual, the coordinator would carry out their SIMFORCE orders. JUDCO's ruling would have no effect unless members chose to observe it or unless JUDCO had worked out some way of making it effective.

Question: Will there be enough subsistence tickets for everybody?

Answer: You will have to wait and see that when the society begins.

Question: Must the owner of a subsistence agency use one of his five tickets for his own subsistence or does he not need one?

Answer: He needs one the same as everybody else unless he buys a Permanent Subsistence Certificate for $25.

Question: Can a person get subsistence even though he does not have a job?

Answer: Yes. Someone might give him a subsistence ticket or he might own a subsistence agency himself.

Question: Can a SIMFORCE arrest someone without a reason?

Answer: Yes, if they follow the procedures described in the manual.

Question: Doesn't SIMSOC create a capitalist society?

Answer: No. It is true that the income for the basic groups is given to individuals but they do not necessarily have to operate as private citizens. You can set up a system of state ownership or ownership by groups and call the head a manager or secretary; or you can allow the individual group heads the freedom to decide for themselves how to use the group's income. It is up to you to create the kind of economic system you think is best. Whatever the system, however, some individual must still be officially designated as the head and the rules do give this person important powers which you will have to come to terms with in some way in any system.

Question: Is the object of the game to keep the National Indicators as high as possible?

Answer: That's one possible objective but not the only one. It's up to you how much you to choose to emphasize the National Indicators compared to other objectives. This is not the kind of game where there is one clear goal of "winning." It's more like life, in that you usually want to achieve several different goals at the same time.

STUDY QUESTIONS (OPTIONAL)

Assignment one.

Answer three or more of the following questions, using events in SIMSOC and the selected readings for illustration, but drawing on other material as well where applicable:

(a) Under what conditions could a society manage to function without a formal agency to administer sanctions for deviance (i.e., a police force)?

(b) What may prevent people in authority from using their authority for selfish ends?

(c) Under what conditions are people most likely to keep agreements which they make and under what conditions are they most likely to break them?

(d) Imagine a situation in which people hold many different goals, some of which conflict with each other. Imagine that there are also certain things that help or hurt everybody equally. Describe several different ways in which a society can get its members to contribute to the general interest, even when this detracts from their pursuit of their private interest.

(e) What factors keep a society from breaking down into a series of small communities that have no contact with each other or whose only contact is to make war on each other? To what extent are these factors present or absent among the different countries of the world?

(f) Some studies of leadership have shown that the persons who work hardest to move the group toward its goals are not the most popular or best-liked persons. Why do you think this is so and what do you think the best-liked persons are likely to contribute to the group?

(g) Under what conditions will efforts at inducing conformity produce nonconformity or deviance by the persons at whom these efforts are directed? Under what conditions are efforts at producing conformity most likely to meet with success?

(h) What kinds of people are most likely to deviate from group norms?

(i) What features would you build into or prohibit from a society if you wanted to keep yourself from being influenced or constrained by others as much as possible? What features would you build into a society or prohibit from a society if you wanted to make sure you could influence others as much as possible?

(j) Some people argue that conflict is always bad for a society, whereas others see it as healthy and making positive contributions. For each of these viewpoints, discuss the conditions under which they are likely to be valid.

(k) Under what conditions will groups within a society rebel and under what conditions will their rebellion be successful?

(l) When will a protest group decide to work within the system rather than trying to overthrow the system?

(m) What determines how effective a government is in putting resources to work to solve a society's problems?

(n) What are some effective mechanisms for handling social conflict in a society?

(o) How do feelings of powerlessness affect one's social interaction with those on whom one is dependent?

(p) How are those with power able to deal with the potential or actual resentment of those who are affected by their power?

(q) Under what conditions do members of a society begin to question basic values and goals that have heretofore been accepted by almost everybody?

(r) What kinds of social institutions foster close interpersonal relations and a sense of community?

Assignment two.

Imagine that you are back at the beginning of SIMSOC, except that you know what you now know. Others are in the state of innocence and confusion which prevailed then. Describe in detail what you would do to achieve any three of the following goals:

(a) to get as many people as possible to participate in the running of the society;

(b) to create conditions under which people can be trusted to keep agreements;

(c) to make yourself the best-liked person in the society;

(d) to create conditions under which you and others will be as free as possible from other people's influence, particularly the influence of societal leaders;

(e) to create conditions under which you would have maximum influence over others; and

(f) to make sure the National Indicators of your society are higher than those of any other SIMSOC that has been run.

Suppose you were trying to achieve all three of your selected objectives at the same time. To what extent do they conflict with each other, and to what extent do the same actions contribute to more than one objective simultaneously (either positively or negatively)?

Finally, suppose that the society were to start again at the point at which it ended. To achieve the same objectives discussed above, would you do anything different from what you described above? If so, what would have to be done differently and why?

Assignment three.

Imagine that you are hired by the superintendent of a large metropolitan school system. Your job is to develop an educational game to teach social science material to high school seniors. Pick any body of material in this course, specify what it is you are intending to teach in the game you develop, and then describe the educational game you would use to teach it. You may wish to read one or both of the following books if you become especially interested in this: Samuel Livingston and Clarice Stoll, *Simulation Games* (New York: The Free Press, 1972), and Michael Inbar and Clarice Stoll, editors, *Simulation and Gaming in Social Science* (New York: The Free Press, 1972). The former is a brief paperback edition which includes a substantial section on how to develop games. The latter is a collection of descriptions by simulation game designers of how they developed their simulations.

SIMSOC
SIMULATED SOCIETY

SELECTED READINGS

The following selections deal with some of the issues that SIMSOC is designed to highlight. You should be able to relate your experiences and observations from SIMSOC to these readings and thus understand their points more thoroughly and personally.

Part 1

On the Use of Simulation Games

What are simulation games? Why do people use them and what do they hope to achieve with them? The selections by Abt and Raser introduce the reader who is unfamiliar with this technique to its basic purpose. They try to make clear what it is about simulation games that gives them their potential as a teaching and a learning device. They also explain how and why any social simulation deliberately ignores certain aspects of reality in order to highlight others.

The Reunion of Action and Thought
Clark C. Abt

Physically inactive thought (mistrusted by Nietzsche) and mentally inactive action (mistrusted by all sensible men) are diseases of civilized man. He often wars without thinking and thinks without reward. Physical action in affluent civilization today is reserved for brutalities, chores, and play. Mental action is practiced chiefly by the physically inactive.

The classic Greek ideal embodied both thought and action, both individuation and participation, *in the same activities.* Today, intense participation in social decision-making is limited to a few individuals appointed, elected, or permitted to represent the larger society. Yet individuals can once again become involved, and thought and action can again be integrated, in games created to simulate these social processes. The zest for life felt at those exhilarating moments of history when men participated in effecting great changes on the models of great ideas can be recaptured by simulations of roles in the form of serious games.

"In dreams begin responsibilities," said the poet, and in games begin realities. Games offer expanded possibilities for action in a mode that, while chiefly mental, includes the felt freedom, intuitive speed, and reactive responses of physical movements.

The word "game" signifies one of those incredibly rich concepts of human activity that have many roots and implications. Even the barest dictionary definition suggests protean significance. "Amusement, diversion" "Fun, sport"—with sport suggesting a physical activity combined with an entertaining mental one. "A procedure for gaining an end," as in playing a waiting game. "A field of gainful activity," like the newspaper game. "A

physical or mental competition conducted according to rules with the participants in direct opposition to each other," a general but misleading definition since the participants need not be in direct opposition. "A situation involving opposing interests given specific information and allowed a choice of moves with the object of maximizing their wins and minimizing their losses," a useful, if incomplete, economic definition. As a verb, "to play for a stake." As an adjective, "having a resolute unyielding spirit," presumably in some serious or sporting conflict.

Consider the words appearing in these definitions: amusement, sport, procedure, gain, activity, competition, rules, participants, opposition, information, moves, object, maximizing, minimizing, win, lose, play, spirit. Some of these words describe the formal structure of games: procedure, rules, participants, information, moves, winning and losing. Others suggest the motivation of the participants: amusement, gain, competition, opposition, maximizing, minimizing, play, spirit. Yet all purposeful human activities involve participants, rules and procedures, success and failure. And indeed, the wide use of "game" as a metaphor for many social, economic, political, and military activities shows how much we assume about the formal similarity between games and real-life activities.

My own quite impressionistic view is that a

game is a particular way of looking at something, anything. This "way of looking" has two main components, a rational, analytic one and an emotional, creative, dramatic one. The game's analytic component sees in certain aspects of life—family, love, friendship, education, profession, commerce, war, politics, partying—common formal or structural characteristics identical to those of games. These formal characteristics include some or all of the game elements of competing actors or roles or players, objectives or goals that are usually unattainable by all actors at once, resources and powers that the actors use to try to gain their objectives, rules or laws or customs that limit or handicap the actions of the actors and tend to balance them so that the outcome tends to be uncertain, and definite conceptions of winning or losing that are important but mercifully impermanent.

The emotional, creative, dramatic component of the game is made up of a curious combination of optimistic beliefs in the luck of "another chance" and a pessimistic respect for the odds, the chanciness of it all. It is basically an existential view of man's acting, despite uncertainty, to achieve conflicting goals that end up mattering less than the action itself. "It's how you play the game. . . ." Ignorance need be no bar to action. It is, also, pessimistic (and romantic) in its view of life as conflict—with others, with nature, with self—but always unresolved oppositions, uncertainties, overcomings of obstacles. And it offers a kind of spiritual conquest of all evils by incorporating them into stimulating adversary roles that are as necessary to the good as the black is to the red—something the religion game developed long ago.

Games also include a no-nonsense operational ethic that allows no real excuse for losing. It has respect for "the money ball-player" who delivers despite obstacles and knows there is no justification—in game terms—for not doing so. This is an ethic of personal responsibility, in which there are no real excuses except "bad luck," which is a viable excuse only once in a while.

Reduced to its formal essence, a game is an *activity* among two or more independent *decision-makers* seeking to achieve their *objectives* in some *limiting context*. A more conventional definition would say that a game is a contest with rules among adversaries trying to win objectives. The trouble with this definition is that not all games are contests among adversaries—in some games the players cooperate to achieve a common goal against an obstructing force or natural situation that is itself not really a player since it does not have objectives.

Of course, most real-life activities involve in-dependent decision-makers seeking to achieve objectives in some limiting context. The autonomy of human wills and the diversity of human motives result in gamelike forms in all human interactions, and in this sense all human history can be regarded as gamelike in nature.

* * *

Games may be played seriously or casually. We are concerned with *serious games* in the sense that these games have an explicit and carefully thought-out educational purpose and are not intended to be played primarily for amusement. This does not mean that serious games are not, or should not be, entertaining. We reject the somewhat Calvinistic notion that serious and virtuous activities cannot be "fun." If an activity having good educational results can offer, in addition, immediate emotional satisfaction to the participants, it is an ideal instructional method, motivating and rewarding learning as well as facilitating it.

The term "serious" is also used in the sense of study, relating to matters of great interest and importance, raising questions not easily solved, and having important possible consequences. None of these aspects of serious games need be associated with their customarily heavy behavioral baggage of piousness and solemnity. Games may be significant without being solemn, interesting without being hilarious, earnest and purposeful without being humorless, and difficult without being frustrating. They may deal with important behavioral problems, and they may concern substantive problems in almost all academic and intellectual fields.

* * *

The need to experiment inexpensively and creatively is pervasive. Most people experiment with psycho-social situations throughout their lives in ways having most of the elements of games. What we are discussing here are the extended and novel applications of a very traditional developmental mode of human behavior. The oxymoron of *Serious Games* unites the seriousness of thought and problems that require it with the experimental and emotional freedom of active play. Serious games combine the analytic and questioning concentration of the scientific viewpoint with the intuitive freedom and rewards of imaginative, artistic acts.

The abstract representation of real life in game form does not render the game any less capable of teaching "true" knowledge. One does not have to be Shakespeare to understand his plays (which are, after all, monumental literary games), but acting in the plays can yield a more vivid and lasting view of Shakespeare than would a teacher's reading of the plays to a class.

Jean Piaget has said, "Knowledge is not a copy of reality. To know an object, to know an event, is not simply to look at it and make a mental copy, or image, of it. To know an object is to act on it. To know is to modify, to transform the object, and to understand the process of this transformation, and as a consequence to understand the way the object is constructed. An operation is thus the essence of knowledge, it is an internalized action which modifies the object of knowledge." He adds, "Intelligence is born of action," and "Anything is only understood to the extent that it is reinvented." People in daily life constantly invent and reinvent situations in order to learn from them. Yet too often people fail to recognize that reinventing a situation in which one has been an actor and perhaps reliving or revising decisions made is, in effect, to play a game. People tend to look for an abstract pattern within the situation or to compare situations in order to come to some new abstract conclusion. Yet they often fail to realize that it is an active situation which has led to their new abstract knowledge.

* * *

Games are effective teaching and training devices for students of all ages and in many situations because they are highly motivating, and because they communicate very efficiently the concepts and facts of many subjects. They create dramatic representations of the real problem being studied. The players assume realistic roles, face problems, formulate strategies, make decisions, and get fast feedback on the consequences of their action. Also, with games one can evaluate the students' performances without risking the costs of having errors made in "real-world" tryouts and without some of the distortions inherent in direct examination.

In short, serious games offer us a rich field for a risk-free, active exploration of serious intellectual and social problems. In games man can once again play the exciting and dynamic roles he always enjoyed before society became so compartmentalized. The role-playing that students undertake in games that simulate life is excellent preparation for the real roles they will play in society in later life.

References
1. Jennings, Frank G. "Jean Piaget: Notes on Learning." *Saturday Review*, May 20th, 1967.

What and Why Is a Simulation?

John R. Raser

Man uses verbal or logical analogies because they are esthetically pleasing or because they communicate vividly: "The vessel ploughed through the water." Analogy, or metaphor, is so deeply embedded in language that we are unaware of all but the most obvious. Verbal and logical analogies might almost be called the foundations of thought. By the use of analogy, what is abstract may be made concrete, and what is complex may be made simple. Thus, in the words of Socrates, Plato told his audience that the just man can be understood more clearly by examining the man "writ large," the just state. John of Salisbury reversed Plato by describing the state as a man, with the king as the head, the soldiers as the arms, and God as the soul. And Jesus told his followers that the man of true faith is like a lily of the field that takes no thought of the morrow.

Such analogies and similes are bridges that enable us to move from the simple, the concrete, and the specific, to the complexities and abstractions with which we wish to grapple. Analogies are tools for turning the *symbolic* into the *iconic*, thus giving form and substance to what is illusive and invisible. Think of the power of the Cross as a Christian symbol, an enormously economical abstraction; and of the even greater emotional and intellectual power of a painting (an "ikon") of the Crucifixion.

When the social scientists speak of "simulation," however, they are restricting the term to a much narrower sense than that used in the paragraphs above. Before it is possible to understand just how and why social scientists use simulation, it is necessary to grasp the exact sense in which they use the word.

A simulation is a model of a system. Other models . . . may attempt to represent a system through verbal means, mathematical means, or pictorial means. Like simulations, they involve the abstraction of certain aspects of the system one is studying and an attempt to replicate these aspects by other means, such as words or mathematical symbols. But the simulation model differs in that it is an *operating* model. Once the variables that have been selected are given values within the simulation and the relations among the variables are specified, the model is allowed to operate. It may operate through the interaction of people who play roles within the model; or it may operate on a computer. The rules given to the human participants in the simulation or the computer program represent the premises of the model. Its operation produces the implications.[1]

As compared with a Tinker Toy model of a molecule, which can represent only static structure, not process, a simulation can be thought of as a *dynamic model*. Simulators, therefore, must try not only to build a model of system *structure*, but also to incorporate system *processes*. In doing so, they abstract, simplify, and aggregate, in order to introduce into the model more clarity than exists in the referent system.

Abstraction and Simplification

What is abstracted? That is, which components and relationships are included in the simulation and which are not? This will depend on the purposes of the simulator; it cannot be decided in a vacuum. Relevance or irrelevance can be determined only within the framework of a particular goal. Let us take, for example, the simulation of an aircraft in flight. If the aim is to study the "lift" provided by a particular type of airframe configuration, then a wooden form shaped like the aircraft in question placed in a wind tunnel will provide the data needed. We can eliminate all the internal workings of the plane, except, perhaps, those needed to provide for the aileron and tail settings that govern its flight. Details such as radio equipment, seats, wiring, fuel tanks, and stewardesses, which, from one point of view, would make the simulation a more complete and accurate representation of an aircraft in flight—and thus more "valid"—are, in fact, only expensive and distracting rubbish. The usefulness and, thus, the "validity" of the simulation are achieved through intelligent abstraction and simplification, not through detailed and accurate representation of the entire system in question.

If, on the other hand, the aim of the simulator is to study human fatigue on an aircraft in flight, then a fairly detailed simulation of the

[1] Sidney Verba, "Simulation, Reality, and Theory in International Relations," World Politics, 16 (1964), p. 491.

This reading is reprinted from John R. Raser, *Simulation and Society*. Boston: Allyn and Bacon, 1969, pp. 5, 10–12, 15–19, 29–30, 32, 35–37, and 43–44. Raser is a political scientist at the Claremont Graduate School and the Western Behavioral Sciences Institute.

interior of the aircraft will be needed, with its space limitations, its physical layout, its vibrations and noises, and its human occupants. The external configuration and air speed can be ignored.

So the design of the simulation is determined by the specific problem to be studied, not by general considerations of "perfect replication." In fact, the entire idea of perfect replication is nonsense. No two things can be identical in *all* respects; they have differing positions in time and/or in space, if nothing else. When we say that a model is a *representation* of something, we imply that the two differ in some respects. It is important to bear in mind that all modeling begins with *abstraction* and *simplification*; they constitute "the name of the game" rather than being inconvenient limitations that simulators could overcome if they had more funds, better facilities, more computer memory-space, or a more comprehensive theory.

It is equally important to recognize that for some purposes a very simple model is preferable to a more complicated one, if only because it is cheaper and easier to manipulate. The difficult questions that model-builders face concern *which* elements, *which* relationships, *which* processes should be included, and which can be neglected. It is to answer these questions that modelers cry for better theory. The theory regarding airfoil lift, for example, is so well worked out that the problem could probably be solved in a few minutes on a computer rather than in a wind tunnel. But the theories regarding human fatigue and its relationship to noise, space limitations, the presence or absence of other people, or the activity being engaged in, are so primitive that the simulation builder would be hard put to know just what he should include in his simulation and what he may exclude in order to obtain useful and generalizable results.

In sum, then, simulations tap into different bodies of theory about referent systems, depending on the simulation purposes. It is not possible to judge the merits of a simulation on the basis of its simplicity or complexity except in terms of its purpose. It is certainly possible, however, to judge a simulation according to the validity of the theories or part-theories that it incorporates. A simulation, for example, that attempts to represent the movement of the heavenly bodies in space would be rejected if it were based on the theory that space is filled with ether. Simulation shares the problems of all other scientific endeavors in that the usefulness and generalizability of its results depend on the adequacy and validity of the theory on which it is based.

* * *

Why Simulate?

Why do people build simulations? The primary answers can probably be subsumed under the headings of *economy*, *visibility*, *reproducibility*, and *safety*, although there are certainly other reasons as well.

Economy

It is frequently cheaper to study a given phenomenon in a model or in a simulation than in its natural setting. So whereas constructing and operating a simulation frequently is an extremely expensive proposition, it is usually less so than the alternative of attempting to gain the desired information from the referent world. For example, to build a scale model of an air frame and place it in a wind tunnel, operate the wind tunnel, and make observations of the flow of smoke over the foil under different configurations is time consuming and expensive, but far less so than to build a full size air frame, incorporate it into an aircraft, and to fly it under the same variety of conditions. Experiments can be performed on the model much more economically than on what it models.

Furthermore, experiments performed on a model can eliminate costly mistakes that might cause waste or disaster if not caught. Assume for a moment that our intrepid simulator has been able to overcome all the difficulties we discussed in connection with the harbor simulation, and that it functions properly. Now the construction of a breakwater is contemplated. By adding a model of the proposed breakwater to his simulation of the harbor, he can determine whether its presence will set into motion any new currents or other unforeseen developments which might have undesirable consequences for the harbor as a whole. Lacking this kind of predictive device, the real breakwater might indeed reduce the chop and swell—but at the unanticipated cost of depositing a sand bar requiring monthly dredging of the navigational channel!

So there are two senses in which the use of simulation may be economical. First, because it is usually cheaper to experiment with a model than with the real thing; and, second, because costly mistakes can be avoided by "running it through in advance."

Visibility

Using a simulation frequently increases the visibility of the phenomenon under study in two ways. First, the phenomenon may be physically more accessible, and hence more readily observed. Sitting behind a glass and watching smoke flow past an air foil in a wind tunnel is much easier than trying to measure the airflow past the wing of a plane in flight. Watching a silt deposit build up in a table top replica of a harbor is much easier than trying to measure what is occurring under 80 feet of muddy sea water. In fact, the "accessibility gap" may be so wide in some instances that observation of the phenomenon under study may be virtually impossible in nature, but extremely easy in a simulation. A working model of the solar system is one example; another example is the computer simulation of nuclear warfare that enables strategists to study the amount of destruction resulting from differences in weather conditions, weapons yield and reliability, time of warning, and extent of preparation.

A second way that simulation may increase the visibility of the phenomenon under study is by bringing it to the foreground, highlighting it, *clarifying* it. It is difficult to study the circulation of blood in a living organism, for the system of which it is a part is so complex that interference with it may radically affect the entire system. But in a *simulation* of blood circulation, it is possible to block the flow of blood at various points and observe the results.

Frequently, the phenomenon under study is so confused and chaotic that it is hard to make any sense of it. Consider the student who wishes to test the basic principles of international relations, who wants to look at world affairs in order to understand them. What does he need to look at? How shall he decide what is relevant? Where shall he start, what should he observe? The United Nations? The daily newspapers? The International Court of Justice? The flows of international trade? The national military postures? The thousands of intergovernmental and private agencies? If he tries to become *au courant* with all the elements of international politics, he will almost certainly end up confused and exhausted.

But if someone has built a simulation of international relations that incorporates most of the salient elements in simplified and explicit form, the student can study it and so gain a grasp of general outlines, an operating framework, upon which he can then elaborate the details in which he is particularly interested. For him, the simulation has functioned to *simplify* a system whose complexity obscures specific phenomena. Hydraulic models of the economic system or little plastic digital computers for children serve this same purpose of clarifying and simplifying the complex by eliminating all but the salient and relevant phenomena. So simulations aid visibility by making certain kinds of phenomena more accessible for observation and measurement, and by introducing clarity into what is otherwise complex, chaotic, or confused.

Reproducibility

Simulations allow scholars to reproduce chains of events that they could not otherwise observe repeatedly. There are at least two reasons for wanting to reproduce events. The first reason involves the element of *chance.* For example, suppose a researcher wants to find out how long passengers will have to wait for buses at the peak rush hour. He could station observers in the bus terminal for 360 days in a row, and through an hour by hour count, gain some understanding of those elements of chance which simply cannot be predicted, such as how many buses will be stopped at how many red lights, or how many passengers will not have the correct change at ticket windows. But a computer simulation of the operation of a bus terminal is not only far more economical, but also allows the researcher to build the element of chance into his simulation, run it repeatedly, and learn that the wait will be "X" minutes under given conditions with a probability of, say, .86 that it will be no more than "X plus 1" and no less than "X minus 1" minutes. These probabilities can be derived only by letting the simulation run often enough to allow all the possible outcomes to occur, and by observing the frequencies with which they do in fact occur.

Also, of course, simulations allow the student to reproduce many times a situation that might never occur again in real life: this aspect enables him to examine certain variables and relationships with respect to their influence on the outcome of the real life situation. It enables him, in effect, to play the fascinating historical game, "What might have happened if . . . ?"

In the terminology of research, simulation allows us to observe the effects of different kinds of manipulation of the input variables: it is possible to change assumptions, to alter the input parameter values, and to modify the relationships among elements of the system. For example, in the simulation of a nuclear exchange, we might want to ask, "What difference does 15 minutes' warning as opposed to 30 minutes' warning make in the amount of destruction? What difference does it make in the severity of the retaliation that will be suffered if the counterforce missiles are only 70% reliable instead of 90% reliable?" Changing input variables is closely related to the technique of allowing chance to operate in a random fashion, except that in this case we alter the variables in ways that interest us. We might ask, as another example, "What difference will it make in the international system if the chief of state of one of the major powers is highly paranoid as opposed to self-confident and trusting?

So simulations are valuable because they

allow phenomena to be reproduced, and thus (1) enable the experimenter to derive statistical probabilities when the outcome is uncertain, and/or (2) enable him to vary numerous aspects of the system in ways that yield profitable insights into how the system operates. In other words, simulations allow controlled experiments to be made that would otherwise be impossible.

Safety

Frequently, propositions may be tested in simulations more safely than in the real world. There are two senses in which this is true. The first is best illustrated by the "flight trainer" for prospective pilots, or by the "reflex test" equipment sometimes used to determine whether a given person is qualified to operate certain machines safely. These are essentially training or testing simulations—laboratories for measuring or increasing human skill. The safety features of such simulations are obvious. Pilot error in the flight trainer may result in a scowl from the instructor, but it won't produce a fiery death or the smashup of a multimillion-dollar aircraft. Discovering that one's reflexes are slow may be humiliating, but it is better to discover it in a laboratory than at 70 miles per hour on a superhighway.

Not only do simulations allow us to avoid putting human beings in dangerous situations, but they also allow us to study dangerous situations themselves without actually creating them. The simulation of a thermo-nuclear exchange is one example. The computer simulation of a controlled nuclear reaction is another example; it produces information about tolerances of stability without risking the hazards of a real reactor's going "critical." So simulations are used for safety purposes, both to protect human beings while they are being trained or studied, and to produce laboratory analogues of dangerous phenomena that we need to study.

The decision to use a simulation may be governed by one or another of these features of economy, visibility, reproducibility, and safety, depending on the research situation. Still other reasons for using simulations are that participation in a simulation deepens the involvement of the subjects, and that simulations offer an opportunity to stage "future events" so that they may be analyzed and "played through." These other reasons for simulating will be elaborated more fully in the context in which they occur.

So far, we have discussed simulations without drawing a distinction between those used in the physical sciences and those used by social scientists. In many cases, the distinction is not clear cut—the computer simulation of a bus terminal is an example—for both physical and human behav-

ioral factors must be built into the model. However, most of the examples given so far have been drawn from the physical sciences and from engineering, because in many ways the problems are more straight-forward and the examples clearer. In a sense, I have attempted to use a principle of simulation in this chapter, by using the more simple to provide a model for understanding the more abstract and complex. The following section deals with the special problems and promises of simulation and games in the social sciences.

* * *

The Gaming Approach to Simulation

In a simulation, the rules for translating external variables into simulation variables are highly formal; in more colloquial language, the rules are tight and tough. All substitutions and analogies must be defended; the relations between variables must be carefully specified; the operation of the simulation must be governed by mathematical rules. Clearly, then, the translation of variables must be based on adequate theory and data.

In a "game," according to my definition, there is more leeway with respect to analogical consistency and strictness. The rules for translating "real life" variables into simulation variables are less demanding, so it is possible to "play around" a bit and "make do."

* * *

Thus, *the game can serve as a "pre-simulation," to be used both as a laboratory for studying basic principles of human behavior and as an admittedly inadequate framework for conducting research leading to improvement of the framework itself.*

This "gaming" approach to simulation building is one that a colleague refers to as "messing around" in science. This is not a disparaging phrase; "messing around" is a legitimate way to increase knowledge. In fact, some philosophers of science have argued that this approach to building a body of knowledge about human social behavior is sounder and more productive than the more traditional methods.

* * *

The "gaming" approach to simulation-construction is similar to lifting oneself up by one's bootstraps or, perhaps more accurately, to rebuilding an airplane while it is in flight. Although this may at first seem like an exercise in absurdity, there are sound reasons for advocating it as a research strategy. But whether we turn to games as "pre-simulations"—as a means of elaborating and refining theory that can then be embodied in a simulation devoid of human participants—or whether we use games as a laboratory for studying the behavior of human subjects, we confront certain basic epistemological questions.

* * *

The kind of "knowing," which comes from the recognition of patterns and thus of the sub-units of those patterns, is called *distal* knowledge. We confront a collection of fragments—bits of punctiform data, each of which is uninterpretable—and suddenly we see the entire pattern or context. Common expressions used to describe this experience include "insight," "revelation," "seeing how it all fits together," and "having it suddenly all make sense." They all express the recognition that when an entire context or pattern is grasped, *each part of the pattern* is also more clearly apprehended. In a sense, we may say that the whole is greater than the sum of its parts.

* * *

Now we can use pattern-recognition not only in understanding concrete physical phenomena, but also in handling abstractions—in testing concepts and in building theory. An idea acquires new meaning when it is set in the context of other ideas; then, both idea and context enrich and illuminate each other. Scientists increasingly recognize that the inclusion of theories and part-theories in a larger construct is a powerful technique for enhancing data-gathering and theory-testing, *even though the scientists may lack confidence in the absolute validity of many of the theories included in the construct.* As Donald T. Campbell observes, the certainty of identifying any single part is facilitated by a prior identification of the whole, even if the prior identification is uncertain and partially erroneous.

We are now back to our starting point; this is the process in science we referred to earlier as "messing around." It is the process involved in constructing a "game" that you hope eventually to develop into a simulation. Instead of waiting to build a construct (simulation) until you are certain of the nature of all its elements, you build a game that requires tentatively postulating the entire model. By watching the behavior of the operating sub-parts of the tentative model and by noting how they "fit" with its other parts, you can check and refine both the sub-parts and the model as a whole.

* * *

These arguments point directly to "games" as ideal laboratory environments, if we are interested in the interaction between a human being and the system of which he is a part. Games provide a powerful research tool for generating information. As knowledge about basic human behavior increases, the game evolves towards its end point—simulation.

References
1. Campbell, Donald T. "Pattern Matching as an Essential in Distal-Knowing." In *The Psychology of Egon Brunswick,* ed. K. R. Hammond. (New York: Holt, Rinehart & Winston), 1966.
2. Verba, Sidney. "Simulation Reality and Theory in International Relations." *World Politics* 16 (1964).

Part 2

Social Protest and Social Change

Typically, a group emerges in SIMSOC that is radically discontented with the existing situation in the society. Such groups have many analogues in a real society and they experience the same dilemmas that protest groups face in the real world. Should they work within the system, pursuing moderate strategies that do not alienate those whom they wish to influence? Should they pursue more dramatic and militant strategies in the spirit of confrontation politics? Should they express their frustration and anger even if this does not necessarily bring about the changes they desire? Can they trust their own leaders not to become a new oppressor in different garb?

The readings in this section examine the issue of protest primarily from the standpoint of groups seeking social change. Lipsky views protest as a resource of the powerless and analyzes it as an instrument of change rather than an expression of frustration or anger. It is, as he points out, an instrument with important limitations but it may be the only instrument available to some groups. Warren discusses the moral dilemma between the desire to achieve a society that one *knows* is better and the respect for the integrity of others who honestly may want something different. Gurr takes a dual perspective, asking both how reformist and revolutionary groups should act to achieve their objectives and how the establishment should act to block such change. Gamson also takes a dual perspective, arguing that political trust in the leaders of a society can be a handicap to a discontented group that desires change even as it gives a society's leaders sufficient power to take effective action on the outstanding problems in the society.

Protest as a Political Resource

Michael Lipsky

The frequent resort to protest activity by relatively powerless groups in recent American politics suggests that protest represents an important aspect of minority group and low income group politics. At the same time that Negro civil rights strategists have recognized the problem of using protest as a meaningful political instrument, groups associated with the "war on poverty" have increasingly received publicity for protest activity. Saul Alinsky's Industrial Areas Foundation, for example, continues to receive invitations to help organize low income communities because of its ability to mobilize poor people around the tactic of protest. The riots which dominated urban affairs in the summer of 1967 appear not to have diminished the dependence of some groups on protest as a mode of political activity.

This article provides a theoretical perspective on protest activity as a political resource. The discussion is concentrated on the limitations inherent in protest which occur because of the need of protest leaders to appeal to four constituencies at the same time. As the concept of protest is

This reading is reprinted from Michael Lipsky, "Protest as a Political Resource." *American Political Science Review* 62 (December, 1968), pp. 1144–58. Footnotes have been deleted and the style of references have been changed. Lipsky is a political scientist at MIT.

developed here, it will be argued that protest leaders must nurture and sustain an organization comprised of people with whom they may or may not share common values. They must articulate goals and choose strategies so as to maximize their public exposure through communications media. They must maximize the impact of third parties in the political conflict. Finally, they must try to maximize chances of success among those capable of granting goals. The tensions inherent in manipulating these four constituencies at the same time form the basis of this discussion of protest as a political process. It is intended to place aspects of the civil rights movement in a framework which suggests links between protest organizations and the general political processes in which such organizations operate.

1. "Protest" Conceptualized

Protest activity as it has been adopted by elements of the civil rights movement and others has not been studied extensively by social scientists. Some of the most suggestive writings have been done as case studies of protest movements in single southern cities. These works generally lack a framework or theoretical focus which would encourage generalization from the cases. More systematic efforts have been attempted in approaching the dynamics of biracial committees in the South, and comprehensively assessing the efficacy of Negro political involvement in Durham, N.C. and Philadelphia, Pa. In their excellent assessment of Negro politics in the South, Matthews and Prothro have presented a thorough profile of southern Negro students and their participation in civil rights activities. Protest is also discussed in passing in recent explorations of the social-psychological dimensions of Negro ghetto politics and the still highly suggestive, although pre-1960's, work on Negro political leadership by James Q. Wilson. These and other less systematic works on contemporary Negro politics, for all of their intuitive insights and valuable documentation, offer no theoretical formulations which encourage conceptualization about the interaction between recent Negro political activity and the political process.

Heretofore the best attempt to place Negro protest activity in a framework which would generate additional insights has been that of James Q. Wilson. Wilson has suggested that protest activity be conceived as a problem of bargaining in which the basic problem is that Negro groups lack political resources to exchange. Wilson called this "the problem of the powerless."

While many of Wilson's insights remain valid, his approach is limited in applicability because it defines protest in terms of mass action or response and as utilizing exclusively negative inducements in the bargaining process. Negative inducements are defined as inducements which are not absolutely preferred but are preferred over alternative possibilities. Yet it might be argued that protest designed to appeal to groups which oppose suffering and exploitation, for example, might be offering positive inducements in bargaining. A few Negro students sitting at a lunch counter might be engaged in what would be called protest, and by their actions might be trying to appeal to other groups in the system with positive inducements. Additionally, Wilson's concentration on Negro civic action, and his exclusive interest in exploring the protest process to explain Negro civic action, tend to obscure comparison with protest activity which does not necessarily arise within the Negro community.

Assuming a somewhat different focus, protest activity is defined as a mode of political action oriented toward objection to one or more policies or conditions, characterized by showmanship or display of an unconventional nature, and undertaken to obtain rewards from political or economic systems while working within the systems. The "problem of the powerless" in protest activity is to activate "third parties" to enter the implicit or explicit bargaining arena in ways favorable to the protesters. This is one of the few ways in which they can "create" bargaining resources. It is intuitively unconvincing to suggest that fifteen people sitting uninvited in the Mayor's office have the power to move City Hall. A better formulation would suggest that the people sitting in may be able to appeal to a wider public to which the city administration is sensitive. Thus in successful protest activity the *reference publics* of protest *targets* may be conceived as explicitly or implicitly reacting to protest in such a way that target groups or individuals respond in ways favorable to the protesters.

It should be emphasized that the focus here is on protest by relatively powerless groups. Illustrations can be summoned, for example, of activity designated as "protest" involving high status pressure groups or hundreds of thousands of people. While such instances may share some of the characteristics of protest activity, they may not represent examples of developing political resources by relatively powerless groups because the protesting groups may already command political resources by virtue of status, numbers or cohesion.

It is appropriate also to distinguish between the relatively restricted use of the concept of protest adopted here and closely related political strategies which are often designated as "protest" in popular usage. Where groups already possess sufficient resources with which to bargain, as in the case of some economic boycotts and labor strikes, they may be said to engage in "direct confrontation." Similarly, protest which represents efforts to "activate reference publics" should be distinguished from "alliance formation," where third parties are induced to join the conflict, but where the value orientations of third parties are sufficiently similar to those of the protesting group that concerted or coordinated action is possible. Alliance formation is particularly desirable for relatively powerless groups if they seek to join the decision-making process as participants.

The distinction between activating reference publics and alliance formation is made on the assumption that where goal orientations among protest groups and the reference publics of target groups are similar, the political dynamics of petitioning target groups are different than when such goal orientations are relatively divergent. Clearly the more similar the goal orientations, the greater the likelihood of protest success, other things being equal. This discussion is intended to highlight, however, those instances where goal orientations of reference publics depart significantly, in direction or intensity, from the goals of protest groups.

Say that to protest some situation, A would like to enter a bargaining situation with B. But A has nothing B wants, and thus cannot bargain. A then attempts to create political resources by activating other groups to enter the conflict. A then organizes to take action against B with respect to certain goals. *Information concerning these goals must be conveyed through communications media* (C, D, and E) to F, G, and H, which are B's *reference publics.* In response to the reactions of F, G, and H, or in anticipation of their reactions, B responds, *in some way,* to the protesters' demands. This formulation requires the conceptualization of protest activity when undertaken to create bargaining resources as a political process which requires communication and is characterized by a multiplicity of constituencies for protest leadership.

A schematic representation of the process of protest as utilized by relatively powerless groups is presented in the following figure. In contrast to a simplistic pressure group model which would posit a direct relationship between pressure group and pressured, the following discussion is guided by the assumption (derived from observation) that protest is a highly indirect process in which communications media and the reference publics of protest targets play critical roles. It is also a process characterized by reciprocal relations, in which

Schematic Representation of the Process of Protest by Relatively Powerless Groups

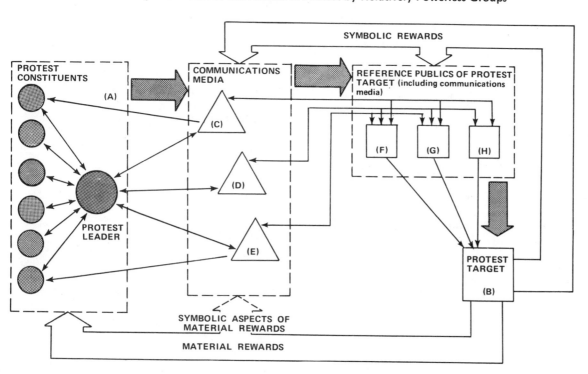

protest leaders frame strategies according to their perception of the needs of (many) other actors.

In this view protest constituents limit the options of protest leaders at the same time that the protest leader influences their perception of the strategies and rhetoric which they will support. Protest activity is filtered through the communications media in influencing the perceptions of the reference publics of protest targets. To the extent that the influence of reference publics is supportive of protest goals, target groups will dispense symbolic or material rewards. Material rewards are communicated directly to protest constituents. Symbolic rewards are communicated in part to protest constituents, but primarily are communicated to the reference publics of target groups, who provide the major stimuli for public policy pronouncements.

The study of protest as adopted by relatively powerless groups should provide insights into the structure and behavior of groups involved in civil rights politics and associated with the "war on poverty." It should direct attention toward the ways in which administrative agencies respond to "crises." Additionally, the study of protest as a political resource should influence some general conceptualizations of American political pluralism. Robert Dahl, for example, describes the "normal American political process" as

> one in which there is a high probability that an active and legitimate group in the population can make itself heard effectively at some crucial stage in the process of decision.

Although he agrees that control over decisions is unevenly divided in the population, Dahl writes:

> When I say that a group is heard "effectively" I mean more than the simple fact that it makes a noise; I mean that one or more officials are not only ready to listen to the noise, but expect to suffer in some significant way if they do not placate the group, its leaders, or its most vociferous members. To satisfy the group may require one or more of a great variety of actions by the responsive leader: pressure for substantive policies, appointments, graft, respect, expression of the appropriate emotions, or the right combination of reciprocal noises.

These statements, which in some ways resemble David Truman's discussion of the power of "potential groups," can be illuminated by the study of protest activity in three ways. First, what are the probabilities that relatively powerless groups can make themselves heard effectively? In what ways will such groups be heard or "steadily appeased"? Concentration on the process of protest activity may reveal the extent to which, and the conditions under which, relatively powerless groups are likely to prove effective. Protest undertaken to obstruct policy decisions, for example, may enjoy greater success probabilities than protest undertaken in an effort to evoke constructive policy innovations.

Second, does it make sense to suggest that all groups which make noises will receive responses from public officials? Perhaps the groups which make noises do not have to be satisfied at all, but it is other groups which receive assurances or recognition. Third, what are the probabilities that groups which make noises will receive tangible rewards, rather than symbolic assurances? Dahl lumps these rewards together in the same paragraph, but dispensation of tangible rewards clearly has a different impact upon groups than the dispensation of symbolic rewards. Dahl is undoubtedly correct when he suggests that the relative fluidity of American politics is a critical characteristic of the American political system. But he is less precise and less convincing when it comes to analyzing the extent to which the system is indeed responsive to the relatively powerless groups of the "average citizen."

The following sections are an attempt to demonstrate the utility of the conceptualization of the protest process presented above. This will be done by exploring the problems encountered and the strains generated by protest leaders in interacting with four constituencies. It will be useful to concentrate attention on the maintenance and enhancement needs not only of the large formal organizations which dominate city politics, but also of the ad hoc protest groups which engage them in civic controversy. It will also prove rewarding to examine the role requirements of individuals in leadership positions as they perceive the problems of constituency manipulation. In concluding remarks some implications of the study of protest for the pluralist description of American politics will be suggested.

II. Protest Leadership and Organizational Base

The organizational maintenance needs of relatively powerless, low income, ad hoc protest groups center around the tension generated by the need for leadership to offer symbolic and intangible inducements to protest participation when immediate, material rewards cannot be anticipated, and the need to provide at least the promise of material rewards. Protest leaders must try to evoke responses from other actors in the political process, at the same time that they pay attention to participant organizational needs. Thus relatively deprived groups in the political system not only receive symbolic reassurance while material rewards from the system are withheld, but protest leaders have a stake in perpetuating the notion that relatively powerless groups retain political efficacy despite what in many cases is obvious evidence to the contrary.

The tension embraced by protest leaders over the nature of inducements toward protest participation accounts in part for the style adopted and goals selected by protest leaders. Groups which seek psychological gratification from politics, but cannot or do not anticipate material political rewards, may be attracted to militant protest leaders. To these groups, angry rhetoric may prove a desirable quality in the short run. Where groups depend upon the political system for tangible benefits, or where participation in the system provides intangible benefits, moderate leadership is likely to prevail. Wilson has observed similar tendencies among Negro leaders of large, formal organizations. It is no less true for leadership of protest groups. Groups whose members derive tangible satisfactions from political participation will not condone leaders who are stubborn in compromise or appear to question the foundations of the system. This coincides with Truman's observation:

> Violation of the "rules of the game" normally will weaken a group's cohesion, reduce its status in the community, and expose it to the claims of other groups.

On the other hand, the cohesion of relatively powerless groups may be strengthened by militant, ideological leadership which questions the rules of the game and challenges their legitimacy.

Cohesion is particularly important when protest leaders bargain directly with target groups. In that situation, leaders' ability to control protest constituents and guarantee their behavior represents a bargaining strength. For this reason Wilson stressed the bargaining difficulties of Negro leaders who cannot guarantee constituent behavior, and pointed out the significance of the strategy of projecting the image of group solidarity when the reality of cohesion is a fiction. Cohesion is less significant at other times. Divided leadership may prove productive by bargaining in tandem, or by minimizing strain among groups in the protest process. Further, community divisions may prove less detrimental to protest aims when strong third parties have entered the dispute originally generated by protest organizations.

The intangible rewards of assuming certain postures toward the political system may not be sufficient to sustain an organizational base. It may be necessary to renew constantly the intangible rewards of participation. And to the extent that people participate in order to achieve tangible benefits, their interest in a protest organization may depend upon the organization's relative material success. Protest leaders may have to tailor their style to present participants with tangible successes, or with the appearance of success. Leaders may have to define the issues with concern for increasing their ability to sustain organizations. The potential for protest among protest group members may have to be manipulated by leadership if the group is to be sustained.

The participants in protest organizations limit the flexibility of protest leadership. This obtains for two reasons. They restrict public actions by leaders who must continue to solicit active participant support, and they place restraints on the kinds of activities which can be considered appropriate for protest purposes. Poor participants cannot commonly be asked to engage in protest requiring air transportation. Participants may have anxieties related to their environment or historical situation which discourages engagement in some activities. They may be afraid of job losses, beatings by the police, or summary evictions. Negro protest in the Deep South has been inhibited by realistic expectations of retribution. Protests over slum housing conditions are undermined by tenants who expect landlord retaliation for engaging in tenant organizing activity. Political or ethical mores may conflict with a proposed course of action, diminishing participation.

On the other hand, to the extent that fears are real, or that the larger community perceives protest participants as subject to these fears, protest may actually be strengthened. Communications media and potential allies will consider more soberly the complaints of people who are understood to be placing themselves in jeopardy. When young children and their parents made the arduous bus trip from Mississippi to Washington, D.C. to protest the jeopardizing of Head Start funds, the courage and expense represented by their effort created a respect and visibility for their position which might not have been achieved by local protest efforts.

Protest activity may be undertaken by organizations with established relationship patterns, behavior norms, and role expectations. These organizations are likely to have greater access to other groups in the political system, and a demonstrated capacity to maintain themselves. Other protest groups, however, may be ad hoc arrangements without demonstrated internal or external relationship patterns. These groups will have different organizational problems, in response to which it is necessary to engage in different kinds of protest activity.

The scarcity of organizational resources also places limits upon the ability of relatively powerless groups to maintain the foundations upon which protest organizations develop. Relatively powerless groups, to engage in political activity of any kind, must command at least some resources. This is not tautological. Referring again to a continuum on which political groups are placed according to their relative command of resources, one may draw a line somewhere along the continuum representing a "threshold of civic group political participation." Clearly some groups along the continuum will possess some political resources (enough, say, to emerge for inspection) but not enough to exercise influence in civic affairs. Relatively powerless groups, to be influential, must cross the "threshold" to engage in politics. Although the availability of group resources is a critical consideration at all stages of the protest process, it is particularly important in explaining why some groups seem to "surface" with sufficient strength to command attention. The following discussion of some critical organizational resources should illuminate this point.

Skilled professionals frequently must be available to protest organizations. Lawyers, for example, play extremely important roles in enabling protest groups to utilize the judicial process and avail themselves of adequate preparation of court cases. Organizational reputation may depend upon a combination of ability to threaten the conventional political system and of exercising statutory rights in court. Availability of lawyers depends upon ability to pay fees and/or the attractiveness to lawyers of participation in protest group activity. Volunteer professional assistance may not prove adequate. One night a week volunteered by an aspiring politician in a housing clinic cannot satisfy the needs of a chaotic political movement. The need for skilled professionals is not restricted to lawyers. For example, a group seeking to protest an urban renewal policy might require the services of architects and city planners in order to present a viable alternative to a city proposal.

Financial resources not only purchase legal assistance, but enable relatively powerless groups to conduct minimum programs of political activities. To the extent that constituents are unable or unwilling to pay even small membership dues, then financing the cost of mimeographing flyers, purchasing supplies, maintaining telephone service, paying rent, and meeting a modest payroll become major organizational problems. And to the extent that group finances are supplied by outside individual contributions or government or foundation grants, the long-term options of the group are sharply constrained by the necessity of orienting group goals and tactics to anticipate the potential objections of financial supporters.

Some dependence upon even minimal financial resources can be waived if organizations evoke passionate support from constituents. Secretarial help and block organizers will come forward to work without compensation if they support the cause of neighborhood organizations or gain intangible benefits based upon association with the group. Protest organizations may also depend upon skilled non-professionals, such as college students, whose access to people and political and economic institutions often assist protest groups in cutting across income lines to seek support. Experience with ad hoc political groups, however, suggests that this assistance is sporadic and undependable. Transient assistance is particularly typical of skilled, educated, and employable volunteers whose abilities can be applied widely. The die-hards of ad hoc political groups are often those people who have no place else to go, nothing else to do.

Constituent support will be affected by the nature of the protest target and whether protest activity is directed toward defensive or assertive goals. Obstructing specific public policies may be easier than successfully recommending constructive policy changes. Orientations toward defensive goals may require less constituent energy, and less command over resources of money, expertise and status.

III. Protest Leadership and Communications Media

The communications media are extremely powerful in city politics. In granting or withholding publicity, in determining what information most people will have on most issues, and what alternatives they will consider in response to issues, the media truly, as Norton Long has put it, "set . . . the civic agenda." To the extent that successful protest activity depends upon appealing to, and/or threatening, other groups in the community, the communications media set the limits of protest action. If protest tactics are not considered significant by the media, or if newspapers and television reporters or editors decide to overlook protest tactics, protest organizations will not succeed. Like the tree falling unheard in the forest, there is no protest unless protest is perceived and projected.

A number of writers have noticed that the success of protest activity seems directly related to the amount of publicity it receives outside the immediate arena in which protest takes place. This view has not been stated systematically, but hints can be found in many sources. In the literature on civil rights politics, the relevance of publicity represents one of the few hypotheses available concerning the dynamics of successful protest activity.

When protest tactics do receive coverage in the communications media, the way in which they are presented will influence all other actors in the system, including the protesters themselves. Conformity to standards of newsworthiness in political style, and knowledge of the prejudices and desires of the individuals who determine media coverage in political skills, represent crucial determinants of leadership effectiveness.

The organizational behavior of newspapers can partly be understood by examining the maintenance and enhancement needs which direct them toward projects of civic betterment and impressions of accomplishment. But insight may also be gained by analyzing the role requirements of reporters, editors, and others who determine newspaper policy. Reporters, for example, are frequently motivated by the desire to contribute to civic affairs by their "objective" reporting of significant events; by the premium they place on accuracy; and by the credit which they receive for sensationalism and "scoops."

These requirements may be difficult to accommodate at the same time. Reporters demand newsworthiness of their subjects in the short run, but also require reliability and verifiability in the longer run. Factual accuracy may dampen newsworthiness. Sensationalism, attractive to some newspaper editors, may be inconsistent with reliable, verifiable narration of events. Newspapers at first may be attracted to sensationalism, and later demand verifiability in the interests of community harmony (and adherence to professional journalistic standards).

Most big city newspapers have reporters whose assignments permit them to cover aspects of city politics with some regularity. These reporters, whose "beats" may consist of "civil rights" or "poverty," sometimes develop close relationships with their news subjects. These relationships may develop symbiotic overtones because of the mutuality of interest between the reporter and the news subject. Reporters require fresh information on protest developments, while protest leaders have a vital interest in obtaining as much press coverage as possible.

Inflated reports of protest success may be understood in part by examining this relationship between reporter and protest leader. Both have role-oriented interests in projecting images of pro-

test strength and threat. In circumstances of great excitement, when competition from other news media representatives is high, a reporter may find that he is less governed by the role requirement of verification and reliability than he is by his editor's demand for "scoops" and news with high audience appeal.

On the other hand, the demands of the media may conflict with the needs of protest group maintenance. Consider the leader whose constituents are attracted solely by pragmatic statements not exceeding what they consider political "good taste." He is constrained from making militant demands which would isolate him from constituents. This constraint may cost him appeal in the press. However, the leader whose organizing appeal requires militant rhetoric may obtain eager press coverage only to find that his inflamatory statements lead to alienation of potential allies and exclusion from the explicit bargaining process.

News media do not report events in the same way. Television may select for broadcast only thirty seconds of a half-hour news conference. This coverage will probably focus on immediate events, without background or explanatory material. Newspapers may give more complete accounts of the same event. The most complete account may appear in the weekly edition of a neighborhood or ethnic newspaper. Differential coverage by news media, and differential news media habits in the general population, are significant factors in permitting protest leaders to juggle conflicting demands of groups in the protest process.

Similar tensions exist in the leader's relationships with protest targets. Ideological postures may gain press coverage and constituency approval, but may alienate target groups with whom it would be desirable to bargain explicitly. Exclusion from the councils of decision-making may have important consequences, since the results of target group deliberations may satisfy activated reference publics without responding to protest goals. If activated reference publics are required to increase the bargaining position of the protest group, protest efforts thereafter will have diminished chances of success.

IV. Protest Leadership and "Third Parties"

I have argued that the essence of political protest consists of activating third parties to participate in controversy in ways favorable to protest goals. In previous sections I have attempted to analyze some of the tensions which result from protest leaders' attempts to activate reference publics of protest targets at the same time that they must retain the interest and support of protest organization participants. This phenomenon is in evidence when Negro leaders, recognized as such by public officials, find their support eroded in the Negro community because they have engaged in explicit bargaining situations with politicians. Negro leaders are thus faced with the dilemma that when they behave like other ethnic group representers they are faced with loss of support from those whose intense activism has been aroused in the Negro community, yet whose support is vital if they are to remain credible as leaders to public officials.

The tensions resulting from conflicting maintenance needs of protest organizations and activated third parties present difficulties for protest leaders. One way in which these tensions can be minimized is by dividing leadership responsibilities. If more than one group is engaged in protest activity, protest leaders can, in effect, divide up public roles so as to reduce as much as possible the gap between the implicit demands of different groups for appropriate rhetoric, and what in fact is said. Thus divided leadership may perform the latent function of minimizing tensions among elements in the protest process by permitting different groups to listen selectively to protest spokesmen.

Another way in which strain among different groups can be minimized is through successful public relations. Minimization of strain may depend upon ambiguity of action or statement, deception, or upon effective inter-group communication. Failure to clarify meaning, or falsification, may increase protest effectiveness. Effective intra-group communication may increase the likelihood that protest constituents will "understand" that ambiguous or false public statements have "special meaning" and need not be taken seriously. The Machiavellian circle is complete when we observe that although lying may be prudent, the appearance of integrity and forthrightness is desirable for public relations, since these values are widely shared.

It has been observed [by Wilson] that "[t]he militant displays an unwillingness to perform those administrative tasks which are necessary to operate an organization. Probably the skills of the agitator and the skills of the administrator . . . are not incompatible, but few men can do both well." These skills may or may not be incompatible as personality traits, but they indeed represent conflicting role demands on protest leadership. When a protest leader exhausts time and energy conducting frequent press conferences, arranging for politicians and celebrities to appear at rallies, delivering speeches to sympathetic local groups, college symposia and other forums, constantly picketing for publicity and generally making "contacts," he is unable to pursue the direction of office routine, clerical tasks, research and analysis, and other chores.

The difficulties of delegating routine tasks are probably directly related to the skill levels and previous administrative experiences of group members. In addition, to the extent that involvement in protest organizations is a function of rewards received or expected by individuals because of the excitement or entertainment value of participation, then the difficulties of delegating routine, relatively uninteresting chores to group members will be increased. Yet attention to such details affects the perception of protest groups by organizations whose support or assistance may be desired in the future. These considerations add to the protest leader's problem of risking alienation of protest participants because of potentially unpopular cooperation with the "power structure."

In the protest paradigm developed here "third parties" refers both to the reference publics of target groups and, more narrowly, to the interest groups whose regular interaction with protest targets tends to develop into patterns of influence. We have already discussed some of the problems associated with activating the reference publics of target groups. In discussing the constraints placed upon protest, attention may be focused upon the likelihood that groups seeking to create political resources through protest will be included in the explicit bargaining process with other pressure groups. For protest groups, these constraints are those which occur because of class and political style, status, and organizational resources.

The established civic groups most likely to be concerned with the problems raised by relatively powerless groups are those devoted to service in the public welfare and those "liberally" oriented groups whose potential constituents are either drawn from the same class as the protest groups (such as some trade unions), or whose potential constituents are attracted to policies which appear to serve the interest of the lower class or minority groups (such as some reform political clubs). These civic groups have frequently cultivated clientele relationships with city agencies over long periods. Their efforts have been reciprocated by agency officials anxious to develop constituencies to support and defend agency administrative and budgetary policies. In addition, clientele groups are expected to endorse and legitimize agency aggrandizement. These relationships have been developed by agency officials and civic groups for mutual benefit, and cannot be destroyed, abridged or avoided without cost.

Protest groups may well be able to raise the

saliency of issues on the civic agenda through utilization of communications media and successful appeals or threats to wider publics, but admission to policy-making councils is frequently barred because of the angry, militant rhetorical style adopted by protest leaders. People in power do not like to sit down with rogues. Protest leaders are likely to have phrased demands in ways unacceptable to lawyers and other civic activists whose cautious attitude toward public policy may reflect not only their good intentions but their concern for property rights, due process, pragmatic legislating or judicial precedent.

Relatively powerless groups lack participation of individuals with high status whose endorsement of specific proposals lend them increased legitimacy. Good causes may always attract the support of high status individuals. But such individuals' willingness to devote time to the promotion of specific proposals is less likely than the one-shot endorsements which these people distribute more readily.

Similarly, protest organizations often lack the resources on which entry into the policy-making process depends. These resources include maintenance of a staff with expertise and experience in the policy area. This expertise may be in the areas of the law, planning and architecture, proposal writing, accounting, educational policy, federal grantsmanship or publicity. Combining experience with expertise is one way to create status in issue areas. The dispensing of information by interest groups has been widely noted as a major source of influence. Over time the experts develop status in their areas of competence somewhat independent of the influence which adheres to them as information-providers. Groups which cannot or do not engage lawyers to assist in proposing legislation, and do not engage in collecting reliable data, cannot participate in policy deliberations or consult in these matters. Protest oriented groups, whose primary talents are in dramatizing issues, cannot credibly attempt to present data considered "objective" or suggestions considered "responsible" by public officials. Few can be convincing as both advocate and arbiter at the same time.

V. Protest Leadership and Target Groups

The probability of protest success may be approached by examining the maintenance needs of organizations likely to be designated as target groups. For the sake of clarity, and because protest activity increasingly is directed toward government, I shall refer in the following paragraphs exclusively to government agencies at the municipal level. The assumption is retained, however,

that the following generalizations are applicable to other potential target groups.

Some of the constraints placed on protest leadership in influencing target groups have already been mentioned in preceding sections. The lack of status and resources that inhibit protest groups from participating in policy-making conferences, for example, also helps prevent explicit bargaining between protest leaders and city officials. The strain between rhetoric which appeals to protest participants and public statements to which communications media and "third parties" respond favorably also exists with reference to target groups.

Yet there is a distinguishing feature of the maintenance needs and strategies of city agencies which specifically constrains protest organizations. This is the agency director's need to protect "the jurisdiction and income of his organization [by] . . . [m]anipulation of the external environment" [see Sayre and Kaufman]. In so doing he may satisfy his reference groups without responding to protest group demands. At least six tactics are available to protest targets who are motivated to respond in some way to protest activity but seek primarily to satisfy their reference publics. These tactics may be employed whether or not target groups are "sincere" in responding to protest demands.

1. Target groups may dispense symbolic satisfactions. Appearances of activity and commitment to problems substitute for, or supplement, resource allocation and policy innovations which would constitute tangible responses to protest activity. If symbolic responses supplement tangible pay-offs, they are frequently coincidental, rather than intimately linked, to projection of response by protest targets. Typical in city politics of the symbolic response is the ribbon cutting, street corner ceremony or the walking tour press conference. These occasions are utilized not only to build agency constituencies, but to satisfy agency reference publics that attention is being directed to problems of civic concern. In this sense publicist tactics may be seen as defensive maneuvers. Symbolic aspects of the actions of public officials can also be recognized in the commissioning of expensive studies and the rhetorical flourishes with which "massive attacks," "comprehensive programs," and "coordinated planning" are frequently promoted.

City agencies establish distinct apparatus and procedures for dealing with crises which may be provoked by protest groups. Housing-related departments in New York City may be cited for illustration. It is usually the case in these agencies that the Commissioner or a chief deputy, a press secretary and one or two other officials devote whatever time is necessary to collect information, determine policy and respond quickly to reports of "crises." This is functional for tenants, who, if they can generate enough concern, may be able to obtain short-cuts through lengthy agency procedures. It is also functional for officials who want to project images of action rather than merely receiving complaints. Concentrating attention on the maintenance needs of city politicians during protest crises suggests that pronouncements of public officials serve purposes independent of their dedication to alleviation of slum conditions.

Independent of dispensation of tangible benefits to protest groups, public officials continue to respond primarily to their own reference publics. Murray Edelman has suggested that:

> Tangible resources and benefits are frequently not distributed to unorganized political group interests as promised in regulatory statutes and the propaganda attending their enactment.

His analysis may be supplemented by suggesting that symbolic dispensations may not only serve to reassure unorganized political group interests, but may also contribute to reducing the anxiety level of organized interests and wider publics which are only tangentially involved in the issues.

2. Target groups may dispense token material satisfactions. When city agencies respond, with much publicity, to cases brought to their attention representing examples of the needs dramatized by protest organizations, they may appear to respond to protest demands while in fact only responding on a case basis, instead of a general basis. For the protesters served by agencies in this fashion it is of considerable advantage that agencies can be influenced by protest action. Yet it should not be ignored that in handling the "crisis" cases, public officials give the appearance of response to their reference publics, while mitigating demands for an expensive, complex *general* assault on problems represented by the cases to which responses are given. Token responses, whether or not accompanied by more general responses, are particularly attractive to reporters and television news directors, who are able to dramatize individual cases convincingly, but who may be unable to "capture" the essence of general deprivation or of general efforts to alleviate conditions of deprivation.

3. Target groups may organize and innovate internally in order to blunt the impetus of protest efforts. This tactic is closely related to No. 2 (above). If target groups can act constructively in the worst cases, they will then be able to pre-empt protest efforts by responding to the cases which best dramatize protest demands. Alternatively, they may designate all efforts which jeopardize agency reputations as "worst" cases, and devote extensive resources to these cases. In some ways extraordinary city efforts are precisely consistent with protest goals. At the same time extraordinary efforts in the most heavily dramatized cases or the most extreme cases effectively wear down the "cutting-edges" of protest efforts.

Many New York City agencies develop informal "crisis" arrangements not only to project publicity, as previously indicated, but to mobilize energies toward solving "crisis" cases. They may also develop policy innovations which allow them to respond more quickly to "crisis" situations. These innovations may be important to some city residents, for whom the problems of dealing with city bureaucracies can prove insurmountable. It might be said, indeed, that the goals of protest are to influence city agencies to handle every case with the same resources that characterize their dispatch of "crisis" cases.

But such policies would demand major revenue inputs. This kind of qualitative policy change is difficult to achieve. Meanwhile, internal reallocation of resources only means that routine services must be neglected so that the "crisis" programs can be enhanced. If all cases are expedited, as in a typical "crisis" response, then none can be. Thus for purposes of general solutions, "crisis" resolving can be self-defeating unless accompanied by significantly greater resource allocation. It is not self-defeating, however, to the extent that the organizational goals of city agencies are to serve a clientele while minimizing negative publicity concerning agency vigilance and responsiveness.

4. Target groups may appear to be constrained in their ability to grant protest goals. This may be directed toward making the protesters appear to be unreasonable in their demands, or to be well-meaning individuals who "just don't understand how complex running a city really is." Target groups may extend sympathy but claim that they lack resources, a mandate from constituents, and/or authority to respond to protest demands. Target groups may also evade protest demands by arguing that "If-I-give-it-to-you-I-have-to-give-it-to-everyone."

The tactic of appearing constrained is particularly effective with established civic groups because there is an undeniable element of truth to it. Everyone knows that cities are financially undernourished. Established civic groups expend great energies lobbying for higher levels of funding for their pet city agencies. Thus they recognize the validity of this constraint when posed by city officials. But it is not inconsistent to point out that funds for specific, relatively inexpensive programs, or for the expansion of existing programs, can often be found if pressure is increased. While constraints on city government flexibility may be extensive, they are not absolute. Protest targets nonetheless attempt to diminish the impact of protest demands by claiming relative impotence.

5. Target groups may use their extensive resources to discredit protest leaders and organizations. Utilizing their excellent access to the press, public officials may state or imply that leaders are unreliable, ineffective as leaders ("they don't really have the people behind them"), guilty of criminal behavior, potentially guilty of such behavior, or are some shade of "left-wing." Any of these allegations may serve to diminish the appeal of protest groups to potentially sympathetic third parties. City officials, in their frequent social and informal business interaction with leaders of established civic groups, may also communicate derogatory information concerning protest groups. Discrediting of protest groups may be undertaken by some city officials while others appear (perhaps authentically) to remain sympathetic to protest demands. These tactics may be engaged in by public officials whether or not there is any validity to the allegations.

6. Target groups may postpone action. The effect of postponement, if accompanied by symbolic assurances, is to remove immediate pressure and delay specific commitments to a future date. This familiar tactic is particularly effective in dealing with protest groups because of their inherent instability. Protest groups are usually comprised of individuals whose intense political activity cannot be sustained except in rare circumstances. Further, to the extent that protest depends upon activating reference publics through strategies which have some "shock" value, it becomes increasingly difficult to activate these groups. Additionally, protest activity is inherently unstable because of the strains placed upon protest leaders who must attempt to manage four constituencies (as described herein).

The most frequent method of postponing action is to commit a subject to "study." For the many reasons elaborated in these paragraphs, it is not likely that ad hoc protest groups will be around to review the recommendations which emerge from study. The greater the expertise and the greater the status of the group making the study, the less will protest groups be able to influence whatever policy emerges. Protest groups lack the skills and resource personnel to challenge expert recommendations effectively.

Sometimes surveys and special research are undertaken in part to evade immediate pressures. Sometimes not. Research efforts are particularly necessary to secure the support of established civic groups, which place high priority on orderly procedure and policy emerging from independent analysis. Yet it must be recognized that postponing policy commitments has a distinct impact on the nature of the pressures focused on policymakers.

VI. Conclusion

In this analysis I have agreed with James Q. Wilson that protest is correctly conceived as a strategy utilized by relatively powerless groups in order to increase their bargaining ability. As such, I have argued, it is successful to the extent that the reference publics of protest targets can be activated to enter the conflict in ways favorable to protest goals. I have suggested a model of the protest process which may assist in ordering data and indicating the salience for research of a number of aspects of protest. These include the critical role of communications media, the differential impact of material and symbolic rewards on "feedback" in protest activity, and the reciprocal relationships of actors in the protest process.

An estimation of the limits to protest efficacy, I have argued further, can be gained by recognizing the problems encountered by protest leaders who somehow must balance the conflicting maintenance needs of four groups in the protest process. This approach transcends a focus devoted primarily to characterization of group goals and targets, by suggesting that even in an environment which is relatively favorable to specific protest goals, the tensions which must be embraced by protest leadership may ultimately overwhelm protest activity.

At the outset of this essay, it was held that conceptualizing the American political system as "slack" or "fluid," in the manner of Robert Dahl, appears inadequate because of (1) a vagueness centering on the likelihood that any group can make itself heard; (2) a possible confusion as to which groups tend to receive satisfaction from the rewards dispensed by public officials; and (3) a lumping together as equally relevant rewards which are tangible and those which are symbolic. To the extent that protest is engaged in by relatively powerless groups which must create resources with which to bargain, the analysis here suggests a number of reservations concerning the pluralist conceptualization of the "fluidity" of the American political system.

Relatively powerless groups cannot use protest with a high probability of success. They lack organizational resources, by definition. But even to create bargaining resources through activating third parties, some resources are necessary to sustain organization. More importantly, relatively powerless protest groups are constrained by the unresolvable conflicts which are forced upon protest leaders who must appeal simultaneously to four constituencies which place upon them antithetical demands.

When public officials recognize the legitimacy of protest activity, they may not direct public policy toward protest groups at all. Rather, public officials are likely to aim responses at the reference publics from which they originally take their cues. Edelman has suggested that regulatory policy in practice often consists of reassuring mass publics while at the same time dispensing specific, tangible values to narrow interest groups. It is suggested here that symbolic reassurances are dispensed as much to wide, potentially concerned publics which are not directly affected by regulatory policy, as they are to wide publics comprised of the downtrodden and the deprived, in whose name policy is often written.

Complementing Edelman, it is proposed here that ʹin the process of protest symbolic reassurances are dispensed in large measure because these are the public policy outcomes and actions desired by the constituencies to which public officials are most responsive. Satisfying these wider publics, city officials can avoid pressures toward other policies placed upon them by protest organizations.

Not only should there be some doubt as to which groups receive the symbolic recognitions which Dahl describes, but in failing to distinguish between the kinds of rewards dispensed to groups in the political system, Dahl avoids a fundamental question. It is literally fundamental because the kinds of rewards which can be obtained from politics, one might hypothesize, will have an impact upon the realistic appraisal of the efficacy of political activity. If among the groups least capable of organizing for political activity there is a history of organizing for protest, and if that activity, once engaged in, is rewarded primarily by the dispensation of symbolic gestures without perceptible changes in material conditions, then rational behavior might lead to expressions of apathy and lack of interest in politics or a rejection of conventional political channels as a meaningful arena of activity. In this sense this discussion of protest politics is consistent with Kenneth Clark's observations that the image of power, unaccompanied by material and observable rewards, leads to impressions of helplessness and reinforces political apathy in the ghetto.

Recent commentary by political scientists and others regarding riots in American cities seems to focus in part on the extent to which relatively deprived groups may seek redress of legitimate grievances. Future research should continue assessment of the relationship between riots and the conditions under which access to the political system has been limited. In such research, assessment of the ways in which access to public officials is obtained by relatively powerless groups through the protest process might be one important research focus.

The instability of protest activity outlined in this article also should inform contemporary political strategies. If the arguments presented here are persuasive, civil rights leaders who insist that protest activity is a shallow foundation on which to seek long-term, concrete gains may be judged essentially correct. But the arguments concerning the fickleness of the white liberal, or the ease of changing discriminatory laws relative to changing discriminatory institutions, only in part explain the instability of protest movements. An explanation which derives its strength from analysis of the political process suggests concentration on the problems of managing protest constituencies. Accordingly, Alinsky is probably on the soundest ground when he prescribes protest for the purpose of building organization. Ultimately, relatively powerless groups in most instances cannot depend upon activating other actors in the political process. Long-run success will depend upon the acquisition of stable political resources which do not rely for their use on third parties.

References

Clark, Kenneth. *Dark Ghetto*. New York: Harper and Row, 1965.

Dahl, Robert A. *A Preface to Democratic Theory*. Chicago: University of Chicago Press, 1956.

Dahl, Robert A. *Who Governs?* New Haven: Yale University Press, 1961.

Edelman, Murray. *The Symbolic Uses of Politics*. Urbana: University of Illinois Press, 1964.

Long, Norton. "The Local Community as an Ecology of Games." In *The Polity*, ed. Charles Press. Chicago: Rand McNally, 1962.

Matthews, Donald, and Prothro, James. *Negroes and the New Southern Politics*. New York: Harcourt, Brace and World, 1966.

Sayre, Wallace, and Kaufman, Herbert. *Governing New York City*. New York: Russell Sage Foundation, 1960.

Truman, David B. *The Governmental Process*. New York: Alfred A. Knopf, 1953.

Wilson, James Q. *Negro Politics*. New York: The Free Press, 1960.

Wilson, James Q. "The Strategy of Protest: Problems of Negro Civic Action." *Journal of Conflict Resolution* 3: 291–303.

Truth, Love, and Social Change
Roland L. Warren

There are two kinds of values to which people orient themselves in thinking about social change. They can be depicted in their extreme form, as will be indicated presently. In this extreme form they become mutually exclusive, although we are seldom aware of this. Most of us carry both orientations around with us, applying them in different admixtures in this case or that—so far as I can see without a systematic examination of their inter-relation, and thus without recognition that, pressed beyond a certain threshold, they are in fact incompatible. Our orientation toward these two kinds of values has important implications for the whole question of channeling social change, and the posture we take—as individuals, as groups, as organizations, as nation-states—toward social changes that are on the fringe of feasibility. Such changes involve issues which at a particular point in history become increasingly relevant: so much so that people find themselves taking sides as to whether they want the change or whether they do not, and they find themselves believing that their side-taking has something to do with the outcome, so that it becomes more than relevant, it becomes fateful.

The Conflict of Truth and Love

The two basic orientations toward change can be termed "truth" and "love." By truth is meant here not the truth of the dispassionate scientist, aloof from the world of events as he pursues knowledge, but rather the impassioned conviction of the zealot, the person who is convinced he has come upon some fundamental moral value and wishes to see it embedded in the warp and woof of events. His truth is that of the prophets of old, who prefaced their statements: Thus saith the Lord. They saw this normative truth as something greater than themselves, yes, greater than those who opposed them—something whose authenticity called to them with absolute conviction, something that must override less important things, something for which they were willing to sacrifice their own happiness, their lives, if need be, as well as others'. This is the sense in which I am using the word "truth"—the conviction that we somehow represent the fundamental order of things in calling for the changes that we propose to bring to the social order.

I am using "love" in a special sense, too. I am using it roughly in the sense of the Latin *caritas* and the Greek *agape*, and Corinthian I. I am using it not in the affective sense, but in the appreciative sense, as a relationship of infinite appreciation and respect, perhaps best expressed in the concept of Stoic and Jew and Christian alike that all men are brothers, being children of the same loving Father. However it is described—and I use this language only figuratively—it constitutes roughly a commitment to the infinite value of each human being, and the corollary, expressed by the philosopher Kant in more formal terms, that human beings are to be considered as ends, rather than merely as means.

As I say, most people live comfortably with these two commitments, often honoring them more in the breach than in the observance, until they are confronted with a situation where the two values meet each other head on over an important issue, and they are faced with the problem of deciding whether they are to force their truth—of compelling value—on the person who disagrees, or whether, out of love for him in the sense of respect for his infinite worth as an autonomous individual, they are going to seek a *modus vivendi* with him which will prevent them from acting in an unloving way but will leave them, in Browning's words, with a sense of the unlit lamp and the ungirt loin.

Truth and love come into conflict distressingly often, not least in the field of social change. When we speak of channeling social change, do we really mean getting people to jump through our hoops?

There are at least two issues involved here. One is the question of whether we really know enough about social change to know whether it can be channeled, and if so, whether we have the knowledge necessary to do the actual channeling. The other plummets us into the value questions. If we can channel change, and do so, we must presumably guide change in accordance with some preconceived end. But whose end? On the other hand, if we do not have a preconceived end or goal, can we really be serious when we use a term like channeling, which means guiding?

Finally, if it is our end toward which we wish to bend the course of events, are we not in effect trying to get people to jump through our hoops? Are we not, in effect, saying that we want to help people decide things for themselves so long as they decide them in our way, but that if there is any danger that they may decide them in some way

This reading is reprinted from Roland L. Warren, *Truth, Love, and Social Change.* © 1971 by Rand McNally & Company, Chicago, pp. 273–76 and 279–98. Warren is a sociologist at the Heller School of Social Welfare at Brandeis University.

unacceptable to us, we must set limits? Do we show sweet reasonableness and willingness to negotiate *within* the channel while at the same time exposing the iron fist of compulsion if people decide they would prefer to go *outside* the channel?

A consideration of the strain and turmoil in this generation indicates the complex interrelation of these two sets of questions. We have not yet found a way to revise national boundaries and in other ways accommodate changes in power, aspiration, and international configuration without resort to war. Such changes occur peacefully, within or outside of international institutions set up for this specific purpose, only when great power coalitions are present to enforce the peaceful changes on lesser powers.

On a different level, we appear unable to make a serious impact on the bundle of tormenting problems at the center of our great cities. We have poured billions of dollars into low-income housing and have attempted through federal policy to desegregate our Negro ghettos, both with highly equivocal results.

On both the international level and the community level we see the confusion raised by the uncertainty of our ability to control change and of how the direction of change shall be established. With great-power agreement, many things are possible in the United Nations. Similarly, where major parties to the community dialogue have achieved consensus, the way is open for prompt action, and we seem to know how to proceed. Unfortunately, on both levels, circumstances that permit important problems to be solved in an atmosphere of consensus as to goals among the principal parties are few indeed.

Most of the great issues of our day have become issues because they involve a variety of interests and points of view, passionately held. The passionately held point of view which differs from our own we tend to think of as resistance to change, and we look for some pathology behind the inability or refusal of our opponent to see the wisdom of our own view. Reflecting the large changes in viewpoint in which our century is engulfed—and over which we have little if any control—we tend increasingly to look at the viewpoint of our opponent from a causal rather than a moralistic approach. His condition is thereby transformed in our minds from one of deliberate malice to one of pathology. Instead of being evil, he is simply sick. We seem unwilling to admit to ourselves—and to proceed with the necessary implications—that there are genuine conflicts of interest and genuine conflicts in value—two different but related things. Not all interests can be reconciled by increasing trust and intercommunication, although no doubt some of them can. Nevertheless, our global remedy for conflict of interest appears to be based on the false premise that such interest conflicts are at least theoretically reconcilable but that such reconciliation is prevented by faulty communication, faulty reasoning, and pathological traits of the individual or nation, which prevent them from adopting the necessary posture of goodwill and rationality which would produce agreement and permit necessary and desirable changes to occur without conflict. Although the differences are extremely great, they are not necessarily irreconcilable, we assume.

Part of our difficulty is that we don't recognize the hard fact of conflicts over interests and values. Our apparent inability to face this fact squarely, and thus realistically to go about getting on with things, lies in our implicit adherence to a great Socratic truth—or perhaps, if all its implications are considered, one should call it a great nontruth—namely, that the truth is one, and that it is discoverable and demonstrable through some such reasoning process as the Socratic dialectic. Ultimately, then, it is only ignorance that keeps you and me from acknowledging the same basic set of values, and once you have overcome your ignorance, you will see that your interests and mine coincide. For our true interests lie compatibly in the realization of the same set of values, which cannot be considered to imply anything but the same real situation for all men.

Now, this is patent nonsense. Yet it holds us immobilized. It keeps us looking for the fool's gold of agreement in situations where we will never find it, and it keeps us explaining away the disagreement in terms of ignorance, malice, or pathology. We have taken this same nonsense over into our Jewish-Christian theology, and assumed that in some ultimate sense, all people have the same set of values and that all valid values can be realized simultaneously. We appreciate Greek tragedy, but do not understand its fateful lesson—that values of loyalty and honor and love and religion often conflict with each other in most fatal ways, and that such conflicts cannot be reasoned away.

* * *

Inducement of Change, Resistance to Change

There are two modes of viewing change, the passive and the active. The passive mode, in this case, is analogous to the passive mode in grammar. It implies that ego is on the receiving end. The individual is the object of change. The active mode, on the other hand, puts ego, the subject of the sentence, on the initiating end. The individual is the initiator of change. Change is seen as resulting from ego's behavior. Obviously, both modes have their validity, but let us pursue further the active mode of change, that which considers change as the object, at least in part, of human volition.

It is interesting that in doing so, most of us tend to empathize with the individual who is trying to bring about the change. One might just as readily empathize with other individuals in the environment who oppose the change, but we do not customarily react in this fashion. We seem to be conditioned to assuming that change is good and that the person who resists it therefore constitutes a problem. Why do we do this? I suppose there are at least two reasons. The first is syntax. We tend to identify ourselves with the subject of the sentence, rather than with the object. The other is more complex. We (the "we" being people who deliberate at all about such things) tend to take a problem-oriented view toward society, an essentially utopian view which looks at the situation, recognizes aspects of it that are less than satisfactory, and begins to think about altering the more unsatisfactory aspects.

Actually, the opposite basic orientation is equally appropriate. We could look at society and see the great merits in the existing situation and be concerned with preserving it so as not to lose its merits in the uncertain search for improvement.

The tendency to empathize with the change agent and to see the change resister as a problem begs the question in a highly naïve way. Often, when we say someone is resisting peaceful change, the case actually is that he is not resisting peaceful change at all, he is simply resisting our change, whether peacefully or nonpeacefully. He doesn't like it. It goes against his own selfish interests, or his larger values, or both. But since our change is by definition right, then we must account for his disagreement.

How will we overcome his resistance? Perhaps we should get to know his culture better, so that our change can be made more palatable to him on his own terms. Perhaps he should be educated, since his disagreement with something which is obviously beneficial is an indication of his ignorance of the true situation. Or perhaps he is sick. He isn't free to think creatively with us. Theoretically, if we could rid him of his illness, he would be able to reason correctly and see the light even as we have seen it.

All of this may of course be so, but it is highly debatable. There are two alternative ways of accounting for his disagreement. The first is to accept our implicit premises that the true and the good are one and that therefore only one of us can be right, but that he happens to be the one who is right, and we are in error. *We* (if you will forgive me the absurdity) are in need of being educated; or perhaps *we* are sick and thus unable to follow his flawless reasoning.

The other explanation is more acceptable from my own point of view. Granted that neither he nor we are ignorant or sick (although either or both may be, of course), he simply disagrees with our evaluation, basing his own on a different scale of values, or on a different set of selfish interests from ours, or both.

Perhaps all I am trying to say is that we should not fall into the naïve blunder of thinking that the problem lies with the person who resists change. It may conceivably be the other way around.

Some Implications of Truth and Love

Let us return now to the original consideration of truth and love as two fundamental modes of orientation toward social change. Actually, the relationship here is not simply one of orientation toward social change, but rather a deep-rooted polarity that permeates many aspects of our lives and extends to the most diverse fields. The truth-love relationship is at one end of a broad, inclusive spectrum. At the other end are orientations toward experience itself, a fundamental epistemological dichotomy perhaps best captured by the difference between what William James calls "knowledge by acquaintance" and "knowledge about." Somewhere in between these extremes there is an area that can be described by the term "savoring of existence" and which extends on one side toward a fundamental orientation toward ways of knowing and on the other toward a fundamental orientation toward change. Let me begin in the middle and work out toward both ends, first in the direction of orientation toward knowing.

Starting in the middle, in the area of "savoring of existence," I shall begin with the lyric poets. This is highly appropriate, since in my judgment that is what lyric poetry is all about. It is the plea of the poet, embodied in words, that we savor existence, not merely exist. The lyric poet therefore points out to us the immediate sense of color and smell and taste in the countryside or on the city streets, in a mansion or in a hovel. Or he takes the everyday occurrence, the everyday emotions, and holds them up to us in a way that attracts us to their immediate qualities, not thinking of them as task-oriented events, but rather as visceral experiences. And so we see in a direct and intense way a field of daffodils, or the boom and bustle of the young, energetic city of Chicago, or we are invited to share the experience, the inner tone, of a man's love for a woman.

What a contrast from a different use of words—a use that describes facts about situations, or points out their logical interrelationships, or seeks, within the situation, to pursue some goal outside of the situation, to concentrate on those aspects of the situation that have to be dealt with in order to achieve something else!

As we move from this set of alternatives within a situation—savoring it for its immediacy, for its flavor, or pursuing it for understanding, for rational ordering—over toward two alternative ways of knowing (not a far move at all), it is interesting to note the variation among philosophers in their ways of approaching their subject matter. At the one extreme are the philosopher-poets, at the other the philosopher-scientists. On the one hand there is the long line of attempts through word pictures to inquire into the essence of reality. One thinks of Plato's cave analogy, or of the charioteer in the tenth book of the *Republic.* How different from Aristotle, who is in turn much more analytical, much more prosaic, much more systematic, emphasizing logical interrelationships almost to the exclusion of the attempt to portray a sense of the immediate reality. One does not expect poetry from Aristotle. But think of the other poetic philosophers, of Nietzsche, of Santayana, and others who deliberated in a mode that was essentially poetic. They wanted to give full value to one side of the duality indicated by Pascal, himself an interesting admixture of the two: The heart has its reasons which reason itself does not understand.

They contrast markedly with another line of philosophers, represented by Aristotle's great adapter, Thomas Aquinas, and by Descartes, Spinoza, and most contemporary philosophers of science.

Bergson recognized not only this duality in ways of knowing, but also the partial incompatability of what he contrasted as reason and intuition. Opting for the latter, he insisted that only intuitively could nature's essence, which was process rather than state, be captured. Reason can only break up reality into categorical chunks for purposes of analysis. It can put these chunks together again in only a mechanical way. In doing so, it loses its grasp on the reality of process, the *élan vital.* Only through intuition can man encounter the essential flow of reality.

It is interesting that English does not have two forms of the verb "to know" which account for this basic difference in approaching reality. Many other languages, particularly the Western European ones, do have a pair of terms corresponding to the

distinction being made here: the Latin *scire* and *noscere,* the German *wissen* and *kennen,* the French *savoir* and *connaître,* and so on. It is these pairs that William James indicated through his use of the somewhat clumsy terms "knowledge about" and "knowledge by acquaintance."

Having explored the end of the continuum that has to do with the dichotomy in ways of knowing, let us move toward the other end, which has to do with our relation to other people, particularly in regard to social change and to the alternative emphasis on truth or love in respect to it.

Buber gives a striking depiction of the alternatives in his description of the I-thou relationship and the I-it relationship. The one is to the whole person the other only to a part of the person. And similarly, the one relates the whole self, the other only part of the self. The one relationship looks to the other person as a being of infinite worth in itself.

> But this is the exalted melancholy of our fate, that every *Thou* in our world must become an *It.* . . . As soon as the relation has been worked out, or has been permeated with a means, the *Thou* becomes an object among objects—perhaps the chief, but still one of them, fixed in its size and its limits.

Here we see an implied reference to Kant's dictum of treating humanity in oneself or in another always as an end, never as merely a means. Buber describes the first alternative, man as an end, the I-Thou relationship, in terms of love.

> Love ranges in its effect through the whole world. In the eyes of him who takes his stand in love, and gazes out of it, men are cut free from their entanglement in bustling activity. Good people and evil, wise and foolish, beautiful and ugly, become successively real to him; that is, set free they step forth in their singleness, and confront him as *Thou.*

The Prophet and the Reconciler

Now it seems to me that the way of truth, in the sense of moral truth as I described it earlier, is addressed not to the whole other person, but only to a part of him. It seeks to bend the other person to one's own purposes—an utterly indefensible effort except for the assurance conveyed by psychological certainty of one fact: that one's own purpose is of transcendent value—or, in religious language, is God's purpose. "Thus spake the Lord!"

This sense of inner certainty that the ideals for which one is striving are sanctified, that they are God's truth, is best exemplified in the Biblical prophets. For them, it had a number of implications. First, they were sure they were right, for the Lord had spoken to them. Second, they considered the truths that God had spoken as being of the highest value, more valuable than their own comfort, safety, or life. They therefore showed extreme courage in proclaiming God's truth, often under extreme antagonism aroused by their proclamations. Third, they seemed to be so charged with the importance of their message that they hardly raised the question of a loving relationship to their fellow men. Theirs was not the way of understanding and reconciliation. How could they understand and reconcile themselves to evil? Their mission was to condemn evil, and to condemn the evildoer as well. "Wherefore, O harlot, hear the word of the Lord," says Ezekiel to Jerusalem, and proceeds to document his accusation in hardly conciliatory terms.

Many of the prophets of old and their latter-day counterparts have suffered beatings, imprisonment, and worse because of the antagonism they created. One can hardly withhold the observation that much of the antagonism might have been mitigated by a more conciliatory approach, or, as some modern change agents might put it, by more attention to process and less to task. But psychological certitude about knowing the truth has a way of going to extremes, of sacrificing other values to this truth, and of combatting viciously those who cannot be swayed to it.

Hence the way of truth has led to the condemnation of Socrates, the crucifixion of Jesus, the burning of Giordano Bruno, the excommunication of Spinoza, Calvin's tyranny in Geneva, and a host of other instances of the pursuing of one's own truth, experienced as *the* truth, to the sacrifice of other values, and—especially important for our discourse—to the sacrifice of love. It is needless to tell others or ourselves that a sense of psychological certitude is no guarantee of truth. He who finds himself afire with the zeal of allegiance to a commanding ideal needs no further certitude.

If we think of the prophet as a sort of ideal type who maximizes truth, we can set up a corresponding ideal type, particularly in controversial issues such as the prophet engages in, which maximizes love. That ideal type can be designated as the reconciler. The reconciler, as he faces a dispute, is more concerned with reestablishing an amicable relationship between the contestants than he is with the question of which truth triumphs. In order to be effective as a reconciler, he must persuade both parties to the dispute that he wishes them not ill but good. They must be able to consider him as unprejudiced—not in the sense that he may not have any convictions in the issue at stake, but rather that he can be utterly relied upon not to allow his own personal predilections to influence his relationship to either of the parties as he attempts to resolve their conflict.

He cannot function as a reconciler while he affirms the good of one side and the evil of the other. To the extent that he does so, he has stepped over into the role of the prophet and vitiated his role as reconciler.

But by the same token, to the extent that he holds his own conception of the truth in abeyance, seeking not to impose what he thinks is the right solution but rather engaging in a process of helping the contenders agree on a resolution, he is submitting to a constraint on his own ability to prophesy, to proclaim God's truth.

There does not appear to be any way out of this dilemma. The individual either seeks to impose his way or subordinates his commitment to what he considers the right way to a conflicting commitment to amity.

Truth and love cannot be maximized simultaneously. The prophet maximizes truth, but at the expense of love. The reconciler maximizes love, but at the expense of his own truth. It is possible to take various positions in between, all of which involve maximizing neither.

All of us experience this incompatibility on various issues with which we are confronted. How far shall we enforce our truth on the antagonist? But the problem is not a vexing one on all issues in which we find ourselves in disagreement with someone else. For on many of these issues, although we have an opinion, we do not feel so strongly about it that we must have our way. We are willing to go along with whatever resolution is found.

Moving farther along in the direction of our concern with social change, we find here also two disparate emphases that seem to permeate the gamut of change postures and issues. One has to do with accomplishing a particular outcome, achieving a particular task. The goal is clear, and the problem is only to acquire the necessary support from other parties for its accomplishment. This task orientation corresponds to the prophetic one, to the emphasis on truth.

The other, equally relevant in considering purposive social change, may be called process orientation. It emphasizes not the accomplishment of this or that specific task, but rather the building of a set of relationships among the principal parties, encouraging communication and discussion among them, so that they will then set for themselves whatever goals they may wish to set. The emphasis is on the man-to-man relationship, not on the task to be accomplished. It is not organized toward tasks, toward people as means, as "its," toward rationality, toward truth, but rather toward process, toward people as ends, as "thous," toward sentiment, toward love.

I do not want to overstress this series of dichotomies. What I have sought to do so far is to string these various beads along on two strings. On the one string, the truth string, has been knowledge about, reason, the systematic philosophers, logical exposition, the I-It relationship, the prophet, and task orientation in social change. On the other string, the love string, has been knowledge by acquaintance, intuition, the poetic philosophers, lyric poetry, the I-Thou relationship, the reconciler, and process orientation in social change.

In doing so, of course, I am implying that the dilemma we face in purposive change is not an isolated phenomenon, but part of a dualism that runs through the whole question of our relation to our fellow men and our ways of comprehending reality. And I have been explicit on one other related point—that there truly is a conflict between truth and love, and that in matters where positions are strongly held, it is illusory to assume that the problem is merely one of helping both sides to see or find the one truth, in a Socratic sense, and much more realistic to acknowledge deep-rooted and abiding differences of interest and value that rational deliberation can seldom be expected to reconcile.

This is not to say that true agreement is impossible when two or more parties hold different points of view. We have seen the contrary much too often to believe that. Mary P. Follett's book on *Creative Experience* is not only a strong logical argument for the possibility of "emergent" resolutions which each side of a controversy can affirm even more readily than they affirmed their initial conflicting positions; it is also replete with illustrations of cases in which this has occurred. I am asserting, though, that we cannot expect either that it always will occur or that it is always possible for it to occur.

Task Goals and Process Goals in Change

Let us examine another aspect of the truth-love problem, the question of task orientation and process orientation in purposive change, from the standpoint of the change agent in the community. By change agent I simply mean any person or group, professional or nonprofessional, inside or outside a social system, which is attempting to bring about change in that system. To take the classic example, let the change agent be a public health worker who is attempting to introduce in-

oculation against a contagious disease. He has his goal already established. It was established, let us assume, not by people of the community who felt a strong need and desire for inoculation, but rather by an outside health organization's determination to seek to prevent deaths from the contagious disease in that community by means of a mass inoculation program.

Let us contrast this public health worker with a different type of change agent, a general-purpose community development worker. This worker does not have a task-oriented goal. He is not concerned primarily with whether a bridge gets built or illiteracy is reduced by 20 percent through an intense literacy campaign or a mass inoculation program takes place. The community development worker is concerned with engaging in a process with community people through which they will come into closer relation to one another and will begin to form viable patterns for decision-making and to utilize these patterns for making their own decisions as to what goals they care to pursue, and in what order, and then to go about implementing the decisions they have made.

Two decades or so of community development work have indicated that there is indeed an abiding problem whether to emphasize specific preconceived tasks or rather to emphasize community growth in decision-making ability. The difficulty, of course, lies in the fact that it is always much more satisfying to be able to show tangible indications of task accomplishment; the accomplishment achieved through stimulating local people to make their own decisions and implement them may be painfully slow in coming, and may evaporate as soon as the community worker leaves the scene.

Since community development has been conceived primarily as a means toward national social and economic development, which involves goal-setting at a level more inclusive than the community, thus establishing specific goals and quotas for various communities, it is readily apparent why the task-oriented approach has won out over the process-oriented approach in most community development ventures. Putting this another way, most ventures are fairly explicit about the dual goals of the accomplishment of specific tasks *and* the social process of enhancing community decision-making capacity. But when the chips are down, it is the task goals that hold sway, and rather than attempting to help community people decide what they themselves want, the change agent attempts to persuade community people to do what he wants.

It is interesting that community change agents tell each other in their literature that they should be emphasizing process rather than task, but they also keep admitting that task continues to eclipse process. Somehow they assume that this is not good community development, or at least that it is not democratic community development. Some of the theorists seem to be quite clear that they favor the emphasis on process, even when the chips are down and there is precious little task performance to show for it.

Others, however, can't bring themselves to make this decision. They seem to think it is possible both to help people do what they themselves want to do and at the same time to ensure that specific goals get accomplished. They assume not only that the people, because they are now confronting their problems rationally or democratically, or because various barriers to free communication within the community have been broken down in the community development process, will be able to make viable decisions, but that these viable decisions will somehow magically correspond to what some outside agency (the national plan) thinks the community should be doing. They are often disappointed.

Of course, there are some change agents who are simply committed to task accomplishment, and acknowledge no special commitment to building any sort of more viable or more democratic or more anything relationships among the people of the community. The task-oriented community worker corresponds to the truth line, while the process-oriented community worker corresponds to the love line. As we have seen, the man who tries to combine them does not have it easy.

Conflict, Consensus, and Change

Since we are on the community level let us consider a different but related kind of problem in the community setting. The problem is usually described in terms of the alternatives of conflict strategies and consensus strategies in bringing about community changes. As is well known, recent years have seen an eruption of controversy within American communities involving such issues as birth control, fluoridation, urban renewal, and civil rights. Any of these issues is an excellent example of the "dilemma of partisans," as Wayne A. R. Leys has called it: the dilemma of having to choose between seeking to force one's way on others and renouncing one's own good in favor of amity with opponents.

The trend in the last decade has been noticeably in the direction of affirming conflict as a desirable state of affairs, or at least as an indispensible prerequisite to the accomplishment of worthwhile goals that are not in accordance with the interests of some power structure or other. The way of trying to work through consensus, through moral appeal, through persuasion has seemed too slow for many advocates of social change.

The body of practice theory that has had most directly to do with the social aspects of planning for change in the community is the branch of social work called community organization. Until comparatively recently, its model for change called for cooperation with community people in establishing decision-making channels, definite goals, and choosing and implementing appropriate courses of action. Let us recall Murray G. Ross's definition:

> Community organization is a process by which a community identifies its needs or objectives, orders (or ranks) them, develops the confidence and will to work at them, finds the resources (internal and/or external) to deal with them, takes action in respect to them, and in so doing extends and develops cooperative and collaborative attitudes and practices in the community.

This definition assumes that a community has only one set of needs or objectives, and that these are the same for all its varied inhabitants and interest groups. I have commented earlier on the questionable nature of this assumption. The definition goes on to describe a process of goal setting and implementation based on a consensus of all the principal parties. It does not take conflict situations into account.

Yet some of the most important issues confronting American communities are rife with conflicting viewpoints.

The implicit assumption of consensus as a basis for purposive change is apparent in the structure of such community planning agencies as the old-style councils of social agencies or the newer community welfare councils. They have been based on a commitment to consensus, and as a result have tended to be relatively conservative organizations. They have in general avoided controversy by means of limiting their membership essentially to like-minded persons, coming overwhelmingly from the middle class (to the relative exclusion of Negroes, the poor, labor unions), and they have also tended to shun direct confrontation with "controversial" questions such as birth control, the organization of protest groups among the poor, and open housing. Likewise, they have avoided conflict tactics, such as demonstrations, picketing, and so on, as "inappropriate." Such tactics are indeed inappropriate to an organization with a strong commitment to consensus.

Recently there has been a change in intellectual climate within the profession of community organizers, partly because of the increasing realization that the most important issues that cry for resolution do involve controversy, partly because there has been a growing number of leaders in the field who have come out for a positive, task-oriented role on the part of the community organizer, rather than simply that of an enabler. The community organizer no longer merely seeks consensus among community people. He attempts to achieve a consensus for the goals that he, for whatever reason, thinks are worthwhile.

It is perhaps justified to say that he has moved over toward truth and away from love.

Apathy and Opposition as Obstacles to Change

In some of my own research on processes of purposive change at the community level, it has been interesting to note an important difference between two kinds of community action. By community action I mean temporary, sporadic efforts to further some community purpose, such as to establish a new art museum or to institute a new set of social services or to attract a new industry to the community. Such projects as I have in mind usually start with relatively few people, who expand their circle as they move on with the project, in order to avail themselves of the resources of other people and groups, and, once the goal of the project is developed—the new art museum is established, the new social services are instituted, the new industry has come to town—they either dissolve their coalition or transform it in some way into a formal organization.

In one review of thirty-five action projects of this general type which a colleague and I made, it was apparent that there were two kinds of change efforts. In the first kind, the principal problem confronting the change agents was that of setting up a viable coalition to work toward its specific objective, and to hold this coalition together long enough to acquire the necessary resources and apply them effectively to the goal. In these cases, the principal obstacle seemed to be apathy. Most people either didn't care or were in only mild agreement with the goals of the change agents. Interest had to be generated and sustained in order to acquire the needed resources and apply them to the objective.

In the other kind of action project, the principal obstacle was not apathy, but opposition. People were interested, people cared, but they were divided into two groups: those who supported the change agent's objective and those who opposed it.

We found that these two kinds of change

efforts took different forms with regard to a number of variables, including the type of change strategy employed, the types of goals they set for themselves, the stance of key leaders regarding the proposed change, and even the success or failure of the change venture.

There are certain implications here for the channeling of social change. In the first cases, those in which there was general consensus in approving the change goal but where the problem was apathy, not only was it possible to work with collaborative techniques in bringing about change, but the use of these techniques apparently contributed favorably to the outcome by serving to stimulate people's interest and support through participation in decision-making.

In much of our thinking about channeling social change, we tend to assume that all channeling problems are of this first type—the need to exchange views, to stimulate interest, to iron out differences, to pull together.

But this happy model does not fit all cases. For in the others, those in which there is dissensus regarding values or interests or both, there are real differences that cannot be dissolved by bringing people together for face-to-face talks, or by bringing them into the decision-making process, or by other processual means. Of course, one might coopt them by permitting them a voice in goal-setting as an investment in their subsequent support of the change effort, but the price may be too high. That is, they may not lend their support unless the project's goals are changed so radically as to defeat the purposes of the change agent.

Putting this another way, the change agent is faced with the problem posed earlier—he must either force his values on others or give them up in the interests of amity. He can achieve his goal only by defeating the opposition. He is in a zero-sum situation. You win, I lose, or vice versa.

Now let me point out one of the weaknesses of this study, for it has implications for the channeling of social change. The analysis I have just made leaves out an important variable—the strategy of the change agent. It more or less assumes that if there is opposition, you must either fight or give up your goal. It leaves no room for the third alternative, which is mutual give-and-take in the search for a solution acceptable to both sides. Let me say that we approached this particular study with this third possibility in mind, and we found relatively little evidence of the process in the cases investigated. We had little difficulty in classifying all the cases into either the consensus or the dissensus category.

Nevertheless, let me make an observation about this possible third category, which seems so hopeful yet so elusive. I have indicated that there are many change situations in which consensus is not only possible but actually realized, but that there are others in which it is not realized and perhaps not even possible. Earlier I asserted the fallacy of assuming that this second category never exists, of assuming that there is only one consistent, valid set of values, and that thus all men can find agreement on this one set of values and its implications, if only they are well informed and if they are psychologically freed from the personal deficiencies that interfere with finding the truth and affirming it. I indicated that this was a sort of Socratic conception that was untenable.

The third possibility—that agreement can be found through a creative process of interaction, so that an emergent truth, rather than a preexisting truth, can be discovered and can form the basis for consensus in what was earlier opposition—is simply a modification of the first position, and it still retains the weaknesses of that position. Rather than saying, with Socrates, that agreement is possible because there is only one truth and we shall find it, it says, with Hegel, that agreement is possible because there is only one truth, which we shall create in the synthesis of our conflicting partial viewpoints. Now this may be possible occasionally, but if we are to be realistic, we must acknowledge that many situations do not fit this model, and that a lot of people get hurt before the conflict gets itself resolved in a long-range historical synthesis. We can hardly be satisfied with a complacent view that history is the unfolding of absolute reason and that newer and ever higher syntheses will work themselves out as the centuries go by. This position, wherein everything that is is right, as Hegel put it, is hardly more tenable to the person deeply concerned with the misery that social change problems bring in their wake than is Pangloss' vapid assurance that everything is for the best in this best of all possible worlds, or the assurance of the social Darwinists that progress is a built-in process and will take place automatically if only we don't tamper with the social organism.

Dynamic Pluralism

There must be an alternative to the way of the loveless prophet and the truthless reconciler, but the idea of the creative synthesis of opposing viewpoints, while helpful and perhaps applicable in some cases, does not completely fill the gap. We must confront head on the problem of change situations where there is abiding opposition, and where not everyone can be satisfied. We can neither take nor even allow the way of pushing one's own value in total disregard of other values, either

one's own or others', nor can we take the way of failing to cope rapidly and radically with the problems that beset us merely because we cannot reach perfect agreement as to how to proceed.

This implies the need for neither consensus nor knock-down, drag-out conflict, but for a creative confrontation, a dynamic pluralism, if you will. To me, this seems to place a high priority not on glossing over differences, but quite the contrary, on emphasizing differences. It would imply a sense of discomfort not when people have not reached consensus, but when they have. By the same token, it must imply, if we are not to be at each other's throats or destroy the firm ground on which we claim to stand, the strengthening of the ground rules of the process of opposition—channeling, if you will, this opposition, keeping it within the bounds of an acceptable and tolerable confrontation, rather than letting it engulf all other values and all other parties. We need the mechanisms that will encourage the prophet in proclaiming his truth, but will not permit him to destroy himself and the rest of us if we do not care to accept it. We need mechanisms that will permit and channel the seeking of agreement, but which will not suppress important parts of the whole picture in the name of an illusory consensus. We need mechanisms that will fall short of satisfying every party to every controversy, but which will assure the right of the dissatisfied to be heard and to continue their efforts to persuade the rest of us.

Although my own principal frame of reference is the local geographic community, I think the above needs, which seem to me to fit the community context, likewise fit other contexts. These include the international context, where abiding differences in ideology and national interest preclude perfect agreement on all important issues, and where so often nations pursue their own interests and ideological positions with the loveless zeal of the prophet. They include the field of issue resolution on the national scene, and other political decision-making contexts; formal organizations of various types; and informal groups, including the family.

Some Preconditions for Dynamic Pluralism

If we need to encourage different points of view, if we need to encourage the confrontation of these points of view, if we can feel easier about not achieving agreement before moving ahead in compelling decisions, and if we need strong ground rules for making decisions that not all parties will completely welcome—if we are to have a dynamic pluralism, is it possible to consider some of the preconditions for such a state of affairs?

The problem is how to encourage that confrontation of strongly held viewpoints, of at least partially opposed interests, which is necessary for change, without literally or figuratively killing one another off.

Let us consider some of the preconditions for such a state of affairs.

1. The first precondition is to find ways of overcoming the simplistic dichotomization built into verbal language forms. Either-or, for or against, right or wrong, true or false, good guys or bad guys—they form patterns of thinking that encourage the worst in the prophet, namely, his temptation to see the moral differences in such extreme form that hostility and coercion appeal to him as means for assuring that his truth, which is of course God's truth, will prevail. This tendency to see things along a single dimension often makes differences of degree seem differences of kind, excludes consideration of other aspects that should be taken into account in evaluating possible courses of action, and thus operates to vitiate whatever possible basis may exist for creative synthesis or compromise or at least a *modus vivendi.*

In our individual struggles to think more inclusively, to assess complex situations and alternatives, we are terribly handicapped by this trick that our language plays on us. Mathematics and symbolic logic afford alternatives to verbal language in only the most limited cases. In others, we shall have to continue to talk to each other in highly imprecise language that burdens us with thinking in highly imprecise fashion.

But there are many things that can be done. Children, as they learn language in their formal schooling, can be taught to express relationships in a discriminating fashion; they can be taught to avoid reification, making things out of words; they can be taught to express dichotomous statements in terms of continua, and in other ways learn to employ language in ways that help elucidate the problem under analysis, rather than obscuring the nuances.

2. A second precondition is to assure fluidity among the parties to various issues, so that they find themselves in different combinations of collaboration and opposition as they confront different issues. One might describe this suggestion as emphasizing the value of coalitions, in preference to alliances. In this distinction, a coalition is thought of as a temporary collaborative relationship among a number of autonomous actors in order to further their common interests respecting a specific ad hoc goal. An alliance, on the other hand, is a more permanent collaborative relationship among a number of autonomous actors in order to further their common interests on a wide range of goals. The coalitional arrangement not only permits the individual party greater flexibility in choosing his collaborative partners according to a number of separate issues, but also makes it more difficult for a bloc to maintain discipline within its membership as it seeks to include more and more issues under the headings of "ours" and "theirs." The type of pluralism I described above is furthered by the coalitional type of arrangement. Let me give only two examples, one theoretical, the other practical.

The theoretical example is taken from Karl Marx. His prediction of ultimate revolution of the proletariat in the most advanced capitalist countries was based on his assumption that class consciousness would grow as the proletariat became increasingly oppressed. Capitalist society would become even more polarized than he found it in nineteenth-century England into an exploitative class of capitalists and an exploited class of workers. This polarization would affect so many aspects of life that an ultimate confrontation would be inevitable.

Part of the reason the predicted revolution has not occurred in the advanced capitalist countries is that the predicted polarization has not occurred. Rather, people of various incomes and in various relationships to the instruments of production have found themselves in a plurality of coalitions on issues that did not divide along worker-owner lines, but along lines of religion, geography, political preference, and so on. Society never became polarized into two hostile alliances.

My other illustration is the recent breakup of the two major power blocs, the Warsaw Pact countries and the NATO countries. There are no doubt differences of opinion on the matter, and it is of course difficult to separate out other developments that have altered the international field. But many people, including me, believe that the situation in which the two blocs were monolithically arrayed under the clear hegemony of the Soviet Union and the United States respectively was a highly dangerous one, more dangerous than the existing situation, and that it was dangerous precisely because each powerful bloc leader could feel confident of his ability to command the collaborative loyalty of his whole bloc on all major issues that separated the two blocs. And, parenthetically, there were too many major issues that did.

As the situation becomes more confused, as bloc leaders lose their inordinate control over bloc members, as bloc members begin to form loose coalitions across bloc lines, as issues get sorted out along lines that do not coincide with bloc lines, states leave their complete dependence on alliances and engage in more discrete, less inclusive ad hoc coalitions based on ad hoc interests. Let me emphasize the point: a coalition is preferable to an alliance as a context for collaboration in a world that makes pluralistic tolerance a necessity.

3. The next suggestion may simply beg the question, but there may at least be some advantage to being explicit about it: new techniques must be found for effecting peaceful change in situations where full agreement cannot be reached. Let me give three examples:

The first is the adjustment of international boundaries. We know, for example, that in many of the newly formed African states, the national boundaries were set merely as a continuation of lines drawn on a map in highly adventitious fashion at some point or other in history. We know that boundary changes would be highly desirable here and perhaps in other parts of the world, but how to effect them? Must it be through war? Or, in order to prevent war, must we maintain boundaries that work hardship and make little sense?

Example two is the settlement of labor disputes. Airline, railroad, and postal strikes, as well as strikes in major industries, can have drastic effects on the entire economy. When their secondary costs are added up, the means seem fantastically disproportionate to the ends. So far, we have come up with mediation, conciliation, the cool-off, arbitration, calling in the national guard, and applying presidential and other governmental pressures as means of settling wage disputes. Like the Wise Men in *Amahl and the Night Visitors*, "we still have a long way to go."

The third example is the civil rights revolution and its attendant violence. Whether or not it is true—as I believe it is—that ghetto riots and calls to violence by the fringe of the Black Power movement are responses to the failure of the white man to respond to moral pressure, it is nevertheless also true that rioting is a poor way of bringing about social change, even if it seems the only effective way open. It seems to me that the extent to which the black revolution will remain substantially nonviolent—as it has been, surprisingly, in the past— will be determined by the ability of blacks and whites to devise ways of bringing about equality of opportunity rapidly enough to meet the rising expectations of blacks for social justice.

In each of these examples there are important conflicts of interest. But in other areas of controversy, important conflicts of interest are amenable to legislative, judicial, or other types of issue resolution that are not so costly as wars, strikes, and race riots. There is a technological aspect, in addition to the moral one. Of course, another alternative in each of these cases is no change, the status quo. But in each case, the status quo becomes increasingly untenable, and one thing becomes certain: The status quo will not survive. The issue cannot be status quo or change. The issue is only: Will change come peacefully, and at a not inordinate cost generated by the process of reallocation itself?

4. If we are to have a creative pluralism, still a fourth prerequisite must be met. We must devise ways of adjusting our formal systems to accommodate new power relationships among the actors; ways, again, which will not be excessively costly. One obvious area in which this adaptation of formal mechanisms is particularly important is the international field. The United Nations must somehow find ways to deal realistically with shifts that have taken place among the great powers since the permanent membership of the Security Council was determined, and thereby to compensate for the inadequacy of equal representation of unequal states in the General Assembly. But the most obvious example of nonadaptation of the formal mechanism to accommodate changes in power is the absence of the People's Republic of China from the United Nations and from its Security Council.

At the local level, a particularly challenging change in power relationships is occurring through the emergence on the city scene of a new source of power—organized blacks. Just what form this exercise of power will take in its informal aspects, and how this power will be incorporated into the deliberative bodies that set or help set community policy, remain to be seen. But here, as elsewhere, the issue is not status quo versus change. The issue is how we will achieve the change that will accommodate the community's institutional structure to the growing power of black citizens as they become organized, develop an explicit position on community issues, act through representatives, and take their place at the hard bargaining table where powerful interest groups hammer out community policy. Will ways be devised to incorporate them rapidly into the important decision mechanisms, or will they have to fight their way in at considerable cost to themselves and to whites?

5. A fifth prerequisite for tolerant pluralism will have to be a willingness to float with situations rather than forever insisting on controlling them. The days of the Pax Romana or the Pax Britannica or the Pax Americana are largely past. Great powers can be expected to wield inordinate influence; but their attempts to control all situations with prophetic zeal can only lead to the extravagant side costs that are so apparent in Vietnam, costs not only to the Vietnamese, but to the rest of the world as well, insofar as they constitute barriers to the solution of still other problems that

are also important, problems of atomic nonproliferation in international relations, problems of the urgent tasks of the Great Society, whose programs are being rolled back at home. If peaceful ways of resolving problems of true conflict of interest are to be taken seriously, then it must logically follow that not all nations, or even all great powers, will be satisfied with all issue resolutions. The quest for total control, the aspiration of any country to police the world can only create excessive costs.

6. We need to improve our knowledge in at least three ways:

First, improved knowledge through better communication is needed to explore those situations, referred to earlier, which seem like stubborn conflicts of basic interest but in which ways may possibly be found to avoid the zero-sum situation, ways that both sides can affirm. This may not be possible in every case; but without trying, we will never know. And without the kind of communication that illuminates possible pathways to agreement which lie in the shadow, we can't even try. This is no cure-all, but a full exploration of possibilities for mutual agreement would seem an obvious course of action.

Ironically, as conflict grows, communication between the parties tends to narrow rather than widen. A process of sealing off the parties from interaction except in a conflict situation begins to take place, with the result that less and less opportunity presents itself to explore possible ways to agreement. As tension mounts, the willingness to explore paths to agreement is interpreted increasingly as a sign of disloyalty, while partisans on both sides call for victory in the name of the prophetic truth they claim to represent. Yet there is indication, even at the national level, that the readiness to take steps toward such exploration is a variable that can be widened. In such instances, of course, the good offices of third parties can be invaluable.

Second, we need better data about the issues at stake, about the effect that alternative courses of action might have, about how seriously the other party takes the controversy, about where he is willing to compromise and where he is not.

Third, we need better understanding, in a scientific sense, of conflict and conflict-resolving processes. Much of the research on war and peace is related to this in that it gives a more precise way of calculating the moves an opponent may make, particularly in a zero-sum situation. There is some indication that such knowledge is already being used to devise strategies of deterrence that, though hardly a cure for war, have nevertheless enabled the great powers to move more knowledgeably and therefore more cautiously through improved calculation of the anticipated ripostes of the opponent. On a quite different level, we have much knowledge, but need a great deal more, on the genesis of long-time hatreds between particular peoples, on the psychological concomitants of extreme nationalism, on the relation of frustration and relative deprivation to aggression of various types, on the possibilities of escalation of disarmament, rather than armament, and so on through a long list.

Here again a note of caution is in order. Knowledge can be used for various ends, and there is no guarantee that scientific knowledge of any type will be used for worthy ends. The presence of improved knowledge is itself no guarantor of peaceful change, though I count myself among those who believe it is an aid.

Finally, we need to take into consideration the various aspects of both conflict and cooperation.

It would seem to me that every situation in which conflict or cooperation becomes an issue has at least four components, none of which should be neglected:

First, there is a structural component. The situation may be so structured that a principal party can protect its vital interests only through conflict and violence; or, on the other hand, it may be so structured that other courses of action are open.

Second, there is the matter of interests. We have already considered situations where interests conflict and situations where they do not, and have asserted that some situations involve interest conflicts that are real and enduring and cannot be resolved to the complete satisfaction of all parties.

Third, there are the personal aspects. There is little doubt that if the leaders of the United States and the Soviet Union in 1962 had had personal characteristics different from those they in fact had, the outcome of the Cuban missile crisis might have been fatefully different. It is quite apparent that some people are more predisposed toward hostile aggressiveness than others, and that some of these predispositions may be culturally induced.

Fourth, there are the processual elements in the situation. Given the structural, interest, and personal elements, it is still possible that because of faulty communication, or types of interactional strategy that are less than optimal, solutions that would have been really satisfactory to both sides may never emerge as genuine possibilities; or, on the other hand, through adroit strategies and good communication, what seemed like a zero-sum conflict may turn out to be resolvable to the satisfaction of all parties, and at relatively modest side costs.

[Acknowledging] the importance of each of these components in interactional situations prevents us from affirming or denying partial solutions that are offered as panaceas for war, or for violence, or for other excessive costs of conflict resolution. Education for peace, development of well-adjusted personalities, setting up adequate international machinery, developing a cosmopolitan culture, assuring adequate communication, employing the "appropriate" strategies for conflict resolution—all are relevant, but by the same token, all are misleading as go-it-alone candidates for resolving change peacefully. Every situation where change must be undertaken under conditions of conflict of interests has the four aspects mentioned above, and none of them should be neglected.

Truth, Love, and Social Change

Let me summarize this discourse briefly by saying that it explores the concepts of truth and love in relation to purposive social change, relating truth to the specific goal that the change agent desires, but on which other people may have deep disagreements, and relating love to the contrary value that most of us acknowledge, a value that admonishes us not to impose our truth on others in these deep interest conflicts, out of respect for their value as autonomous human beings. We cannot do both principles complete justice at the same time, even though there are occasional instances when a conciliatory approach may show paths to agreement where none seemed previously to exist. In effect, I have suggested not a solution to this dilemma, but rather a *modus vivendi*, an uneasy resolution in which different truths may compete for acceptance, and resolutions short of full agreement may become implemented.

In conclusion, I should like to return to Buber's dichotomy between the I-Thou relationship and the I-It relationship, the one loving, the other exploitative; the one seeing one's fellow human as an end, the other seeing him as merely a means. If there is any validity in the preceding discourse, it indicates that in most important situations involving alternative courses of social change, neither relationship can be completely relevant. What is more troublesome, they are, in Buber's presentation, essentially incompatible.

Someone has suggested that we need to think of a third kind of relationship—an I-You relationship. It is not the relationship of the I-Thou in the sense of an immediate relationship of love for one's fellow human, particularly for one's opponent. Nor need it be that of the I-It, in the sense of seeing one's fellow human only as an object for manipulation to one's own purposes.

Between the two, can there not be a whole broad spectrum of morally responsible relationships that are neither pure love nor pure manipulation, which seek indeed to persuade, but never to coerce the conscience; which do not love, but nevertheless respect; which are concerned with task, but are not oblivious of process; which behave in anticipation of the future, but with a sense of living in the present; which seek to understand, but also to experience directly; which have a trace of the prophetic, but also a trace of the reconciler?

I may not be capable of considering everyone at all times as a Thou (Buber himself implies that this is God's role), but that need not free me to consider anyone as simply a pawn to be manipulated. There is an intermediate stage between the category of "friends" and that of "the masses." It is that of Yous, to whom one responds if not with love, then with integrity; if not by walking a second mile, at least by walking a first.

It seems to me that there is such a possibility, and that this is perhaps best categorized in Buber's terms as the I-You relationship, and that far from being nonexistent, it is the modal type of relationship into which human beings come. It is a relationship in which I cannot always follow my own truth and reach agreement with my neighbor, but it is at least a way in which we can live together in a richer and more colorful world than we could if truth and love always went hand in hand. Above all, it is a world of dynamic pluralism, a world in which you will always put a question mark beside my Q.E.D., a world in which, because you and I cannot both have our way, we are forced into compromise. We need to find ways of channeling change which will assure that you and I will reach the optimum agreement possible, but that our remaining disagreement will neither immobilize us nor result in our destroying each other and those around us.

References
1. Buber, Martin. *I and Thou.* (New York: Scribner), 1952.
2. Follett, Mary. P. *Creative Experience.* (New York: Longmans, Green), 1924.
3. Ross, Murray G. *Community Organization: Theory and Principles.* (New York: Harper) 1955.
4. Warren, Roland L., and Hyman, Herbert H. "Purposive Community Change in Consensus and Dissensus Situations." *Community Mental Health Journal,* 2 (Winter 1966).

Strategies of Conflict
Ted Robert Gurr

In a society characterized by intense levels of discontent, three rather different kinds of motives with respect to political violence are likely to be found. The primary motive of the incumbent political elite is usually to minimize violence and maximize order in both the short and long run. The most intensely discontented dissidents probably want to maximize violence in satisfaction of their anger, however they may rationalize the impulse. Other dissidents, including many of the less intensely discontented and the moralists, are likely to want to minimize relative deprivation more than to act out their anger for its own sake; their motivations are primarily instrumental. The process model and the general causal models suggest optimum policies for each of these groups.

A Strategy for Incumbents

The objective attributed here to the typical incumbent elite is to maintain stability, whether or not it maximizes the satisfactions of other citizens. To minimize the potential for collective violence, these are the kinds of alternatives open to it: first, to minimize change in group value positions, in other words to maintain the status quo in the distribution of social, economic, and political goods. If the elite is committed to progress, or willy nilly caught up in it, the benefits of that progress should be evenly distributed. No group, at least no discontented group, should gain less rapidly than others. Limited resources may preclude significant progress for all groups; or developmental policy may dictate that an entrepreneurial or bureaucratic class get more of what there is to get. In the face of such necessities, discontent can be reduced by increasing the number and scope of value opportunities for the less advantaged groups. People who have little can be satisfied at least temporarily if they have the means to work toward their goals—if they have a degree of control over their resources and destinies, if they can acquire the skills they need to advance themselves, if they face no discriminatory barriers to progress. The opportunities must have at least some payoff, of course. If they do not, hopes soured have more devastating effects for stability than hopes never pursued.

Even if discontent is widespread, a ruling elite can reduce the likelihood of violence against itself by symbolically reinforcing its legitimacy, censoring those who agitate against it, and providing diversionary means for the expression of hostility.

Concessions to the discontented help also, but they must be equitably distributed among all the discontented, on pain of antagonizing those who get little: concessions are most effective if they contribute to the capacity of the discontented to help themselves.

If politicized discontent is relatively mild, the optimum pattern for maintaining coercive control is to minimize the men and resources devoted to internal security, and to apply sanctions with both consistency and leniency. If discontent is severe, consistency of sanctions is even more essential; sanctions applied randomly or inequitably are certain to intensify opposition. The combination of leniency and minimal surveillance will not deter intensely angered men, however, and without close surveillance no consistent sanctions can be imposed against them. The best strategy then is to maximize surveillance but to maintain a policy of relative leniency. Such a policy is likely to increase hostility to a lesser degree than maximum surveillance and severe sanctions in combination. It also is likely to "keep the lid on" long enough so that remedial action can be taken. The courses of remedial action include the judicious distribution of goods and means outlined above. They also include the establishment or expansion of effective organizational frameworks in which those goods and opportunities can be put to work, and provision of regular channels for expressing and remedying grievances.

A Strategy for Revolutionaries

The "revolutionary" motive assumed here is the violent destruction of the old order, a motive that is almost always rooted in an irreconcilable hatred of the old that is best satisfied by violence. There may be good utilitarian reasons for such a motive as well: some ruling elites are adamantly opposed to change, responding with unmitigated repression to expressions of popular discontent. In such circumstances dissidents are likely to have only two options: acquiescence or revolution. The regime that responds to their demands only with suppression will intensify their hostility, and is thus likely to speed its own destruction. The tac-

This reading is reprinted from Ted Robert Gurr, *Why Men Rebel.* © 1970 by Princeton University Press (Princeton Paperback, 1971), pp. 351-357. Reprinted by permission of Princeton University Press. Gurr is a political scientist at Northwestern University.

tics outlined here for revolutionaries are those most likely to ensure that destruction.

If discontent is intense and widespread in a society, revolutionary tasks are simplified; if not, there are means by which it can be increased. Ideological appeals offer the best means, to the extent that their content is designed to justify new aspirations and specify means toward their attainment. Any relatively disadvantaged group is a potential audience for such appeals. The existence of objective deprivation is far from being a sufficient condition for the effectiveness of appeals, however. The groups most likely to respond are those that already have been exposed to change and are already discontented with some aspect of their lives. One of the best indicators of a potential for conversion to revolutionary expectations is group experience of absolute decline in value position; such a decline indicates more certainly the existence of discontent than a neo-Marxian judgment that group members ought to be discontented because they have less than others. Relatively disadvantaged people who have recently begun to interact with more prosperous groups, or who have been regularly in contact with such groups and regularly subordinated, also are susceptible to conversion. The closer their association with more advantaged groups, and the less their objective (and subjective) opportunities for improving their own status, the more easily they can be persuaded of the justifiability of aspirations for a better life and the necessity for revolutionary action to attain it. Subordinated urban classes, new migrants to cities, and people on the margins of expanding modern economies make better potential recruits for revolutionary movements than rural peoples still caught in the unchanging web of traditional life.

The most effective revolutionary appeals offer means and justifications that are compatible with the discontents and cultural experience of their potential audience. They facilitate revolutionary violence insofar as they convince their listeners that the ruling elite is responsible for discontent, unwilling and unable to alleviate it, and committed to policies that victimize the oppressed. The symbolic and manifest demonstration that revolutionary violence can be carried out and can be successful reinforces appeals' effectiveness. The revolutionary cause is enhanced if the regime can be induced to take repressive action that confirms such ideological assertions. The fact of violent revolutionary agitation often impels such action: media may be censored, civil liberties restricted, dissident leaders jailed and their organizations suppressed, public benefits diverted from dissident followers. The short-range effect of such

policies may be to minimize the dissident capacity for action; the more enduring effect is to confirm the accuracy of revolutionary appeals, thus justifying more intense opposition in the future.

Unless a regime is very weak, it is incumbent on revolutionaries to organize for group defense and eventual assault. Organization should be flexible enough to adapt to and survive regime repression, broad enough in scope so that it can mobilize large numbers of people for action or at least make it difficult for them to support the regime. Organizational resources should be devoted primarily to coercive means and to agitational activities rather than the satisfaction of the material deprivations of leaders and their followers. Dissident organizations otherwise tend to become ends in themselves, providing intrinsic satisfactions that blunt the revolutionary impulse. Participation in revolutionary organization should provide sufficient interpersonal values—especially the sense of comradeship and shared purpose—to ensure the enduring commitment of followers, but require enough sacrifices in the service of its long-range purposes to justify and intensify continued opposition to the regime. It must also provide, of course, some minimum of security for its followers; they must feel that they have a fair chance of survival as well as of success. The coercive capacities of revolutionaries can be enhanced by subversion or demoralization of regime forces, solicitation of external support, and establishment of isolated base areas among sympathizers—to the extent that such tactics are feasible.

The trump card of revolutionaries is violence itself. Even if their coercive capacities are low relative to the regime, selective terrorism can be used to demonstrate the incapacity of the regime to defend its citizens. Such terrorism is dysfunctional to the revolutionary cause if it affects neutral or innocent people; it is more effective if directed against those who are widely disliked. Violence is most effective if it invites severe but inconsistent retaliatory responses by the regime, which have the effect of alienating those who might otherwise support the elite. Open revolutionary warfare is the final tactic of revolutionaries, but is difficult to organize in the modern state, extraordinarily costly, and uncertain of success. It is a last resort against strong regimes, an unnecessary one against weak ones, a first resort only when regimes are already weakening and revolutionary capabilities high.

A Strategy for the Discontented

Most discontented men are not revolutionaries. They may be angry, but most of them probably prefer peaceful means for the attainment of their goals to the privations and risks of revolutionary action. Assuming that their primary motive is to increase their well-being rather than to satisfy anger through violence, their optimum strategy lies intermediate between those of elites who would maintain order and of revolutionaries who would destroy that order to establish a new one. The discontented are not likely to be concerned with minimizing or equalizing rates of group progress, tactics that regimes might choose to use, or with intensifying discontent. Their objective is to improve their own lot as much as possible. To do so they must seek new means and resources. Political violence is not thereby excluded from their repertory of tactics towards that end; given their circumstances, some violence may be necessary. But one of their primary tactical concerns, whether or not they resort to violence, is to minimize retaliatory action in response to their actions.

Given the existence of a potential for collective violence, the optimum policy of the discontented is not to increase the potential for political violence as such but to put the potential to constructive purposes. The symbolic appeals of dissident leaders should be of two kinds, one set designed to mobilize potential followers, another to justify their claims to the regime and the social groups from which they are most likely to gain concessions. Limited political violence in such a context has several uses. It can dramatize claims, provide an outlet for the hostility of followers and thereby enhance institutional support for dissident organizations, and may signal to the regime the threat of more disruptive violence if claims are not met. But it is a risky tactic, more risky in some political systems than others. Violence tends to stimulate counter-violence, a principle that applies to both dissidents and their opponents. The threat of violence has the same effect. A regime so challenged may consequently devote more resources to coercive control than to remedial action. The obligation on dissident leaders is therefore to be as careful and judicious in the use of violence as elites must be in their use of counter-force. Perhaps the best tactic of leaders of dissident groups, if violence occurs at all, is to represent it as the excesses of their followers, whom they are capable of controlling if provided with concessions.

The extent to which leaders can in fact control the actions of their followers, and make effective use of whatever means and resources they obtain, is determined by their degree of institutional support. Whereas the first task of revolutionaries is to intensify discontent and focus it on the political system, the most essential task of pragmatic dissidents thus is to organize: to expand the scope of their organizations, elaborate their internal structure, develop the sense and fact of common purpose, and maximize the use of their collective resources, not for violent action but for value-enhancing action. The establishment of such organizations can provide many intrinsic satisfactions for members: a sense of control over their own affairs, a feeling of community and purpose, status for leaders and security for followers. Such organizations are much more likely than unorganized collectivities to take effective political action, to get whatever can be gotten through conventional political bargaining processes. If token violence is to be used in a calculated risk to increase bargaining power, it can be most effectively used if institutional support is high. Most important, whatever value opportunities and resources are obtained, through bargaining or otherwise, are most efficiently used to satisfy discontents in a well-developed organizational context.

If dissident organizations are effective in devising means and obtaining resources for remedial action, they will seldom remain long in opposition. They are likely to become firmly fixed in the existing political order, their leaders incorporated in its ruling elite. But if regimes are adamantly hostile and repressive in the face of the claims of dissident organizations, as they are in too many nations, those organizational capacities can be turned to revolutionary ends. If revolution is accomplished, the result is ultimately the same: dissident leaders become the elite of the new order they have established, their organizations the backbone of that order, and their followers, those who survive, the new loyalists. The dissidents can best judge if the costs of such a course are worth the gains; theirs are the lives at stake.

The Importance of Trust

William A. Gamson

Probably few need convincing that political discontent is important but it is important for two different reasons—one from a social control and the other from an influence perspective.

Trust as the creator of collective power. "In wartime," Winston Churchill told his parliamentary critics during a censure debate, "if you desire service, you must give loyalty." Others have urged the necessity of the same exchange in peacetime. Parsons has made the argument most directly and fully. Authorities must necessarily make a series of decisions under conditions of uncertainty. "Effectiveness, therefore, necessitates the capacity to make decisions and to commit resources, *independently of specific conditions prescribed in advance* . . . by some kind of prior agreement" (Parsons, 1961, p. 52). In other words, for authorities to be effective they must have a good deal of freedom to commit resources without the prior consent of those who will be called on ultimately to supply those resources. Such freedom to invest or spend the resources they have "borrowed" from members allows leaders to generate additional resources and thus, in theory, provide the lenders with a generous return in the form of public goods or increased resources.

> Like economic firms, units specializing in political function are dependent on the return of the power they have 'spent' or 'invested' through their decisions about the allocation of resources. This return, analogous to that from consumers' spending, takes the form of the constituency's satisfaction or dissatisfaction with these decisions, and it thus directly affects the leadership's capacity to make further commitments (Parsons, 1961, p. 53).

The effectiveness of political leadership, then, depends on the ability of authorities to claim the loyal cooperation of members of the system without having to specify in advance what such cooperation will entail. Within certain limits, effectiveness depends on a blank check. The importance of trust becomes apparent: the loss of trust is the loss of system power, the loss of a generalized capacity for authorities to commit resources to attain collective goals.

Authorities may, of course, use such power unwisely and, as a result, experience a loss of credit which reduces it. This is well illustrated by the changed conditions of trust in the Johnson administration from 1964 to 1967. In the summer of 1964 when the President's credit rating was high, he asked and received from Congress a generalized grant of authority in the form of the "Bay of Tonkin" resolution. Following an ambiguous incident off the coast of North Vietnam, a trusting Congress agreed to give the President a wide latitude in making military commitments in Southeast Asia. An overwhelming election victory in November, 1964, increased such latitude even further. At that point, the President had a virtually unlimited capacity to make commitments. He might have used his credit to extricate the United States from its involvement in Vietnam at that time. Doing this would have involved some risks including the possibility of events which would have made the administration vulnerable to opposition charges of "appeasement" or "softness." However, the President's high credit at this point might have made such risks tolerable had he chosen this course. Instead, he used his extraordinary latitude to make a full-scale commitment of U.S. military forces and prestige to the prosecution of the war.

The consequence of such a choice was a heavy erosion of trust which reduced the President's freedom of action substantially. Such a loss was indicated by congressional refusal in the spring of 1967 to grant the President broad freedom to make commitments in Latin America without prior congressional consultation and approval. Another rough but useful indicator of the President's credit may be found in the percentage approving his conduct in response to the poll question, "Do you approve or disapprove of the way [the incumbent] is handling his job as President?" President Johnson's poll ratings suffered a substantial drop in the years following his decision to engage the United States as a full-scale belligerent in Vietnam. How much the unpopularity of the Vietnam war contributed to this drop and how much was a result of other actions is a matter of conjecture. The point here is not the cause but the effect of such a loss of confidence. The President became increasingly less free to take actions which would remove past errors and conceivably restore his credit rating. Thus, distrust breeds conditions for the creation of further distrust.

Just as an incumbent administration may suffer a loss of effectiveness through a decline in political trust toward its personal leadership, a set of authorities or regime may experience a similar

This reading is reprinted from William A. Gamson, *Power and Discontent.* Homewood, Ill.: The Dorsey Press, 1968, pp. 42–48.

decline. A well-functioning government is, like a well-functioning bank, " 'insolvent' at any given moment with respect to its formal obligations if there is insistence on their fulfillment too rapidly" (Parsons, 1964, p. 60). The decline of trust has the effect of encouraging groups to demand explicit fulfillment. The presentation of demands by one group stimulates their presentation by others. Thus, it is possible for the loss of trust to encourage a "deflationary" spiral akin to a run on the bank. Parsons points to such a process as an essential part of the dynamics of revolution. Furthermore, under conditions of acute discontent, the government may be forced to divert resources urgently needed to meet its existing commitments in order to manage social control problems. This simply decreases its general capacities further. Coleman suggests another possible source of deflation with similar consequences. He argues,

> It may be useful, . . . to conceive of loyalty to country as a kind of commodity foundation upon which large accounts of trust [are] drawn. The trust [is] necessary in order that the country's work get done (as evidenced, for example, by the breakdown in State Department functioning when loyalty reviews were instituted [during the McCarthy era]). The run on the accounts of trust occurred when there was suddenly believed to be a weaker commodity foundation of loyalty than previously supposed (Coleman, 1963, p. 76).

Political trust, then, is a kind of "diffuse support" which "forms a reservoir of favorable attitudes or good will that helps members to accept or tolerate outputs to which they are opposed or the effect of which they see as damaging to their wants" (Easton, 1965, p. 273). When the supply in the reservoir is high, the authorities are able to make new commitments on the basis of it and, if successful, increase such support even more. When it is low and declining, authorities may find it difficult to meet existing commitments and to govern effectively.

Trust as the source of inactivity. If trust provides opportunities for authorities, it may provide problems for potential partisan leaders. The problems center around the conversion of potential influence into effective action and around what might be called the "apathy" problem. Inactivity or lack of concern may have different meanings. When local newspapers urge a citizen to vote for any candidate as long as he votes they are urging an act of diffuse support for the regime. Nonvoting as a means of withholding such support has never been better expressed than in comedian Mort Sahl's advice to voters in the 1960 Presidential election to "Vote 'No,' and keep the White House empty for another four years."

One meaning nonparticipation may have, then, is an expression of political alienation. This interpretation is supported by evidence from many countries that nonvoters tend to be less educated, lower status, nonorganizational members and in other ways less integrated into the society than are voters. However, there is also evidence that participation increases in times of crisis. "In Germany and Austria," Lipset points out (1960, p. 189), "the normally high turnout reached its greatest heights in 1932–33, in the last elections before the destruction of the democratic system itself." This suggests that some people were not participating earlier because they were satisfied with things then and began participating because they were upset and concerned. Apparently, inactivity can be a sign of confidence as well as alienation. Or it may simply be a sign of irrelevance of politics and government for many people much of the time.

The "apathy" problem, then, has a different meaning for authorities and potential partisans. For the former, it is related to diffuse support; for the latter, it is related to their ability to influence. High trust in authorities implies some lack of necessity for influencing them. From the standpoint of potential partisans, a loss of trust in authorities may mean that solidary group members become more politically active, join organizations and contribute increasing time and money to influencing authorities.

Interest groups face two simultaneous problems and must consider their actions in the light of both. On the one hand, they are concerned with influencing authorities and producing favorable policies. On the other hand, they must maintain, or in many cases, create the support of a constituency. In this latter objective, they are in some respects competing with authorities for the support of a constituency. If trust is sufficiently high, interest groups may appear to be unnecessary mediators of solidary group interests. Why put time, energy, and money into an organization aimed at influencing authorities if these men can already be counted on to be responsive to the group's needs? A loss of trust in authorities may have the consequence of increasing the resources of interest groups by making the necessity of using them to influence authorities more apparent to solidary group members.

The trust variable makes the relation between successful influence and building the support of a constituency a highly complicated one. In many cases, the two goals of interest groups are complementary, successful influence stimulating member support and increased support stimulating more effective influence. However, with a relatively unorganized constituency, the problem of mobilizing support is likely to dominate the concerns of the interest group and short-run influence may be willingly sacrificed to this goal. In such cases, defeats may actually be preferred to victories if they occur in ways that diminish trust in authorities and increase group solidarity and personal investment in interest groups.

This has been explicitly argued by some individuals actively engaged in efforts to organize the urban poor into community unions.

> Organizers must always keep in mind that it is occasionally more important to lose on a specific issue or in a specific confrontation. If the first time Mrs. Jones . . . confronts the "power structure" she wins, her reaction may be to become satisfied with her present level of effectiveness and power. But if she and her neighbors lose the first time, the next time they confront the same or a different official, they may well have doubled their people power (under proper motivation by an organizer) thus strengthening the power of the parent organization.[1]

[1] *Quoted from an unpublished paper by Conrad E. Egan.*

The moral that "nothing succeeds like failure" is not intended but only the more modest one that effects on political trust of constituents may be, quite properly, a more important determinant of partisan group strategy under some circumstances than the likelihood of immediate influence on authorities.

Failure and frustration are frequently debilitating and demoralizing and increases in discontent can have an effect that is the opposite from mobilizing people. More specifically, a combination of high sense of political efficacy and low political trust is the optimum combination for mobilization—a belief that influence is both possible and necessary.

References

Coleman, James S. "Comment on 'On the Concept of Influence'." *Public Opinion Quarterly* 27:63–82.

Easton, David. *A Systems Analysis of Political Life.* New York: John Wiley & Sons, 1965.

Lipset, Seymour Martin. *Political Man.* Garden City, N.Y.: Doubleday & Co., 1960.

Parsons, Talcott. "Some Reflections on the Place of Force in Social Process." In *Internal War,* ed. Harry Eckstein. New York: The Free Press, 1964.

Parsons, Talcott et al. *Theories of Society.* New York: The Free Press, 1961.

Part 3

Social Control

Too little power in the hands of anybody may be as much a problem for a society as too much power in the hands of a few. The powerless, change-oriented group may see only its own helplessness and assume that power must lie elsewhere in the hands of a "power elite." Indeed, sometimes this is the case but, in some SIMSOCs, the problem is not tyranny or domination by a few but lack of sufficient authority for anyone to govern. If there is no one in a society who can make decisions that anyone will pay attention to or observe, then it is difficult to handle any problems that require planning and coordination of resources. A basic problem in SIMSOC as in any real society is the creation of enough legitimacy to mobilize resources to solve societal problems.

For the leaders of a protest group, discontent is an opportunity—it makes it possible to mobilize people on behalf of desired social changes. But, for those who are attempting to gain sufficient legitimacy to govern, discontent presents a problem in social control. They may tell themselves, "Here I am knocking myself out for the good of the society and all I get is a lot of attacks and criticism instead of appreciation and cooperation." From their standpoint, the problem is how to win compliance with their policies—a problem of social control.

The readings in this section focus on the issue of gaining compliance. They have a common thrust—that the threat of force or its actual employment has limited utility. It is just not possible to govern effectively for any length of time if one has to constantly enforce decisions by punishing noncompliance. The short selection by Dahl puts the issue very succinctly. When legitimacy is low, leaders must use other political resources to secure compliance but, in democracies, they are not permitted to acquire sufficient resources to enforce their policies through naked power. Legitimacy is a necessity of effective governance. But what of a prison, a limiting case where the inmates do not accept the legitimacy of their custodians? Surely force must be the key here. Sykes points out that, even in this extreme case, force alone is far from a sufficient means to gain daily compliance with prison rules. Force is used when the normal way of exercising social control breaks down. This does not deny its role—inmates know it can and will be employed if necessary as a last resort—but even a prison cannot be governed without primary, daily reliance on many other kinds of social control. The selection by Gamson discusses some of the methods of control available to authorities and the problems that different types engender.

Legitimacy and Authority
Robert A. Dahl

How do leaders win compliance for their policies? A leader has certain resources at his disposal—money, police, privileges, weapons, status, and so on. He can use these resources to obtain compliance for his policies. Suppose a leader wished to enforce a policy requiring all peasants to give up their land-holdings and enter collective farms. He could use his resources to increase the rewards for those who comply or to increase the disadvantages to those who failed to comply. Thus he could act in one or more of four ways:

To encourage compliance, he could	*To discourage noncompliance, he could*
1. Increase rewards for complying.	3. Decrease rewards from other alternatives.
2. Decrease disadvantages of complying.	4. Increase disadvantages of other alternatives

Now during any brief period, the more of his resources he uses to secure compliance for one policy, the less he has available for securing compliance with other policies. In general, then, leaders have some interest in economizing on their political resources. Resources are not, in any case, limitless.

Individuals have internal sources of rewards and deprivations as well as external sources. Examples of internalized rewards are the feeling that one has done a good job, followed the dictates of conscience, done what is right, performed one's duty, and so forth; conversely, internalized penalties include the feeling that one has done a bad job, violated one's conscience, committed an evil act, and so on. Now from a leader's point of view, the more that citizens comply with policies because of internal rewards and deprivations, the less resources he needs to allocate to create external rewards and deprivations. If a leader could win compliance for his policies simply by transmitting information as to what he wanted citizens to do, with no external rewards or deprivations whatsoever, securing compliance would be all but costless.

When a political system is widely accepted by its members as legitimate, and when the policies of its officials and other leaders are regarded as morally binding by citizens, then the costs of compliance are low. Conversely, when legitimacy and authority are low, leaders must use more of their money, police, privileges, weapons, status, and other political resources to secure compliance.

Popular governments—democracies—necessarily require more legitimacy and authority than dictatorships. Political leaders cannot impose a democracy on a people if a majority (or even, in practice, a very large minority) reject democracy as an illegitimate system. Policies that lack authority, like Prohibition in the United States, generally cannot be enforced by naked power. A chief executive would have needed such a great array of coercive power to enforce Prohibition as to constitute a threat to the system itself. In general, then, in democracies political leaders need authority because they are not permitted to acquire sufficient resources to enforce their policies through naked power.

This reading is reprinted from Robert A. Dahl, *Modern Political Analysis.* © 1963, pp. 31–32. Reprinted by permission of Prentice-Hall, Inc., Englewood Cliffs, New Jersey. Dahl is a political scientist at Yale University.

The Defects of Total Power

Gresham M. Sykes

In our examination of the forces which undermine the power position of the New Jersey State Prison's custodial bureaucracy, the most important fact is, perhaps, that the power of the custodians is not based on authority.

Now power based on authority is actually a complex social relationship in which an individual or a group of individuals is recognized as possessing a right to issue commands or regulations and those who receive these commands or regulations feel compelled to obey by a sense of duty. In its pure form, then, or as an ideal type, power based on authority has two essential elements: a rightful or legitimate effort to exercise control on the one hand and an inner, moral compulsion to obey, by those who are to be controlled, on the other. In reality, of course, the recognition of the legitimacy of efforts to exercise control may be qualified or partial and the sense of duty, as a motive for compliance, may be mixed with motives of fear or self-interest. But it is possible for theoretical purposes to think of power based on authority in its pure form and to use this as a baseline in describing the empirical case.

It is the second element of authority—the sense of duty as a motive for compliance—which supplies the secret strength of most social organizations. Orders and rules can be issued with the expectation that they will be obeyed without the necessity of demonstrating in each case that compliance will advance the subordinate's interests. Obedience or conformity springs from an internalized morality which transcends the personal feelings of the individual; the fact that an order or a rule is an order or a rule becomes the basis for modifying one's behavior, rather than a rational calculation of the advantages which might be gained.

In the prison, however, it is precisely this sense of duty which is lacking in the general inmate population. The regime of the custodians is expressed as a mass of commands and regulations passing down a hierarchy of power. In general, these efforts at control are regarded as legitimate by individuals in the hierarchy, and individuals tend to respond because they feel they "should," down to the level of the guard in the cellblock, the industrial shop, or the recreation yard. But now these commands and regulations must jump a gap which separates the captors from the captives. And it is at this point that a sense of duty tends to disappear and with it goes that easily-won obedience which many organizations take for granted in

the naiveté of their unrecognized strength. In the prison, power must be based on something other than internalized morality and the custodians find themselves confronting men who must be forced, bribed, or cajoled into compliance. This is not to say that inmates feel that the efforts of prison officials to exercise control are wrongful or illegitimate; in general, prisoners do not feel that the prison officials have usurped positions of power which are not rightfully theirs, nor do prisoners feel that the orders and regulations which descend upon them from above represent an illegal extension of their rulers' grant of government. Rather, the noteworthy fact about the social system of the New Jersey State Prison is that the bond between recognition of the legitimacy of control and the sense of duty has been torn apart. In these terms the social system of the prison is very similar to a *Gebietsverband*, a territorial group living under a regime imposed by a ruling few. Like a province which has been conquered by force of arms, the community of prisoners has come to accept the validity of the regime constructed by their rulers but the subjugation is not complete. Whether he sees himself as caught by his own stupidity, the workings of chance, his inability to "fix" the case, or the superior skill of the police, the criminal in prison seldom denies the legitimacy of confinement. At the same time, the recognition of the legitimacy of society's surrogates and their body of rules is not accompanied by an internalized obligation to obey and the prisoner thus accepts the fact of his captivity at one level and rejects it at another. If for no other reason, then, the custodial institution is valuable for a theory of human behavior because it makes us realize that men need not be motivated to conform to a regime which they define as rightful. It is in this apparent contradiction that we can see the first flaw in the custodial bureaucracy's assumed supremacy.

Since the officials of prison possess a monopoly on the means of coercion, as we have pointed out earlier, it might be thought that the inmate population could simply be forced into conformity and that the lack of an inner moral compulsion to obey on the part of the inmates could be ignored. Yet the combination of a bureaucratic

This reading is reprinted from Gresham M. Sykes, *The Society of Captives: A Study of a Maximum Security Prison.* © 1958 by Princeton University Press (Princeton Paperback, 1971), pp. 46-58. Reprinted by permission of Princeton University Press. Sykes is a sociologist at the University of Denver.

staff—that most modern, rational form of mobilizing effort to exercise control—and the use of physical violence—that most ancient device to channel man's conduct—must strike us as an anomaly and with good reason. The use of force is actually grossly inefficient as a means for securing obedience, particularly when those who are to be controlled are called on to perform a task of any complexity. A blow with a club may check an immediate revolt, it is true, but it cannot assure effective performance on a punch-press. A "come-along," a straitjacket or a pair of handcuffs may serve to curb one rebellious prisoner in a crisis, but they will be of little aid in moving more than 1200 inmates through the mess hall in a routine and orderly fashion. Furthermore, the custodians are well aware that violence once unleashed is not easily brought to heel and it is this awareness that lies behind the standing order that no guard should ever strike an inmate with his hand—he should always use a night stick. This rule is not an open invitation to brutality but an attempt to set a high threshold on the use of force in order to eliminate the casual cuffing which might explode into extensive and violent retaliation. Similarly, guards are under orders to throw their night sticks over the wall if they are on duty in the recreation yard when a riot develops. A guard without weapons, it is argued, is safer than a guard who tries to hold on to his symbol of office, for a mass of rebellious inmates may find a single night stick a goad rather than a restraint and the guard may find himself beaten to death with his own means of compelling order.

In short, the ability of the officials to physically coerce their captives into the paths of compliance is something of an illusion as far as the day-to-day activities of the prison are concerned and may be of doubtful value in moments of crisis. Intrinsically inefficient as a method of making men carry out a complex task, diminished in effectiveness by the realities of the guard-inmate ratio, and always accompanied by the danger of touching off further violence, the use of physical force by the custodians has many limitations as a basis on which to found the routine operation of the prison. Coercive tactics may have some utility in checking blatant disobedience—if only a few men disobey. But if the great mass of criminals in prison are to be brought into the habit of conformity, it must be on other grounds. Unable to count on a sense of duty to motivate their captives to obey and unable to depend on the direct and immediate use of violence to insure a step-by-step submission to the rules, the custodians must fall back on a system of rewards and punishments.

Now if men are to be controlled by the use of rewards and punishments—by promises and threats—at least one point is patent: The rewards and punishments dangled in front of the individual must indeed be rewards and punishments from the point of view of the individual who is to be controlled. It is precisely on this point, however, that the custodians' system of rewards and punishments founders. In our discussion of the problems encountered in securing conscientious performance at work, we suggested that both the penalties and the incentives available to the officials were inadequate. This is also largely true, at a more general level, with regard to rewards and punishments for securing compliance with the wishes of the custodians in all areas of prison life.

In the first place, the punishments which the officials can inflict—for theft, assaults, escape attempts, gambling, insolence, homosexuality, and all the other deviations from the pattern of behavior called for by the regime of the custodians—do not represent a profound difference from the prisoner's usual status. It may be that when men are chronically deprived of liberty, material goods and services, recreational opportunities and so on, the few pleasures that are granted take on a new importance and the threat of their withdrawal is a more powerful motive for conformity than those of us in the free community can realize. To be locked up in the solitary confinement wing, that prison within a prison; to move from the monotonous, often badly prepared meals in the mess hall to a diet of bread and water; to be dropped from a dull, unsatisfying job and forced to remain in idleness—all, perhaps, may mean the difference between an existence which can be borne, painful though it may be, and one which cannot. But the officials of the New Jersey State Prison are dangerously close to the point where the stock of legitimate punishments has been exhausted and it would appear that for many prisoners the few punishments which are left have lost their potency. To this we must couple the important fact that such punishments as the custodians can inflict may lead to an increased prestige for the punished inmate in the eyes of his fellow prisoners. He may become a hero, a martyr, a man who has confronted his captors and dared them to do their worst. In the dialectics of the inmate population, punishments and rewards have, then, been reversed and the control measures of the officials may support disobedience rather than decrease it.

In the second place, the system of rewards and punishments in the prison is defective because the reward side of the picture has been largely stripped away. Mail and visiting privileges, recreational privileges, the supply of personal possessions—all are given to the inmate at the time of his arrival in one fixed sum. Even the so-called Good Time—the portion of the prisoner's sentence deducted for good behavior—is automatically subtracted from the prisoner's sentence when he begins his period of imprisonment. Thus the officials have placed themselves in the peculiar position of granting the prisoner all available benefits or rewards at the time of his entrance into the system. The prisoner, then, finds himself unable to win any significant gains by means of compliance, for there are no gains left to be won.

From the viewpoint of the officials, of course, the privileges of the prison social system are regarded as rewards, as something to be achieved. That is to say, the custodians hold that recreation, access to the inmate store, Good Time, or visits from individuals in the free community are conditional upon conformity or good behavior. But the evidence suggests that from the viewpoint of the inmates the variety of benefits granted by the custodians is not defined as something to be earned but as an inalienable right—as the just due of the inmate which should not turn on the question of obedience or disobedience within the walls. After all, the inmate population claims, these benefits have belonged to the prisoner from the time when he first came to the institution.

In short, the New Jersey State Prison makes an initial grant of all its rewards and then threatens to withdraw them if the prisoner does not conform. It does not start the prisoner from scratch and promise to grant its available rewards one by one as the prisoner proves himself through continued submission to the institutional regulations. As a result, a subtle alchemy is set in motion whereby the inmates cease to see the rewards of the system as rewards, that is, as benefits contingent upon performance; instead, rewards are apt to be defined as obligations. Whatever justification might be offered for such a policy, it would appear to have a number of drawbacks as a method of motivating prisoners to fall into the posture of obedience. In effect, rewards and punishments of the officials have been collapsed into one and the prisoner moves in a world where there is no hope of progress but only the possibility of further punishments. Since the prisoner is already suffering from most of the punishments permitted by society, the threat of imposing those few remaining is all too likely to be a gesture of futility.

Unable to depend on that inner moral compulsion or sense of duty which eases the problem of control in most social organizations, acutely aware that brute force is inadequate, and lacking an effective system of legitimate rewards and punishments which might induce prisoners to conform to institutional regulations on the grounds of self

interest, the custodians of the New Jersey State Prison are considerably weakened in their attempts to impose their regime on their captive population. The result, in fact, is, as we have already indicated, a good deal of deviant behavior or noncompliance in a social system where the rulers at first glance seem to possess almost infinite power.

Yet systems of power may be defective for reasons other than the fact that those who are ruled do not feel the need to obey the orders and regulations descending on them from above. Systems of power may also fail because those who are supposed to rule are unwilling to do so. The unissued order, the deliberately ignored disobedience, the duty left unperformed—these are cracks in the monolith just as surely as are acts of defiance in the subject population. The "corruption" of the rulers may be far less dramatic than the insurrection of the ruled, for power unexercised is seldom as visible as power which is challenged, but the system of power still falters.

Now the official in the lowest ranks of the custodial bureaucracy—the guard in the cellblock, the industrial shop, or the recreation yard—is the pivotal figure on which the custodial bureaucracy turns. It is he who must supervise and control the inmate population in concrete and detailed terms. It is he who must see to the translation of the custodial regime from blueprint to reality and engage in the specific battles for conformity. Counting prisoners, periodically reporting to the center of communications, signing passes, checking groups of inmates as they come and go, searching for contraband or signs of attempts to escape—these make up the minutiae of his eight-hour shift. In addition, he is supposed to be alert for violations of the prison rules which fall outside his routine sphere of surveillance. Not only must he detect and report deviant behavior after it occurs; he must curb deviant behavior before it arises as well as when he is called on to prevent a minor quarrel among prisoners from flaring into a more dangerous situation. And he must make sure that the inmates in his charge perform their assigned tasks with a reasonable degree of efficiency.

The expected role of the guard, then, is a complicated compound of policeman and foreman, of cadi, counsellor, and boss all rolled into one. But as the guard goes about his duties, piling one day on top of another (and the guard too, in a certain sense, is serving time in confinement), we find that the system of power in the prison is defective not only because the means of motivating the inmates to conform are largely lacking but also because the guard is frequently reluctant to enforce the full range of the institution's regulations. The guard frequently fails to report infractions of the rules which have occurred before his eyes. The guard often transmits forbidden information to inmates, such as plans for searching particular cells in a surprise raid for contraband. The guard often neglects elementary security requirements and on numerous occasions he will be found joining his prisoners in outspoken criticisms of the Warden and his assistants. In short, the guard frequently shows evidence of having been "corrupted" by the captive criminals over whom he stands in theoretical dominance. This failure within the ranks of the rulers is seldom to be attributed to outright bribery—bribery, indeed, is usually unnecessary, for far more effective influences are at work to bridge the gap supposedly separating captors and captives.

In the first place, the guard is in close and intimate association with his prisoners throughout the course of the working day. He can remain aloof only with great difficulty, for he possesses few of those devices which normally serve to maintain social distance between the rulers and the ruled. He cannot withdraw physically in symbolic affirmation of his superior position; he has no intermediaries to bear the brunt of resentment springing from orders which are disliked; and he cannot fall back on a dignity adhering to his office—he is a *hack* or a *screw* in the eyes of those he controls and an unwelcome display of officiousness evokes that great destroyer of unquestioned power, the ribald humor of the dispossessed.

There are many pressures in American culture to "be nice," to be a "good Joe," and the guard in the maximum security prison is not immune. The guard is constantly exposed to a sort of moral blackmail in which the first signs of condemnation, estrangement, or rigid adherence to the rules is countered by the inmates with the threat of ridicule or hostility. And in this complex interplay, the guard does not always start from a position of determined opposition to "being friendly." He holds an intermediate post in a bureaucratic structure between top prison officials—his captains, lieutenants, and sergeants—and the prisoners in his charge. Like many such figures, the guard is caught in a conflict of loyalties. He often has reason to resent the actions of his superior officers—the reprimands, the lack of ready appreciation, the incomprehensible order—and in the inmates he finds willing sympathizers: They too claim to suffer from the unreasonable irritants of power. Furthermore, the guard in many cases is marked by a basic ambivalence toward the criminals under his supervision and control. It is true that the inmates of the prison have been condemned by society through the agency of the courts, but some of these prisoners must be viewed

as a success in terms of a worldly system of the values which accords high prestige to wealth and influence even though they may have been won by devious means; and the poorly paid guard may be gratified to associate with a famous racketeer. Moreover, this ambivalence in the guard's attitudes toward the criminals nominally under his thumb may be based on something more than a *sub rosa* respect for the notorious. There may also be a discrepancy between the judgments of society and the guard's own opinions as far as the "criminality" of the prisoner is concerned. It is difficult to define the man convicted of deserting his wife, gambling, or embezzlement as a desperate criminal to be suppressed at all costs and the crimes of even the most serious offenders lose their significance with the passage of time. In the eyes of the custodian, the inmate tends to become a man in prison rather than a criminal in prison and the relationship between captor and captive is subtly transformed in the process.

In the second place, the guard's position as a strict enforcer of the rules is undermined by the fact that he finds it almost impossible to avoid the claims of reciprocity. To a large extent the guard is dependent on inmates for the satisfactory performance of his duties; and like many individuals in positions of power, the guard is evaluated in terms of the conduct of the men he controls. A troublesome, noisy, dirty cellblock reflects on the guard's ability to "handle" prisoners and this ability forms an important component of the merit rating which is used as the basis for pay raises and promotions. As we have pointed out above, a guard cannot rely on the direct application of force to achieve compliance nor can he easily depend on threats of punishment. And if the guard does insist on constantly using the last few negative sanctions available to the institution—if the guard turns in Charge Slip after Charge Slip for every violation of the rules which he encounters— he becomes burdensome to the top officials of the prison bureaucratic staff who realize only too well that their apparent dominance rests on some degree of co-operation. A system of power which can enforce its rules only by bringing its formal machinery of accusation, trial, and punishment into play at every turn will soon be lost in a haze of pettifogging detail.

The guard, then, is under pressure to achieve a smoothly running tour of duty not with the stick but with the carrot, but here again his legitimate stock is limited. Facing demands from above that he achieve compliance and stalemated from below, he finds that one of the most meaningful rewards he can offer is to ignore certain offenses or make sure that he never places himself in a position where he will discover them. Thus the guard—backed by all the power of the State, close to armed men who will run to his aid, and aware that any prisoner who disobeys him can be punished if he presses charges against him—often discovers that his best path of action is to make "deals" or "trades" with the captives in his power. In effect, the guard buys compliance or obedience in certain areas at the cost of tolerating disobedience elsewhere.

Aside from winning compliance "where it counts" in the course of the normal day, the guard has another favor to be secured from the inmates which makes him willing to forego strict enforcement of all prison regulations. Many custodial institutions have experienced a riot in which the tables are turned momentarily and the captives hold sway over their quondam captors; and the rebellions of 1952 loom large in the memories of the officials of the New Jersey State Prison. The guard knows that he may some day be a hostage and that his life may turn on a settling of old accounts. A fund of good will becomes a valuable form of insurance and this fund is almost sure to be lacking if he has continually played the part of a martinet. In the folklore of the prison there are enough tales about strict guards who have had the misfortune of being captured and savagely beaten during a riot to raise doubts about the wisdom of demanding complete conformity.

In the third place, the theoretical dominance of the guard is undermined in actuality by the innocuous encroachment of the prisoner on the guard's duties. Making out reports, checking cells at the periodic count, locking and unlocking doors—in short, all the minor chores which the guard is called on to perform—may gradually be transferred into the hands of inmates whom the guard has come to trust. The cellblock runner, formally assigned the tasks of delivering mail, housekeeping duties, and so on, is of particular importance in this respect. Inmates in this position function in a manner analogous to that of the company clerk in the Armed Forces and like such figures they may wield power and influence far beyond the nominal definition of their role. For reasons of indifference, laziness, or naiveté, the guard may find that much of the power which he is supposed to exercise has slipped from his grasp.

Now power, like a woman's virtue, once lost is hard to regain. The measures to rectify an established pattern of abdication need to be much more severe than those required to stop the first steps in the transfer of control from the guard to his prisoner. A guard assigned to a cellblock in which a large portion of power has been shifted in the past from the officials to the inmates is faced with the weight of precedent; it requires a good deal of moral courage on his part to withstand the aggressive tactics of prisoners who fiercely defend the patterns of corruption established by custom. And if the guard himself has allowed his control to be subverted, he may find that any attempts to undo his error are checked by a threat from the inmate to send a *snitch-kite*—an anonymous note—to the guard's superior officers explaining his past derelictions in detail. This simple form of blackmail may be quite sufficient to maintain the relationships established by friendship, reciprocity, or encroachment.

It is apparent, then, that the power of the custodians is defective, not simply in the sense that the ruled are rebellious, but also in the sense that the rulers are reluctant. We must attach a new meaning to Lord Acton's aphorism that power tends to corrupt and absolute power corrupts absolutely. The custodians of the New Jersey State Prison, far from being converted into brutal tyrants, are under strong pressure to compromise with their captives, for it is a paradox that they can insure their dominance only by allowing it to be corrupted. Only by tolerating violations of "minor" rules and regulations can the guard secure compliance in the "major" areas of the custodial regime. Ill-equipped to maintain the social distance which in theory separates the world of the officials and the world of the inmates, their suspicions eroded by long familiarity, the custodians are led into a modus vivendi with their captives which bears little resemblance to the stereotypical picture of guards and their prisoners.

The Management of Discontent
William A. Gamson

There are three general ways in which authorities can contain the influence of potential partisans at its source. They can (1) regulate the access of potential partisans to resources and their ability to bring these resources to bear on decision makers, (2) they can affect the situation of potential partisans by making rewards or punishments contingent on attempts at influence, or (3) they can change the desire of potential partisans to influence by altering their attitudes toward political objects.

Insulation

An extremely important set of controls operates by giving potential partisans differential access to authorities and to positions which involve the control of resources that can be brought to bear on authorities. Such selectivity operates at two points—entry and exit.

Selective entry. Not all social organizations can control who is let in but many exercise considerable selectivity. A society cannot, of course, control the characteristics of the infants born into it—at least not until the Brave New World arrives. This absence of selectivity makes the control problems more severe than those encountered by an organization that can control entry.

However, most societies do exercise control over entry through immigration. Normally, they do not ask others for their tired and poor and huddled masses yearning to be free. Once the demand for large quantities of unskilled labor has been met, they are more likely to request doctors and engineers and huddled intellectuals yearning to be rich. Those who are presumed to offer particularly acute control problems are not welcomed. This includes both those who are likely to commit a variety of individual acts of deviance and those who are likely to organize themselves or others into groups that threaten the existing social order. Societies, like other forms of social organization, try to simplify their subsequent control problems by refusing entry to those elements most likely to aggravate such problems.

* * *

Entry is not an all or nothing state. Once in, members may have differential access to resources and communication opportunities. All members of the House of Representatives cannot be members of the Rules Committee or of other committees which command large amounts of resources. One may regard most social systems as possessing a series of entry points each of which offers control opportunities by denying further access to certain categories of potential partisans. In fact, if the population arriving at each gate were sufficiently endowed with the "right" kind of individuals and the process of selection were infallible and produced no errors, there would be no need for any other kind of control. Neither of the conditions above is usually met so that other forms of control must come into play.

Besides denying some potential partisans access to positions that control resources, they may also be denied access to resources in other ways. They may be prevented from acquiring sufficient skill and knowledge for access. Daniel Lerner, for example, describes the Ottoman Imperium as "not merely a variety of illiterate populations but an antiliterate elite, who regulated the daily round of public life by maintaining exclusive control over key points of contact between individuals and their larger environment" (1958, p. 113). A communication system which carried the news orally from the Ottoman center to scattered villages served "as an administrative technique of social control, not as an instrument for shaping enlightened public opinion." Preventing the acquisition of communication skills in a population of potential partisans with serious discontent is an aid in controlling such a population. Keeping such a population physically separated so that no sense of common interest or solidarity can easily develop may also be regarded as a way of preventing potential partisans from organizing and mobilizing potential resources for influence.

Subsequently, the lack of requisite skill and training may serve to justify the denial of access should such disadvantaged groups press for it. Members of such a group might be advised that giving them access in the absence of "proper qualifications" constitutes preferential treatment. Thus, the selective entry may be justified on highly legitimate and widely accepted criteria and this control device may be preserved from becoming the target of pressure *itself.*

Selective exit. Most of the above discussion of selective entry is applicable to selective exit as well. There are some differences worth noting. While some social organizations have small control over whom they let in as members, all have means

This reading is reprinted from William A. Gamson, *Power and Discontent.* Homewood, Ill.: The Dorsey Press, 1968, pp. 116–117, 119–141.

of removing access. Societies may imprison, exile, or put to death members that prove too troublesome to be handled by other control techniques. Even prisons and state mental hospitals isolate some members from the rest; public schools can expel hard-core control problem students.

There is probably some tendency for selectivity in entry and exit to be inversely correlated. *Those organizations which exercise a great deal of control at entry should be less likely to use expulsion as a control device than those organizations which have little control over who gets in.* If they use care in selection and a "low risk" policy of entry, they can afford to be more lenient in subsequent actions, and should need to rely less on such drastic measures as expulsion. Those with little control at the point of entry are likely to have a higher frequency of difficult cases that cannot be handled by other control techniques.

* * *

The removal of access as a social control device is not without its own set of problems. Goffman (1964) has helped call attention to the fact that the use of such devices generates its own necessity for control. The removal of access tends to be regarded by the individuals involved as a mark of failure or repression and is consequently resented. This resentment may lead to action on the part of the victim. In the confidence game example from which Goffman draws his terminology, the "mark" may decide to complain to the police or "squawk." In our more drab terminology, the person who has been removed from access may translate his resentment into influence unless it is dealt with in some way. The devices which a social system uses to help a victim accept his failure quietly are now generally called, following Goffman's provocative article, "cooling-out mechanisms." We should expect any organization which makes widespread use of the removal of access as a control device to employ such mechanisms. For example, the device of "kicking upstairs" involves the removal from access to a position which commands significant resources while assuaging the resultant discontent by an accretion in status. Compulsory retirement at a given age is another device which removes access without creating the danger that the victim will squawk. As with discrimination in entry, discrimination in exit is most effective when it can be accomplished using accepted, universalistic criteria.

Sanctions

Social organizations maintain systems of sanctions to reward the "responsible" and to punish the "irresponsible" or "deviant." If these words carry with them the connotation of desirability and undesirability, it is because we are accustomed to assuming a social control perspective. Whether being responsible is desirable depends on the nature of the social organization to which one is being responsible. Adolph Eichmann was clearly acting responsibly from the standpoint of Hitler's Germany.

* * *

Social structural and normative limits exist on every authority which circumscribe his ability to use his powers as a resource and, hence, operate as a social control. If the limits are sufficiently great and remove from him any discretion in how he may use his authority, then he has no resource at all stemming from his position. Usually, he is left some area of discretion bounded by some set of limits, the violation of which will result in sanctions. If selection mechanisms have failed to prevent an "irresponsible" person from gaining access to resources, sanctions are an additional control that may keep him in line. If he is unmoved by such sanctions, he may be removed from his position. Short of removal, there are a wide variety of sanctions available. One may be passed over for promotion, denied salary increases, given less helpful and prestigeful facilities, and so forth. Daily life can be made exceedingly unpleasant by the noncooperation of associates on whom one is dependent for the performance of one's job. And the threat that one will not be given any benefit of the doubt in the decisions of others can be a powerful deterrent.

Social control is *not* the only consideration in the distribution of inducements and constraints in a social system. Individuals may be rewarded for outstanding performance or for being the son of the company president; they may be punished for their religion or their incompetence. Control is simply one aspect and in many cases may be far from the dominant one. It should be emphasized that this discussion is not intended as a complete explanation of why individuals are given access to resources or are rewarded; rather, it is an attempt to describe the manner in which such things can be and are used for social control, in addition to whatever other uses they may have.

* * *

Persuasion

Persuasion attempts to control the desire rather than the ability to influence. Potential partisans may be persuaded in a variety of ways either that their interest is well served by political decisions or, if not served on a particular occasion, that the procedures by which decisions are made serve their larger interest. Such persuasion may involve emphasizing the collective aspects of decisions, making those aspects which involve conflict appear less salient or important. Thus, potential partisans may be persuaded that the authorities are operating in the interests of the larger collectivity to which both parties belong even if some *relative* disadvantage is involved for their own subgroup. If potential partisans are convinced that the overall system of decision making is unbiased, they will be more willing to accept temporary setbacks in the belief that "things will even out in the long run."

There is an interesting variety of words used to describe this social control technique—some of them highly pejorative and others complimentary. The approving words include education, persuasion, therapy, rehabilitation, and, perhaps more neutrally, socialization. The disapproving words include indoctrination, manipulation, propaganda, and "brainwashing." The choice of words is merely a reflection of the speaker's attitude toward the social system and its agents. If one believes the authorities are faithful agents of a social system which is accorded legitimacy, then they are "socializing" potential partisans when they exercise social control. If one sides with the potential partisans and identifies with their grievances against the authorities, then this latter group is using "manipulation" as a form of control. The behavioral referent, of course, may be identical in both cases; the choice of word reflects two different perspectives on the same relation.

The word persuasion is used in the broadest possible sense to include any technique which controls the orientation of the potential partisan *without* altering his situation by adding advantages or disadvantages. Some examples may help to make this breadth clear. The withholding of information from potential partisans about adverse effects of decisions is a use of persuasion as a means of social control. The withholding of information on fallout from atomic tests in Nevada during the period prior to the nuclear test-ban treaty was apparently done to avoid increasing public pressure for the cessation of such tests. Similarly, almost all social systems try to keep knowledge of their failures from circulating lest it generate pressure for change. Potential partisans who acquire such information (perhaps from allies among the authorities) publicize it for exactly the opposite reason—in the hope that it will mobilize their constituency to action. The selective withholding of information, then, is a technique of social control through persuasion.

Surrounding authorities with trappings of omniscience is another case of this control technique. If the authorities are viewed as distant, awe-inspiring figures possessed of tremendous intelligence and prescience plus access to privileged information that is essential for forming judgments, then the potential partisan may hesitate to challenge a decision even when he feels adversely affected by it.

There is, however, a contrasting technique which *minimizes* social distance between potential partisans and authorities. By personal contact and the "humanization" of authorities, potential partisans may be encouraged to identify with them; this identification, in turn, produces a trust which makes influence appear less necessary. If the people making the decisions are just like me, then I need not bother to influence them; they may be trusted to carry out my wishes in the absence of influence.

Judged strictly as a social control device, awe offers certain protections that the humanization of authority does not. Minimizing the distance between authorities and potential partisans may encourage the development of trust but it also tends to increase access and allow greater opportunities for influence. The control gained by reducing the desire for influence may be offset by the control lost in increasing the capability of influence. Oracular authorities offer no such danger and usually require a minimum of access.

Doing one's duty. A particularly important use of persuasion as a source of control involves the activation of commitments or obligations to the social system. Potential partisans can be persuaded to refrain from trying to change or subvert those decisions that have unpleasant consequences for them by convincing them that they have a "duty" to honor such decisions. The importance of legitimacy for a political system comes from its connection with this control technique. If legitimacy is high, then there is a high potential for activating commitments and other, more costly forms of control may be avoided. For example, if "patriotism" and "the duty to serve one's country" are sufficiently strong, then there is no need for conscription; a voluntary army can be counted on. However, if legitimacy is weak and alienation toward the political system is prevalent, then the call to duty may sound hollow.

Not everyone is as committed to duty as the young hero of *The Pirates of Penzance* who insists on fulfilling his obligation to the pirates to whom he was mistakenly bound in childhood in spite of his strenuous disapproval of their profession. Still, a wide variety of unpleasant commitments may be accepted with good grace when there is a surplus of political trust. A good illustration of the dependence on such trust may be found in the relatively sudden increase in opposition to the Selective Service System. Students who were able to reach graduate school were, for many years, given *de facto* exemptions from compulsory service. As long as American foreign policy was generally supported, the unequal sacrifices demanded from different groups in the society did not become an issue. However, with the erosion of confidence stemming from American policy in Vietnam, not only the bases of deferment but conscription itself has been seriously challenged. In World War II, appeals to duty activated many to enlist voluntarily and those who didn't were quiet about it. During the Vietnam War, the threat of severe sanctions has not deterred open and organized opposition to the draft. In fact, some student groups have themselves attempted to activate commitments to "higher" values by urging the duty *not* to serve. The price authorities pay for losing political confidence is a loss in their ability to activate commitments and the necessity of relying on more costly types of social control.

The activation of commitments, then, depends on the existence of political trust but it becomes an even more powerful control when it is mediated by face-to-face interaction. This point is best demonstrated by a series of social psychological experiments going back to the early 1940's. These experiments, particularly the later ones in the series, have shocked and outraged many people and have stimulated a vigorous debate among social psychologists on the proper ethics in experimenting with human subjects. But whether or not such experiments *should* have been conducted, the fact is that they *have* been and their results are both surprising and instructive.

Jerome Frank (1944) designed a series of experiments aimed at exploring the conditions under which subjects would refuse to continue disagreeable or nonsensical tasks. Under some conditions, the experimenter simply told the subject what he was expected to do and this was sufficient to ensure performance. For example, some subjects were asked to perform the task of balancing a marble on a small steel ball; almost all of them continued to pursue this manifestly impossible task for a full hour with no overt resistance in spite of inward annoyance. Frank quotes one subject: "I was griped all the way through . . . [but] I promised a man I'd help him out and I couldn't see any reason for backing down on my word." In another variation, Frank attempted to get subjects to eat unsalted soda crackers. When they were told that the experiment required them to eat 12 crackers, the subjects all ate them without argument or protest.

However, in another condition, the situation was translated from one of social control to one of influence. Subjects were told, "This is an experiment in persuasion. I am going to try to make you eat 12 crackers in the first row on the tray. Whether you eat them or not is entirely up to you and doesn't affect the experiment one way or the other. But if you resist, I shall try to make you eat them anyway." Under such instructions, considerable resistance was produced and while verbal pressure from the experimenter succeeded in making several subjects eat a few more crackers, less than a third ate all 12 crackers. As an influence situation, the eating of crackers became a test of wills; as a social control situation, it simply involved the activation of the commitments involved in agreeing to be an experimental subject and no resistance was encountered.

At the point of refusal in the influence variation, the experimenter attempted to introduce legitimacy, by saying, "The experiment requires that you eat one more cracker and that will be enough," or "If you eat just one more cracker, that will be enough." These instructions were successful in getting two-thirds of the recalcitrant subjects to take one more cracker. Eating the final cracker was seen as a way of terminating what had become an embarrassing and extremely awkward situation.

Some other experiments show this form of social control even more dramatically. Pepitone and Wallace (1955) asked subjects to sort the contents of a waste basket which contained cigar butts, soiled paper, dirty rags, broken sticks, pieces of glass, damp kleenex tissue, sodden purina chow, and other disgusting debris. The results were essentially the same in a variety of experimental conditions—the subjects snickered and laughed, and then got down to work and sorted the garbage with no strong protestations.

Martin Orne and his associates (1962; 1965) stumbled onto similar results in pursuing research on hypnosis. Orne sought a task which an unhypnotized subject would break off but not because of pain or exhaustion; that is, the task needed to be so boring and meaningless that a normal subject would simply refuse to do it after awhile. He found it extremely difficult to design such a task because of the powerful social control operating in face-to-face interaction with an experimenter who is accorded legitimacy. In one experiment, Orne gave the subjects a huge stack of 2,000 sheets of simple additions, each sheet containing 224 such additions. The simple instruction of "Continue to work; I will return eventually," was sufficient to get them to work for many hours with little decrement in performance. It was necessary for the weary experimenter to break off the task for the even wearier subject might have complied indefinitely. Even the addition of instructions to tear each sheet up into 32 pieces and to throw them away upon completion did not lead to significant resistance. When work stoppage occurred, the return of the experimenter to the room with instructions to continue was sufficient to ensure more work for additional hours.

Thwarted in this attempt to produce a breakdown of social control, Orne moved to more extreme tasks. Is the degree of control in hypnosis, Orne asked, actually any greater than the degree of control which an experimenter exercises over a normal waking subject when this subject accepts the legitimacy of the experimental situation? To test this, Orne and Evans (1965) used a series of tasks which were extremely disagreeable, and potentially harmful to either the subject himself or to others. The experiment called for a special apparatus—a box with a glass screen which could be slid into place and removed but which, because of the lighting and the type of glass, was impossible to see. Hypnotized subjects were compared with a group of unhypnotized subjects who were instructed to pretend they were hypnotized and with other control groups of normal waking subjects.

Initially, subjects were asked to pick up a few harmless objects from the box—with the glass screen not in place, of course. Then, a harmless lizard was placed in the box and subjects were told to pick it up, followed by similar instructions for a 14-inch harmless green snake and a 14-inch venomous black snake, capable of inflicting a mortal wound. However, before the last task and unknown to the subject, the invisible glass screen was silently lowered into place so that subjects who attempted to comply would get only bruised knuckles instead of snake bite.

At this point, the box was removed and the subject watched the experimenter pour concentrated nitric acid into a small shallow beaker. The experimenter dropped a coin into the acid and allowed the subject to watch it dissolve for approximately a minute. He then asked the subject to remove the coin with his bare hand and to plunge both coin and hand into a nearby basin of soapy, lukewarm water. If the subject complied (or if he did not comply, while he was diverted in some fashion), the beaker with acid was switched with one that appeared identical but contained a harmless solution. The experimenter then instructed the subject to throw the acid in the face of the lab assistant who had been helping with various aspects of the experiment. This completed the experiment proper and was followed by a fairly extensive postexperimental interview.

The results show a good deal of compliance with the experimenter's requests in all conditions.

Of the six hypnotized subjects, five complied with all requests; the sixth, a young lady, became hysterical at the sight of the harmless lizard in the beginning and the other tasks were not used. All six of the subjects who were simulating hypnosis complied fully, carrying out all of the experimenter's requests although showing reluctance at a number of points. Of a group of six control subjects who were told that they were normal controls for a hypnosis experiment, five performed the acid tasks and three of the six attempted to pick up the venomous snake.

The latest and most significant work in this genre is that of Stanley Milgram (1963; 1964; 1965). Milgram focused his work on destructive obedience—obedience to demands which injure others. The basic experiment involves a naïve subject who administers what he believes are extremely severe electric shocks to another "subject" who is in fact a confederate of the experimenter. The subject believes that he is participating in an experiment which involves the effect of punishment on learning. He is instructed to raise the shock level administered after each error which the victim makes in a learning task involving the pairing of words. The simulated generator which the subject uses is extremely convincing; it is marked with voltage designations from 15 to 450 which are accompanied by verbal designations of slight shock, moderate shock, strong shock, very strong shock, intense shock, extreme intensity shock, Danger: severe shock, and two more positions ominously marked XXX. When the naïve subject pulls the generator switch, the generator lights and buzzes but, unknown to him, no shock is actually transmitted.

In Milgram's original experiment, the victim-confederate was in an adjacent room providing answers by pushing buttons. At the 300-volt level and again at the 315-volt level, he was instructed to pound on the wall and, thereafter, provide no more answers. Subjects typically turned to the experimenter at that point who advised them to treat no response as an incorrect response and to proceed with the shock schedule. If the subject asked about injury to the victim, the experimenter replied, "Although the shocks can be extremely painful, they cause no permanent tissue damage."

The results of this experiment are startling. Of the 40 subjects, all proceed past the strong and very strong shock readings and none break off before reaching 300 volts. Even more startling, 26 of the 40 reach the maximum level of 450 volts—the XXX category. Such behavior is clearly not sadism. Subjects are under considerable stress and manifest it by sweating, stuttering, uncontrollable laughing fits, trembling, and other manifestations of extreme tension. Milgram quotes one observer:

I observed a mature and initially poised businessman enter the laboratory smiling and confident. Within 20 minutes, he was reduced to a twitching, stuttering wreck who was rapidly approaching a point of nervous collapse. He constantly pulled on his earlobe and twisted his hands. At one point, he pushed his fist into his forehead and muttered "Oh, God. Let's stop it." And yet he continued to respond to every word of the experimenter and obeyed to the end (Milgram, 1963, p. 377).

Why do subjects continue to honor a presumed obligation to an experimenter whom they do not know, to accomplish goals which are at best vague and obscure to them and which at the same time involve virtually gratuitous injury to another human being whom they have no reason to dislike? Variations of the experiment point to the fact that the strength of the obligation is heavily influenced by the physical presence of the experimenter. In one condition with 40 fresh subjects, the experimenter leaves after presenting the initial instructions and gives subsequent orders over the telephone. Where 26 of 40 were fully obedient when the experimenter was present, only 9 of the 40 subjects were fully obedient when the orders were conveyed over the phone. In a number of cases, the subject lied to the experimenter, saying that he was raising the shock level when he was in fact using the lowest level on the board. If the experimenter appeared in person after the subject refused over the telephone, he was sometimes able to reactivate compliance with the simple assertion, "The experiment requires that you continue."

Similarly, when the victim is brought into the same room with the subject, the number of obedient subjects goes down. The conflict becomes more intense for the subject with the experimenter looking at him and clearly expecting him to continue, while the victim very visibly indicates his pain and his desire to participate no longer. Such results suggest that the blindfolding of a condemned prisoner may have another meaning than the one usually attributed to it. It is not so much to protect the victim's feelings that a blindfold is needed but rather to protect the executioner from his surveillance.

The basic mechanism of control accounting for these results is the activation of commitments. By conveying the definition of the situation that the experimenter is a mere agent, carrying out the sometimes unpleasant demands of "research" or "science," he creates a situation where a refusal is an act of deviance. Well-socialized subjects who have volunteered their services find it difficult to commit such an act under the very eyes of the

experimenter, but when they can do it without the embarrassment of a direct confrontation, it is much easier.

Perhaps the most powerful and common means of social control is simply the conveying of expectations with clarity and explicitness coupled with clear and direct accountability for the performance of such expectations. As long as legitimacy is accorded in such situations, individuals will regard their noncompliance as a failure and any interaction which makes such a personal failure salient is embarrassing, unpleasant and something to be avoided.

This point is no less true for complex, modern societies than for small communities. The activation of commitments still depends both on the acceptance of a general obligation and on reminders of what that duty is in specific situations. The connections between the top political leaders in a society and the members of a solidary group may be remote and may pass through many links before they reach a person's boss or neighbor or colleague or whoever else happens to do the reminding. Nevertheless, at the last link in this chain between authorities and potential partisans, the desire to avoid the embarrassment of being derelict under surveillance is a powerful persuader. The possibility of losing such a potent means of control is a strong incentive for any set of authorities to achieve or maintain high trust on the part of potential partisans.

Participation and Cooptation

One of the most interesting and complicated of control mechanisms is cooptation. Essentially, it involves the manipulation of access, but as a control technique it is double-edged. In his classic study of the Tennessee Valley Authority (TVA), Selznick (1953) defined it as "the process of absorbing new elements into the leadership or policy-determining structure of an organization as a means of averting threats to its stability of existence." Earlier I argued that authorities normally will prefer to limit access to those elements most susceptible to control, but cooptation involves yielding access to the most difficult and threatening potential partisans. Why should any organization wish to deliberately create control problems for itself?

This mechanism arises in situations where control is already insufficient. It is a response to anticipated or actual pressure from partisans of such magnitude that it threatens the incumbent authorities and perhaps threatens the continuation of the system itself. Bringing such partisans "inside" does not create control problems; it simply transfers the existing ones to a different arena. In particular, while cooptation removes some of the insulation between potential partisans and authorities, it makes the former subject to other control techniques which were previously not available. Representatives of the partisan group, once inside, are subject to the rewards and punishments that the organization bestows. They acquire a stake in the organization, having gained some control over resources whose continuation and expansion is dependent on the organization's maintenance and growth. New rewards lie ahead if they show themselves to be amenable to some degree of control; deprivation of rewards which they now enjoy becomes a new possibility if they remain unruly.

Besides these changes in the situation of the partisans, they are likely to enjoy some changes in orientation as well. First of all, their attitudes and commitment to the system may change. They may come to identify with the collectivity to such a degree that it will mute and subdue their original loyalty to a hostile outside partisan group which is trying to change the organization.

A desire to increase the potentialities for control lies behind the advocacy of admitting Communist China to the United Nations for many who hold such a position. UN membership is regarded less in terms of the access to influence it provides and more in terms of the control opportunities it offers. A hostile China is viewed as a greater threat outside the United Nations than inside. Once inside, it is argued, China would acquire interests which would make it a partner in maintaining the stability of the international system. It lacks such interests as an "outlaw" with relatively little stake in maintaining peaceful and cooperative relations with other countries.

From the perspective of potential partisans, cooptation must be regarded as a risk. Representatives of coopted groups are likely to be charged with having "sold out" at the least indication that they are pressing the group's demands with less vigor than previously. In fact, there is a tendency for such partisans to regard the entire opportunity for increased access as a form of manipulation. "The more a ruling class is able to assimilate the most prominent men of the dominated classes the more stable and dangerous is its rule," Marx argued. The very act of accepting access by a leader may be taken as evidence of desertion to the enemy either for selfish gain (i.e., as a "fink") or through naïveté (i.e., as a "dupe").

What can a potential partisan group hope to gain by allowing itself and its leaders to be coopted? It can gain increased access to resources which will enhance its influence and bring about outcome modifications. In other words, cooptation does not operate simply as a control device—it

is also likely to involve yielding ground. For this reason, there are likely to be parallel fears on the part of authorities. They may worry that the act of cooptation represents the "nose of the camel" and be fearful of their ability to keep the rest of the camel out of the tent. Far from manipulation, some authorities may regard it as an act of undue yielding to pressure and the rewarding of "irresponsible" behavior.

Both the partisan's and the authority's fears about cooptation are valid fears. Cooptation invariably involves some mixture of outcome modification and social control and the exact mix is difficult to determine in advance. The authority who opposes coopting the hostile element fears that outcome modification will dominate the mix; the partisan who opposes accepting it, fears that the social control element will dominate.

The TVA case described by Selznick (1953) is instructive in this regard. The newly founded organization was faced, in 1933, with a powerfully entrenched existing interest bloc in the Tennessee Valley. This bloc consisted of a complex headed by the Land Grant Colleges, the more prosperous farmers represented by the American Farm Bureau Federation, and the Federal Agricultural Extension Service with its county agents. In some fashion, TVA had to confront this bloc whose territory the new organization was invading. Had TVA been firmly established with assured support of its own, it might have considered a strategy which would have challenged this bloc. In trying to become established, an alternative strategy recommended itself—to coopt the Farm Bureau complex into TVA. This policy was justified under the rubric of the "grass roots policy" which emphasized partnership with local groups in the region. The most significant act of cooptation was the appointment of one of the leaders of the Farm Bureau complex to TVA's three-man board.

One of the consequences of the cooptation strategy was a considerable amount of influence by the Farm Bureau complex over TVA's agricultural policies. Decisions on fertilizer programs, on the degree of emphasis on rural cooperatives, on the place of Negro farmers in the TVA program, were apparently all heavily influenced by this partisan group in the valley. On the other hand, TVA was able to carry out successfully its public power program and a number of other important objectives which might have become the target of active opposition if the Farm Bureau complex had not been coopted. It is never easy to assess whether the "price" in outcome modification was worth it or not, especially since one cannot know what would have happened if cooptation had not been used. The lesson to be drawn from the TVA example is not that it acted wisely or foolishly in coopting the Farm Bureau complex. Rather it is that *any* act of cooptation of potential partisans by authorities is likely to be a mixture of modification and social control and the balance of the mix is problematic and of concern to both parties.

Leed's discussion (1964) of the absorption of nonconforming enclaves again illustrates the double-edged nature of this process. General Chennault and his followers in the period preceding World War II attempted to develop a group of trained fighter pilots (the "Flying Tigers") to furnish air support for Chinese land forces opposing the Japanese. The military had yet to accept, at this time, the full significance of air warfare and tended to regard it as auxiliary to infantry and artillery. Consequently, the allocation of supplies and personnel to Chennault were limited and a variety of other means were used to control and isolate the Flying Tiger group. However, after the U.S. entry into the war, this conflict proved too costly and a different control technique was used to deal with the rebellious group. In July, 1942, the American Volunteer Group of Flying Tigers was transformed into China Air Task Force and inducted into the U.S. Air Force under General Bissell. Later the group became the 14th Air Force under General Stillwell who was instructed to give Chennault full support. This ended the rebellion and removed the acute pressure from this partisan group. Along with the development of military technology and the experiences of the war, this absorption contributed to a major reorientation in the military toward the importance of air warfare. As in the TVA case, cooptation seems to have involved large amounts of influence for the coopted group.

Closely related to the issue of cooptation and protest-absorption is that of participation in decision making. A long line of social psychological experiments in laboratory and field settings has emphasized the importance of participation as a positive factor in the acceptance of decision outcomes. It is not always clear precisely what is meant by participation.

One may emphasize the influence aspects of participation. To increase the participation of a group of potential partisans may mean to increase its influence over decisions. If there is increased satisfaction in such situations, it is because the modified outcomes are closer to what the partisan group desires. It may have very little or nothing to do with the fact of participation itself. If the significance of participation stems from the attendant influence, then we should expect the same increase in satisfaction and commitment that we would get if outcomes were similarly modified without an increase in participation.

Participation has a social control aspect as well. Here it is claimed that the act of participating in a decision process increases commitment and acceptance of decisions even if outcomes are no more satisfactory. The classic case of such alleged "participation" effects is the Hawthorne Study (Roethlisberger and Dickson, 1939) in which output increased following a variety of decisions made by a group of workers. These particular experiments are a weak reed on which to base any conclusion as Carey (1967) demonstrates in an appropriately harsh review. Carey argues that a "detailed comparison between the Hawthorne conclusions and the Hawthorne evidence shows these conclusions to be almost wholly unsupported" (p. 403). But in a later, more careful study of "participation" effects, Coch and French conclude that resistance to changing work methods can be overcome "by the use of group meetings in which management effectively communicates the need for change and stimulates group participation in planning the changes. Such participation results in higher production, higher morale, and better labor-management relations" (1965, p. 459).

Much of the small group work on "democratic" methods of decision making has a strong social control emphasis. As Verba points out,

> Participation is in most cases limited to member endorsement of decisions made by the leader who . . . is neither selected by the group nor responsible to the group for his actions. In group discussions, the leader does not present alternatives to the group from which the members choose. Rather, the group leader has a particular goal in mind and uses the group discussion as a means of inducing acceptance of the goal. . . . As used in much of the small group literature, participatory democratic leadership refers not to a technique of decision but to a technique of persuasion (Verba, 1961, p. 220).

Participation, like cooptation, is most likely to be some mixture of influence and social control. Many of the same issues arise. If the social control emphasis is paramount, partisans are likely to regard the process as pseudo participation and manipulation. But it is not easy to increase participation without also increasing influence. The increased access may be intended to lead to a greater feeling of participation and increased commitment of members, but those who are so admitted may not be very long satisfied with the trappings of influence. When conflicts arise, the new participants may be in an improved position to pursue their interests effectively.

By the use of *selective* participation, authorities may control some partisans by increasing the ability of others to influence. Hard-pressed authorities may welcome influence attempts by rival partisans for such influence may free rather than confine them. Under such circumstances, authorities may encourage increased participation by selected groups despite, or even because of, the increased influence that it will bring. The new pressures can then be pointed to as justification and defense for failure to take the actions desired by the first group; the second group in turn can be brought to appreciate the constraints which their rival places on the authorities.

The playing off of one partisan group against another as a technique of control is an ancient and familiar one. Machiavelli recommended it to his authorities and Simmel developed it in his discussion of the "tertius gaudens," i.e., the third party who draws advantage from the quarrel of two others. It is captured in the admonition to authorities to "divide and rule." Simmel illustrates it by describing the Inca custom of dividing a "newly conquered tribe in two approximately equal halves and [placing] a supervisor over each of them, but [giving] these two supervisors slightly different ranks. This was indeed the most suitable means for provoking rivalry between the two heads, which prevented any united action against the ruler on the part of the subjected territory" (Simmel, 1950, p. 165).

Such a control technique has certain dangers. First, while it may forestall the necessity of immediate outcome modification and increase the temporary maneuverability of authorities, it does not relieve the pressure in the long run and may even intensify it. For the moment, some of the resources of the partisan groups may be redirected into the conflict with each other but the authorities, by definition, control the choices which these groups are attempting to influence. Second, it is typically the case that rival partisan groups have some degree of common interest. If so, they may find it convenient to pool their resources in a temporary coalition. Thus, increased participation may lead to an enhancement of the influence it was intended to prevent.

References

Carey, Alex. "The Hawthorne Studies: A Radical Criticism." *American Sociological Review* 32:403–16.

Coch, Lester, and French, John R. P., Jr. "Overcoming Resistance to Change." In *Basic Studies in Social Psychology*, eds. Harold Proshansky and Bernard Seidenberg. New York: Holt, Rinehart, & Winston, 1965.

Frank, Jerome D. "Experimental Studies of Personal Pressure and Resistance." *Journal of General Psychology* 30:23–64.

Goffman, Erving. "On Cooling the Mark Out: Some Aspects of Adaptation to Failure." In *Interpersonal Dynamics*, eds. Warren Bennis et al. Homewood, Ill.: The Dorsey Press, 1964.

Leeds, Ruth. "The Absorption of Protest." In *New Perspectives in Organizational Research*, eds. William W. Cooper et al. New York: John Wiley & Sons, 1964.

Lerner, Daniel. *The Passing of Traditional Society*. New York: The Free Press, 1958.

Milgram, Stanley. "Behavioral Study of Obedience." *Journal of Abnormal and Social Psychology* 67:371–78.

Milgram, Stanley. "Group Pressure and Action against a Person." *Journal of Abnormal and Social Psychology* 69:137–43.

Milgram, Stanley. "Some Conditions of Obedience and Disobedience to Authority." In *Current Studies in Social Psychology*, eds. Ivan D. Steiner and Martin Fishbein. New York: Holt, Rinehart, & Winston, 1965.

Orne, Martin T. "On the Social Psychology of the Psychological Experiment." *American Psychologist* 17:776–83.

Orne, Martin T., and Evans, Frederick J. "Social Control in the Psychological Experiment." *Journal of Personality and Social Psychology* 1:189–200.

Pepitone, Albert, and Wallace, W., described in Albert Pepitone. "Attributes of Causality, Social Attitudes, and Cognitive Matching Processes." In *Person Perception and Interpersonal Behavior*, eds. Renato Tagiuri and Luigi Petrullo. Palo Alto, Calif.: Stanford University Press, 1958.

Roethlisberger, F. J., and Dickson, W. J. *Management and the Worker*. Cambridge, Mass.: Harvard University Press, 1939.

Selznick, Philip. *TVA and the Grass Roots*. Berkeley: University of California Press, 1953.

Simmel, Georg. *The Sociology of Georg Simmel*, ed. Kurt H. Wolff. New York: The Free Press, 1950.

Verba, Sidney. *Small Groups and Political Behavior*. Princeton, N.J.: Princeton University Press, 1961.

Part 4

Social Conflict:
Its Nature, Functions, and Resolution

Real societies can be torn apart by destructive conflicts and some SIMSOCs have collapsed because of the inability of the participants to deal with the struggles that arose. But we must not conclude from this that conflict is bad for a society. Most social scientists would accept the argument in the selection by Coser that conflict can and frequently does have positive functions. When we talk about healthy conflicts, we have in mind a conflict that is carried on within certain definite limits—moderate conflict. Too little conflict and a society may stagnate; too much conflict and it may fall apart.

Perhaps the most influential theory of how conflicts are kept within acceptable limits is the theory of pluralist democracy. Once again we turn to Dahl for a succinct summary. The factors that lead to moderate rather than severe conflict in Dahl's paradigm are, essentially, the defining conditions of social and political pluralism.

Although one may be able to predict from prior conditions whether severe conflicts will arise, once they begin they frequently have a dynamic of their own. The selection by Boulding focuses on how conflicts can be controlled and, in some cases, resolved. A successful mechanism of conflict resolution is one which extracts the positive value of social conflict while keeping the human costs and the destructive consequences to a minimum. The development of creative mechanisms for handling conflict is a major challenge for any society.

The Functions of Conflict
Lewis Coser

Conflict within a group . . . may help to establish unity or to re-establish unity and cohesion where it has been threatened by hostile and antagonistic feelings among the members. Yet, not *every* type of conflict is likely to benefit group structure, nor can that conflict subserve such functions for *all* groups. Whether social conflict is beneficial to internal adaptation or not depends on the type of issues over which it is fought as well as on the type of social structure within which it occurs. However, types of conflict and types of social structure are not independent variables.

Internal social conflicts which concern goals, values or interests that do not contradict the basic assumptions upon which the relationship is founded tend to be positively functional for the social structure. Such conflicts tend to make possible the readjustment of norms and power relations within groups in accordance with the felt needs of its individual members or subgroups.

Internal conflicts in which the contending parties no longer share the basic values upon which the legitimacy of the social system rests threaten to disrupt the structure.

This reading is reprinted with permission of The Macmillan Co. and Routledge & Kegan Paul Ltd., from Lewis Coser, *The Functions of Social Conflict*, pp. 151–157. © by The Free Press, a Corporation, 1956. Coser is a sociologist at SUNY, Stony Brook, N. Y.

One safeguard against conflict disrupting the consensual basis of the relationship, however, is contained in the social structure itself: it is provided by the institutionalization and tolerance of conflict. Whether internal conflict promises to be a means of equilibration of social relations or readjustment of rival claims, or whether it threatens to "tear apart," depends to a large extent on the social structure within which it occurs.

In every type of social structure there are occasions for conflict, since individuals and subgroups are likely to make from time to time rival claims to scarce resources, prestige or power positions. But social structures differ in the way in which they allow expression to antagonistic claims. Some show more tolerance of conflict than others.

Closely knit groups in which there exists a high frequency of interaction and high personality involvement of the members have a tendency to suppress conflict. While they provide frequent occasions for hostility (since both sentiments of love and hatred are intensified through frequency of interaction), the acting out of such feelings is sensed as a danger to such intimate relationships, and hence there is a tendency to suppress rather than to allow expression of hostile feelings. In close-knit groups, feelings of hostility tend, therefore, to accumulate and hence to intensify. If conflict breaks out in a group that has consistently tried to prevent expression of hostile feelings, it will be particularly intense for two reasons: First, because the conflict does not merely aim at resolving the immediate issue which led to its outbreak; all accumulated grievances which were denied expression previously are apt to emerge at this occasion. Second, because the total personality involvement of the group members makes for mobilization of all sentiments in the conduct of the struggle.

Hence, the closer the group, the more intense the conflict. Where members participate with their total personality and conflicts are suppressed, the conflict, if it breaks out nevertheless, is likely to threaten the very root of the relationship.

In groups comprising individuals who participate only segmentally, conflict is less likely to be disruptive. Such groups are likely to experience a multiplicity of conflicts. This in itself tends to constitute a check against the breakdown of consensus: the energies of group members are mobilized in many directions and hence will not concentrate on *one* conflict cutting through the group. Moreover, where occasions for hostility are not permitted to accumulate and conflict is allowed to occur wherever a resolution of tension seems to be indicated, such a conflict is likely to remain focused primarily on the condition which led to its outbreak and not to revive blocked hostility; in this way, the conflict is limited to "the facts of the case." One may venture to say that multiplicity of conflicts stands in inverse relation to their intensity.

So far we have been dealing with internal social conflict only. At this point we must turn to a consideration of external conflict, for the structure of the group is itself affected by conflicts with other groups in which it engages or which it prepares for. Groups which are engaged in continued struggle tend to lay claim on the total personality involvement of their members so that internal conflict would tend to mobilize all energies and affects of the members. Hence such groups are unlikely to tolerate more than limited departures from the group unity. In such groups there is a tendency to suppress conflict; where it occurs, it leads the group to break up through splits or through forced withdrawal of dissenters.

Groups which are not involved in continued struggle with the outside are less prone to make claims on total personality involvement of the membership and are more likely to exhibit flexibility of structure. The multiple internal conflicts which they tolerate may in turn have an equilibrating and stabilizing impact on the structure.

In flexible social structures, multiple conflicts crisscross each other and thereby prevent basic cleavages along one axis. The multiple group affiliations of individuals makes them participate in various group conflicts so that their total personalities are not involved in any single one of them. Thus segmental participation in a multiplicity of conflicts constitutes a balancing mechanism within the structure.

In loosely structured groups and open societies, conflict, which aims at a resolution of tension between antagonists, is likely to have stabilizing and integrative functions for the relationship. By permitting immediate and direct expression of rival claims, such social systems are able to readjust their structures by eliminating the sources of dissatisfaction. The multiple conflicts which they experience may serve to eliminate the causes for dissociation and to re-establish unity. These systems avail themselves, through the toleration and institutionalization of conflict, of an important stabilizing mechanism.

In addition, conflict within a group frequently helps to revitalize existent norms; or it contributes to the emergence of new norms. In this sense, social conflict is a mechanism for adjustment of norms adequate to new conditions. A flexible society benefits from conflict because such behavior, by helping to create and modify norms, assures it continuance under changed conditions. Such mechanism for readjustment of norms is hardly available to rigid systems: by suppressing conflict, the latter smother a useful warning signal, thereby maximizing the danger of catastrophic breakdown.

Internal conflict can also serve as a means for ascertaining the relative strength of antagonistic interests within the structure, and in this way constitute a mechanism for the maintenance or continual readjustment of the balance of power. Since the outbreak of the conflict indicates a rejection of a previous accommodation between parties, once the respective power of the contenders has been ascertained through conflict, a new equilibrium can be established and the relationship can proceed on this new basis. Consequently, a social structure in which there is room for conflict disposes of an important means for avoiding or redressing conditions of disequilibrium by modifying the terms of power relations.

Conflicts with some produce associations or coalitions with others. Conflicts through such associations or coalitions, by providing a bond between the members, help to reduce social isolation or to unite individuals and groups otherwise unrelated or antagonistic to each other. A social structure in which there can exist a multiplicity of conflicts contains a mechanism for bringing together otherwise isolated, apathetic or mutually hostile parties and for taking them into the field of public social activities. Moreover, such a structure fosters a multiplicity of associations and coalitions whose diverse purposes crisscross each other, we recall, thereby preventing alliances along one major line of cleavage.

Once groups and associations have been formed through conflict with other groups, such conflict may further serve to maintain boundary lines between them and the surrounding social environment. In this way, social conflict helps to structure the larger social environment by assigning position to the various subgroups within the system and by helping to define the power relations between them.

Not all social systems in which individuals participate segmentally allow the free expression of antagonistic claims. Social systems tolerate or institutionalize conflict to different degrees. There is no society in which any and every antagonistic claim is allowed immediate expression. Societies dispose of mechanisms to channel discontent and hostility while keeping intact the relationship within which antagonism arises. Such mechanisms frequently operate through "safety-valve" institutions which provide substitute objects upon which to displace hostile sentiments as well as means of abreaction of aggressive tendencies.

Safety-valve institutions may serve to maintain both the social structure and the individual's security system, but they are incompletely functional for both of them. They prevent modification of relationships to meet changing conditions and hence the satisfaction they afford the individual can be only partially or momentarily adjustive. The hypothesis has been suggested that the need for safety-valve institutions increases with the rigidity of the social structure, i.e., with the degree to which it disallows direct expression of antagonistic claims.

Safety-valve institutions lead to a displacement of goal in the actor: he need no longer aim at reaching a solution of the unsatisfactory situation, but merely at releasing the tension which arose from it. Where safety-valve institutions provide substitute objects for the displacement of hostility, the conflict itself is channeled away from the original unsatisfactory relationship into one in which the actor's goal is no longer the attainment of specific results, but the release of tension.

This affords us a criterion for distinguishing between realistic and non-realistic conflict.

Social conflicts that arise from frustrations of specific demands within a relationship and from estimates of gains of the participants, and that are directed at the presumed frustrating object, can be called realistic conflicts. Insofar as they are means toward specific results, they can be replaced by alternative modes of interaction with the contending party if such alternatives seem to be more adequate for realizing the end in view.

Nonrealistic conflicts, on the other hand, are not occasioned by the rival ends of the antagonists, but by the need for tension release of one or both of them. In this case the conflict is not oriented toward the attainment of specific results. Insofar as unrealistic conflict is an end in itself, insofar as it affords only tension release, the chosen antagonist can be substituted for by any other "suitable" target.

In realistic conflict, there exist functional alternatives with regard to the means of carrying out the conflict, as well as with regard to accomplishing desired results short of conflict; in nonrealistic conflict, on the other hand, there exist only functional alternatives in the choice of antagonists.

Our hypothesis, that the need for safety-valve institutions increases with the rigidity of the social system, may be extended to suggest that unrealistic conflict may be expected to occur as a consequence of rigidity present in the social structure.

Our discussion of the distinction between types of conflict, and between types of social structures, leads us to conclude that conflict tends to be dysfunctional for a social structure in which there is no or insufficient toleration and institutionalization of conflict. The intensity of a conflict which threatens to "tear apart," which attacks the consensual basis of a social system, is related to the rigidity of the structure. What threatens the equilibrium of such a structure is not conflict as such, but the rigidity itself which permits hostilities to accumulate and to be channeled along one major line of cleavage once they break out in conflict.

Conflict: A Paradigm
Robert A. Dahl

The intensity or severity of a political conflict in a republic is indicated by the extent to which people on each side see the other as an enemy to be destroyed; evidence that political disagreements are becoming severe is an increase in threats or actual use of violence, suppression of opponents, civil war, secession, disloyalty, or a marked increase in demoralization, apathy, indifference, or alienation.

The intensity or severity of a political conflict depends on at least four sets of factors:

1. The way in which politically relevant attitudes are distributed among the citizens and leaders.

a. The greater the number of citizens who hold extreme (and opposing) views the more severe a conflict is likely to be. Conversely, the greater the number who hold moderate views, the less severe a conflict is likely to be.

b. The more extreme the views of political leaders and activists in comparison with the views of ordinary citizens, the more severe the conflict; conversely, the more moderate the views of leaders and activists in comparison with other citizens, the less severe the conflict is likely to be.

2. The patterns of cleavage.

The more conflicts accumulate along the same lines of cleavage, the more severe they are likely to be; conversely, the more conflicts intersect along different lines of cleavage, the less severe they are.

3. How much is at stake.

a. The more at stake, the more severe a conflict is likely to be.

b. A conflict in which no contestant can possibly make himself better off except by making other contestants worse off is likely to be more severe than a conflict in which there is a possibility that no contestant need be worse off than before, and some may be better off.

c. Conflicts involving incompatible "ways of life" are bound to be particularly severe.

4. The political institutions.

a. Political institutions and processes are likely to intensify conflicts if they require the groups involved to negotiate but do not provide any acceptable way by which leaders can terminate negotiations and arrive at a decision.

b. Political institutions and processes are likely to intensify conflicts if they make it possible for leaders to make decisions without engaging in negotiations to obtain the consent of the persons, groups, or parties involved.

c. Political institutions and processes are most likely to reduce the intensity of conflicts if they embody widespread agreement on procedures, *both* for negotiating in order to gain consent and for terminating the negotiations and arriving at a decision.

These propositions are summarized in the Table following.

This reading is reprinted from Robert A. Dahl, *Pluralistic Democracy in the United States: Conflict and Consent.* © 1967 by Rand-McNally and Company, Chicago, pp. 279–81.

a paradigm: some factors that moderate or intensify political conflicts

	conflict is more likely to be	
	moderate if:	severe if:
1. The distribution of attitudes is	convergent	divergent
a. Attitudes of citizens are	convergent	divergent
b. Attitudes of political leaders and activists are	convergent	divergent
2. Lines of cleavage are	overlapping (cross-cutting)	non-overlapping (cumulative)
3. Threats to ways of life are	absent	present
a. Privileged groups feel	secure	seriously threatened
b. Aspiring groups feel	successful	frustrated
4. Political institutions provide		
a. Negotiations for consent but not decisions	no	yes
b. Decisions without consent	no	yes
c. Agreed processes for negotiating consent and arriving at decisions	yes	no

Conflict Resolution and Control
Kenneth E. Boulding

In any given social situation or subsystem, we can perhaps postulate an optimum amount or degree of conflict. The concept is hard to specify, but it is of great importance. It relieves us immediately, for instance, from the illusion, if anyone ever possessed it, that conflict in any amount is either bad or good in itself. The evaluation of conflict has two aspects: quantitative and qualitative. In a given situation, we may have too much or too little conflict, or the amount may be just right. There is no simple operational definition of such an optimum; we must rely for our information on a complex structure of attitudes and evaluations. In a given situation, we may also have the wrong kind of conflict. Here again, there is no simple operational definition, but common speech has words that describe these qualitative differences: conflicts may be bitter and destructive, or they may be fruitful and constructive. We shall not argue here whether the qualitative difference can be reduced to quantity—whether, for instance, conflicts that are bad are so simply because there is too much or perhaps too little of them. In the absence of any clear index of the quantity of a conflict, this issue cannot be resolved. The best strategy would seem to be to go as far as we can with the concept of quantity but reserve the right to discover that conflict has more than one dimension and cannot, therefore, wholly be described in terms of simple "more or less."

We may think that a situation has too little conflict because it is dull and lacks drama. Drama is an important value in practically all cultures, and conflict is one of the most important sources of dramatic interest. Most religious and national ideologies, for instance, conceive of the universe as involving a dramatic conflict between the forces of good and evil played out on the stage of the world. In personal life also, the absence of conflict is identified with a dull, featureless existence. The institution of games and sports is evidence that, where a situation does not have enough conflict in it, conflict will be created artifically, either between individuals, as in chess, pairs as in bridge, or teams as in baseball, football, and so on. Prof. F. H. Knight is reported to have said that what people really want in the world is trouble, and if they do not have enough of it, they will create it artificially, the institution of sport being the proof.

On the other hand, there is a great deal of evidence that conflict in its nonsport aspect is usually felt as too much. Even though we may admit that some conflict is good, the word itself has a bias toward the bad. We think of the problem of conflict not usually in terms of how we get more of it but how we get less of it. We think of conflict in terms of family quarrels, separation, and divorce, or racial discrimination and race riots, or industrial disputes and strikes, or political conflict and revolution, or international conflict and war. These things we think of on the whole as bad, as tending to go too far and to get out of hand. Dialectitians like Hegel and Marx may defend conflict as a necessary instrument of change and progress, and sociologists like Simmel and Coser may defend it as an instrument of social integration, but this still has to be a defense against the common prejudice. Conflict is discord, and the opposite of conflict is harmony; the words reveal the evaluational bias in the language and in the common experience. Discord may be necessary to make music interesting and to give it drama, but its significance lies in the ability of the composer to resolve discord into some meaningful harmony, however subtle. The essence of the drama of conflict is likewise its resolution; it is not the conflict as such that makes the drama but the resolution of the conflict as a meaningful process through time. A conflict that went on and on without end and without resolution would lose even dramatic interest; it would eventually become mere noise and confusion. It is the process of conflict toward some kind of resolution which gives it meaning and which makes it good. This is true even in sports and games; a game that went on interminably without any resolution would be intolerable.

We must, therefore, look at the ways in which conflicts are resolved if we are to assess their value and if we are to evaluate the institutions by which they are controlled. What we must look for here is ways in which a particular conflict process moves toward an end. This is not to say, of course, that conflict itself comes to an end, for conflicts are continually being recreated. Each particular conflict, however, can be thought of as having a life cycle: it is conceived and born, it flourishes for a while, and then certain processes that are probably

This reading is abridged from pp. 305–311, 322–324, 326–328, "Conflict Resolution and Control" from *Conflict and Defense* by Kenneth E. Boulding. © 1962 by Kenneth E. Boulding. Reprinted by permission of Harper & Row, Publishers, Inc. Boulding is an economist at the University of Colorado.

inherent in its own dynamic system eventually bring it to an end. Resolution, as we shall see, is only one way of ending conflicts, and, out of the many ways of ending conflicts, it may not always be clear which deserve the reward of being called resolution. Resolved conflicts, however, are clearly a subset of ended conflicts, and we should study the latter first.

The first method of ending conflicts is probably the commonest, though by its very nature it is also the least noticeable. This is the method of *avoidance.* The parties to the conflict simply remove themselves one from another and increase the distance between them to the point where the conflict ceases from sheer lack of contact. A man who cannot get on with his boss quits or is fired. The man who cannot get along with his country emigrates. Teams between whom the conflict has become too bitter for sportsmanship stop playing with each other. Couples who cannot get along divorce. A customer who does not like one store finds another. Two friends who quarrel separate and do not see each other again. A quarrelsome faction within a church splits from it and forms another sect. Ideological or personal conflict within a party splits it, and two parties go off from the fission. Two atoms that cannot get along in a molecule split off and go their separate ways.

Avoidance is the classical method of resolving economic conflicts through pure competition; disputes about bargains are avoided simply because there is always another bargainer to go to. Political disputes are resolved by trading votes and logrolling and by a constant ballet of shifting political partners. Racial disputes are suppressed by segregation and by seeing to it that the races do not mix or only meet under rigid and stereotyped rules of behavior. Class conflict is avoided by cultural differentiation of the classes, with different speech and behavior patterns, so that the classes also do not meet except under formal and stereotyped conditions. International conflict may be mitigated by devices like arms control, which, in effect, move the nations farther apart. Avoidance always involves putting some kind of distance between the parties. The distance need not only be physical distance, though this is the most obvious and commonest form; it may take the form of social distance, as in segregation, or epistemological distance, as when two parties deliberately cultivate ignorance of each other and avoid overt communications. The Catholic-Protestant entente in the United States almost seems to follow this pattern.

The most extreme form of avoidance is *conquest*, the second form of ending conflict, by which one of the parties is, in effect, removed to infinity, or removed from the scene, leaving the victor in sole possession of the field. An interesting asymmetry in the avoidance pattern shows up clearly at this point. There are three forms of avoidance. One party may simply remove himself from the field; the avoiding party here does all the work. Both parties may remove themselves, though this is less likely, as once one party begins to remove himself, there is little incentive for the other to move. The third form is where one party forcibly removes the other. The parent carries the howling child out into the garden and returns to the house. The trade union or the church expels a dissident faction. One nation forces another by threats to withdraw from a field of conflict. This form of avoidance usually involves a good deal more work on the part of the active party than does simple self-removal, as the active party has to remove the other and then return to the field. Conquest is the extreme case of forcible removal, in which the removed party is removed completely. In a quarrel, one man kills another. In a war, one nation exterminates another. One race or group practices genocide on another. Fortunately, these cases are fairly rare, mainly because of the amount of work involved. Conquest, of course, can take place only where one party is conditionally viable with respect to the other. Two parties that are unconditionally viable with respect to each other obviously cannot practice conquest. Even if the parties are not unconditionally viable, the cost of conquest may preclude its attempt, and some other form of conflict conclusion must be practiced.

If the parties can neither conquer nor avoid each other, some form of *procedural* resolution of conflict is likely. In procedural resolution, the parties have to stay together and live with each other; conflict, in general, may not be resolved permanently in so far as the parties continue to exist in contact, but particular conflicts may be resolved simply in the sense that they come to an end as social systems and are replaced by other conflicts and other systems. We may distinguish three types of procedural conflict conclusion. The first is *reconciliation*, in which the value systems of the images of the parties so change that they now have common preferences in their joint field: they both want the same state of affairs or position in the joint field, and so conflict is eliminated. The second is *compromise*, in which the value systems are not identical and the parties have different optimum positions in the joint field; however, each party is willing to settle for something less than his ideal position rather than continue the conflict. In compromise, this settlement is reached mutually by bargaining between the parties themselves. The third type of conflict conclusion is the *award*, in which a settlement is reached because both parties have agreed to accept the verdict of an outside person or agency rather than continue the conflict. The compromise and the award are essentially similar in that they both represent less than the ideal situation for each party; they differ mainly in the method of arriving at the settlement.

To each of the three forms of procedural conflict conclusion, there corresponds an appropriate set of procedures. Thus, reconciliation is the result of conversation, argument, discussion, or debate that leads to convergent modifications of the images of the two parties. Compromise is the end result of a process of bargaining, in which mediation and conciliation may play an important part. An award is the end result of arbitration or legal trial. Neither the three forms of settlement nor the various procedures are completely separate in practice; though there is a tendency for one form to dominate in any particular case. Frequently, however, both reconciliation and compromise go on together; indeed, some reconciliation may be necessary before compromise is possible. Consequently, there are always likely to be elements of discussion and propaganda in bargaining situations. Similarly, in arbitration cases or in court proceedings, there are often elements both of reconciliation and of bargaining before the award is handed down, and the award will not be accepted unless it has been preceded by informal reconciliation and bargaining. One of the most difficult institutional problems in the handling of conflict is how to arrange for the right proportions and the right order of these various elements of the situation. Thus, legal procedings, such as suits, are often a poor way of handling conflicts in industrial relations, because of the difficulty of incorporating the necessary bargaining and reconciling processes in purely legal procedure. The same difficulty in marital conflict has sometimes led to the setting up of special marriage courts in which these more informal procedures can be employed.

* * *

When procedural conflict proves inadequate to deal with the intensity of the conflict in society or when there are no institutions for procedural conflict, violence is likely to result. The study of violence would again require a volume in itself; for all the importance of the phenomenon, there is surprisingly little theoretical or empirical study of it. It is not even easy to define. People can be killed or incapacitated with ulcers, and they can be injured by psychological violence just as effec-

tively as they can with a gun. However, a distinction does not have to be clear to be important, and, at some point, there is a common-sense dividing line between procedural and violent conflict. Violence is most closely associated with conquest as a form of conflict settlement, though violence is descriptive of a conflict process rather than of a conflict settlement. It is quite possible, for instance, for conquest to be nonviolent, that is, for one party to be absorbed in another or for one organization to be dissolved by strictly procedural means. Departments are organized out of existence, countries are federated or united, organizations are laid down, and firms are bankrupted by purely procedural processes, without more than perhaps a trace of legal coercion lurking in the background.

Violence also does not necessarily lead to settlement. Indeed, it is perhaps the major evil of violence that it frequently inhibits settlement; for it often leaves no path to settlement open but conquest, and this may not be possible. Consequently, violence persists as a chronic disease of society; the procedures that might resolve the conflicts are too weak to prevent violence taking over, and violence in itself prevents the conflicts from being resolved and indeed perpetuates them. Violence, for instance, creates an atmosphere in which reconciliation is difficult and in which, indeed, each party is likely to move farther away from the position of the other. It likewise makes compromise difficult; one does not compromise with a man with a gun, and getting a gun oneself does not assist the process of compromise either. One does not negotiate from strength; one may dictate from strength, but one does not negotiate. The only place where violence may have a part to play in conflict settlement is where there is a sufficient monopoly or preponderance of violence in the hands of one party so that settlement can come about through conquest or award. Monopolies or preponderances of violence, however, seem to be unstable: where violence is not legitimated by procedures and constitutions, it tends to raise violence against it. Violence in itself, because it cannot perform the reconciling and compromising function, leads to the suppression rather than the resolution of conflict: it drives conflict underground but does little to eliminate it.

One of the great organizational problems of mankind, then, is the control of violence or, more generally, the control of conflict to the point where procedural institutions are adequate to handle it. The great course of political evolution, from the family to the tribe to the nation to the superpower, and finally, one hopes, to the world government now in its birth pangs is testimony to the ability of human organization to extend conflict control to wider and wider areas. It is hardly too much to say that conflict control is government, and though government has broader functions than this, conflict control is perhaps its most important single task—the one thing which it must perform or cease to be government.

* * *

The two greatest problems of control systems are first, signal detection, that is, how do we know when something needs to be done, and second, implementation, or how do we know what to do. I suspect that the signal-detection problem in conflict control is not so serious as it might seem. The problem is how to detect social situations that are in the early stages of a process that will lead eventually to destructive conflict if it is not checked. In any such detection or perception problem, there is always a chance of error. There are two types of error. We may give a false alarm; that is, we may perceive the situation as requiring action when in fact it does not, and the problem will solve itself without action. We may give out a failed alarm; that is, we may say nothing needs to be done when in fact something should be done. It seems to be almost impossible to correct both these errors beyond a certain point; that is, if our detection system gives very few failed alarms, it will give a lot of false alarms, and we can avoid false alarms only at the cost of increasing the number of failed alarms. If both false alarms and failed alarms are costly this presents a very great dilemma. One suspects, however, that, in conflict control, false alarms are relatively cheap as compared with failed alarms; that is, the consequences of doing something that need not have been done are relatively slight, whereas the consequences of not doing something that should be done may be disastrous. There is no harm, then, in building a detection system that gives very few failed alarms, even if it gives a lot of false alarms: one can be tolerant of the false alarm. This is a very different situation from that posed by violent conflict, where false alarms and failed alarms may be equally fatal.

One would like to see an international organization for the detection of young conflict processes. The idea may seem impractical at the moment because people do not think in these terms; they think of conflicts as uncontrollable acts of God like hurricanes, and the idea of conflict control is a new one, even though the practice is as old as political organization. It was only a few years ago, however, that people thought of depressions and the business cycle in similar terms and talked about economic blizzards. Now the idea of depression control is accepted even in the most conservative circles. Similarly, one may hope that the idea of conflict control may receive equally rapid acceptance, in view of the immense crisis of conflict that we face.

The problem of implementation is, of course, much more difficult, and what to do once an incipient conflict process has been detected depends very much on the nature of the conflict itself. The problem is perhaps easiest in those areas where there are few specialized agencies for the conduct and encouragement of conflict, such as in race relations; here the counterconflict organization such as, for instance, the National Conference of Christians and Jews or the local interracial council can exercise a substantial influence. In labor relations also, conflict control is an important part of the practice of modern industrial relations, and the knowledge of industrial relations processes that has been accumulated in the course of a generation or more of study is now bearing valuable fruit. The problem is most difficult in the case of international relations, where there are specialized agencies for conflict (the armed forces) that have a vested interest in the preservation of conflict or at least of the threat of conflict, simply because conflict is the only reason for their existence as organizations. Even here, however, the sheer enormity of the cost of nuclear warfare is forcing the development of the institutions of conflict control. The current interest in arms control is a straw in the wind, and, in the case of international relations where the armed forces of the world form a social system with a dynamics of its own that is largely independent of the interests of the nations that support these forces, arms control may be nine-tenths of the problem. The problems of organization and of bargaining involved in setting up the institutions of arms control and, more generally, of international conflict control are difficult indeed; but it would be suicide for the human race to believe that they are insoluble. It has been the major theme of this work to show that conflict processes are neither arbitrary, random, nor, incomprehensible. In the understanding of these processes lies the opportunity for their control, and perhaps even for human survival. We cannot claim that our understanding is deep enough, and much work yet needs to be done, but it can and must be claimed that the understanding and, therefore ultimately, the control of these processes is possible. In that lies the present hope for mankind, for, without conflict control, all other hopes for human welfare and betterment are likely to be dashed to the ground.

References

Coser, Lewis. *The Functions of Social Conflict.* New York: The Free Press, 1956.

Schelling, Thomas C. *The Strategy of Conflict.* Cambridge, Mass.: Harvard University Press, 1960.

Part 5

Interpersonal Influence and Leadership

SIMSOC is intended to be a simulation of a society but at the same time it is a relatively small group of individuals engaged in what is frequently a highly intense interaction. Rich and dramatic interpersonal dynamics are produced in the course of most SIMSOCs and some game coordinators choose to make this a major focus of the post-game discussion. This section of readings focuses on one aspect of this interaction—interpersonal influence and the emergence of leadership.

The selection by Blau analyzes the emergence of leadership and power differentiation within a group as an outgrowth of a process of social exchange. It has the merit of linking interpersonal processes to the emergence of more permanent social institutions. Verba examines a special problem of leadership—trying to meet the emotional and human needs of the members of a group while, at the same time, having to push people toward the accomplishment of some task. It is a problem which many groups solve by using different leaders for the social-emotional and instrumental areas; these leaders, however, must cooperate if the group is to be effective. The tension between the two leadership tasks is greatly reduced, Verba points out, if leaders have high legitimacy. Under such conditions, efforts to move the group toward its goal are not regarded by group members as exercises of personal power which cause resentment. Finally, the selection by Weinstein examines the ploys we use to get what we want in social interactions while at the same time we help both ourselves and others to maintain an appropriate social identity or face. Weinstein gives the name "interpersonal tactics" to the simultaneous management of the twin problems of facework and social influence.

Social Exchange, Power, and Leadership*
Peter M. Blau

Unilateral Dependence and Obligations

By supplying services in demand to others, a person establishes power over them. If he regularly renders needed services they cannot readily obtain elsewhere, others become dependent on and obligated to him for these services, and unless they can furnish other benefits to him that produce interdependence by making him equally dependent on them, their unilateral dependence obligates them to comply with his requests lest he cease to continue to meet their needs. Providing needed benefits others cannot easily do without is undoubtedly the most prevalent way of attaining power, though not the only one, since it can also be attained by threatening to deprive others of benefits they currently enjoy unless they submit. The threat of punishment, although it exerts the most severe restraints, creates the dependence that is the root of power indirectly, as it were, while recurrent essential rewards that can be withheld do so

* At the author's request, we have departed from the usual format in this selection and included footnotes rather than references at the end. The footnotes have been renumbered from the original as appropriate.

This reading is reprinted from Peter M. Blau, *Exchange and Power in Social Life*. New York: John Wiley & Sons, 1964, pp. 118–125, and 199–205. Blau is a sociologist at Columbia University.

directly. The government that furnishes needed protection to its citizens, the employer who provides needed jobs to his employees, and the profession that supplies needed services to the community, all make the others dependent of them and potentially subject to their power.

Emerson has presented a schema for examining "power-dependence" relations and their consequences, which can be reformulated to specify the conditions that produce the imbalance of power itself.[1] Individuals who need a service another has to offer have the following alternatives: *First, they can supply him with a service* that he wants badly enough to induce him to offer his service in return, though only if they have the resources required for doing so; this will lead to reciprocal exchanges. *Second, they may obtain the needed service elsewhere*, assuming that there are alternative suppliers; this also will lead to reciprocal exchanges but in different partnerships. *Third, they can coerce him to furnish the service*, provided they are capable of doing so, in which case they would establish domination over him. *Fourth, they may learn to resign themselves to do without this service*, possibly finding some substitute for it, which would require that they change the values that determine their needs. Finally, if they are not able or willing to choose any of these alternatives, they have no other choice but to comply with his wishes, since he can make continued supply of the needed service contingent on their compliance. In the situation specified, the supply of services inevitably generates power. The absence of the first four alternatives defines the conditions of power in general.

This schema can be employed to indicate the conditions of social independence, the requirements of power, the issues in power conflicts, and their structural implications. The conditions of social independence are characterized by the availability of the first four alternatives, which enables people to evade the fifth one of dependence on services from a given source. First, strategic resources promote independence. Specifically, a person who has all the resources required as effective inducements for others to furnish him with the services and benefits he needs is protected against becoming dependent on anyone. The possession of generalized rewards, such as money, is evidently of major significance in this connection,

although wealth is not a perfect safeguard against dependence, since many benefits a person may want, such as fame or love, cannot be obtained for money but only with other resources.

The fact that there are alternative sources from which a needed service can be obtained is a second condition that fosters independence. If there is only one employer in a community, or only one expert consultant in a work group, others are likely to become dependent on him. The situation, however, does not have to be that extreme. As a matter of fact, any commitment to a social relationship entails a degree of dependence by excluding alternatives. An employee presumably remains in a job either because alternative employment opportunities are less attractive to him or because his investment in this job is so great that moving to another would be too costly for him. Whatever the reason, his lack of equally preferable alternatives makes him dependent on his employer.[2] The degree of dependence of individuals on a person who supplies valued services is a function of the difference between their value and that of the second-best alternative open to them. The more employees prefer their own job to any possible alternative, the more dependent are they on their employer and the more power does he have over them. The employer can cut the salary of employees who are very dependent on their job, assign them unpleasant duties, or force them to work harder, and they have no choice but to accept the decisions and to comply. Yet by doing so the employer makes the job less attractive to the employees and other employment opportunities relatively more attractive, decreasing the difference between the present job and alternatives, and thus reducing his employees' dependence on him and his power over them. Generally, the greater the difference between the benefits an individual supplies to others and those they can obtain elsewhere, the greater is his power over them likely to be. Hence, others can increase their independence of a person who has power over them simply by accepting fewer benefits from him—no more than they can get for their services elsewhere—except that this is often not so simple for them.[3]

---

[1] Richard M. Emerson, "Power-Dependence Relations," *American Sociological Review* 27 (1962), 31–41. Suggestive as the underlying conception is, the focus on balancing operations is unfortunate and somewhat confusing inasmuch as it diverts attention from the analysis of power imbalance. His schema deals with the balancing operations consequent to given differences in power-dependence, whereas the reformulation derives power imbalance from the conditions of exchange.

[2] The counterdependence of the small employer on the employee's services may create interdependence and neutralize the small employer's power, but the large employer is not so much dependent on single employees as on a labor force whose turnover can and must be taken into account in management, and his independence of any one employee sustains his power over all of them, unless it is reduced by their collective action.

[3] Accepting a job at a higher salary than one can command in the market, buying from an acquaintance at wholesale prices, gaining acceptance in a more eminent group than one's achievements warrant, and generally obtaining any recurrent benefit that is superior to what could be obtained elsewhere entails dependence and loss of power.

A third condition of independence is the ability to use coercive force to compel others to dispense needed benefits or services. The inability to use force may be due to weakness or to normative restraints that effectively prohibit resort to coercion, or it may be due to the fact that the desired benefit loses its significance if given under duress, as is the case for love and for social approval. Superior coercive power makes people relatively independent of others inasmuch as power includes the ability to prevent others from interfering with one's conduct. Since there is strength in numbers, independence can be won through forming coalitions capable of enforcing demands.[4]

A lack of need for various services constitutes the fourth condition of independence. The fewer the wants and needs of an individual, the less dependent he is on others to meet them. Needs, however, do not remain constant. By providing individuals with goods and services that increase their satisfaction, their level of expectations tends to be raised, and while they were previously satisfied without these benefits, they are now desirous of continuing to obtain them. The development of new needs in this fashion underlies the increasing consumer demand that is an essential element in an expanding economy. But emergent needs serve this function by strengthening the dependence of people on those who can supply the resources required to meet these needs, notably employers. Religious and political ideals derive their driving force in large part from imbuing adherents with values that make the satisfaction of material wants comparatively unimportant and that, consequently, lessen men's dependence on those who can supply material benefits. By reducing material needs, revolutionary ideologies become a source of independent strength and resistance to power.

The fourfold schema can also help to delineate the strategies required to attain and sustain power, which are complementary to the conditions of independence just discussed. To achieve power over others with his resources, a person must prevent others from choosing any of the first four alternatives, thereby compelling them to comply with his directives as a condition for obtaining the needed benefits at his command. This requires, first, that he remain indifferent to the benefits they can offer him in exchange for his. The strategies of power designed to preserve this indifference include denying others access to resources that are vital for the welfare of a group or individual, for example, by fighting attempts of working-class parties to take over the government; securing needed benefits from outside sources rather than subordinates, as illustrated by the gang leader's

disinclination to borrow money from his more affluent followers;[5] and encouraging competition among the suppliers of essential service, for instance, by opposing the formation of unions that would restrict competition for jobs among workers.

A second requirement of power is to assure the continued dependence of others on the services one has to supply by barring access to alternative suppliers of these services. Monopolization of needed rewards is the typical means of achieving this purpose. The only firm in town where jobs can be found, the only child on the block who has a bicycle, the political society that is the sole source of national security and glory, the church that is the only avenue to salvation, and the police that alone can offer protection against violence—all these have power due to their monopoly over important benefits.

The ability to prevent others from resorting to coercive force to effect their demands is a third prerequisite of maintaining power. Discouraging coalitions among subordinates that would enable them to extract demands is a strategy that serves this end, as is blocking their access to political power. Such organizations as unions and working-class parties have two analytically distinct, though actually inseparable, functions in the fight against existing powers. Their success threatens those in positions of power, on the one hand, by making them dependent for essential services on these organizations (for example, for labor supply) and, on the other, by subjecting them to their coercive power (for instance, the union's sit-down strike or the executive power of the labor-party government). Obstructing such coalitions, therefore, protects power against being undermined either by withholding vital services or by employing coercive force. Probably the most important strategies for safeguarding the power that rests on the possession of important resources, however, are support for law and order and resistance against political control of exchange processes. These defenses protect the power potential that resides in superior vital resources not only from the threat of violence but also from being curbed by the legitimate power of the state.

Fourth, power depends on people's needs for the benefits those in power have to offer. Materialistic values, which make money and what it can buy of great significance, strengthen the power of employers. Patriotic ideals, which identify people with the success of their country in war and peace, fortify the power of the government. Religious convictions, which make the blessings of a church

---

[4] Emerson, *op. cit.*, p. 37.

[5] William F. Whyte, *Street Corner Society* (2nd Ed), University of Chicago Press, 1955, pp. 257–258.

and the spiritual counsel of its representatives rewards of great saliency, reinforce the power of church dignitaries. Revolutionary ideologies, which define the progress of a radical movement as inherently valuable for its members, bestow power on the movement's leadership. Groups and individuals in power have a stake in helping to perpetuate and spread the relevant social values and in opposing counterideologies that depreciate these values. Dominant groups whose power rests on different social values have some conflicting interests, therefore, although their common interest in preserving the existing power structure may well override these differences.

The conflict between the powerful (who have an interest in fortifying their power) and the people over whom they have power (who have an interest in strengthening their independence) centers around four types of issues, which again correspond to the four alternatives outlined. First, there is the issue of the resources of subordinates. If their resources were sufficient to obtain the benefits they need in exchange for them, they would cease to be subject to the power of the others. Granted that every single subordinate's resources are inadequate for this purpose, the issue becomes that of pooling the resources of all subordinates who confront a superior or group of superiors to extract demands from him or them. The second issue is that of the alternative opportunities available to subordinates for obtaining needed benefits. Competition among superiors for the services of subordinates increases the subordinates' independence, whereas monopolistic practices increase the superiors' power. These two conflicts are complementary, since the question in both cases is the degree of collective organization permissible to restrain free competition, although it is the organization of the powerless that would husband their resources in one case, and the organization of the powerful that would monopolize needed benefits in the other.

The third conflict is political. At issue here is the use of coercive force in the fight against powers based on superior resources. The prototype is the conflict over the use of the legitimate coercive power of the state to regulate exchange transactions and restrict power that rests on economic strength. Fourth, there is the ideological conflict between social values that intensify the need for the services the powerful have to offer and counterideologies that mitigate this need. In the process of decreasing the need for some services, however, radical ideologies increase the need for others—namely, those that contribute to the reform movement—with the result that ideologies make adherents less dependent on the power of some but more dependent on the power of others.

Finally, tracing the implications of each of the four alternatives leads to the analysis of basic problems of social structure. First, the fact that benefits can be obtained by reciprocating for them with others directs attention to the study of exchange processes and the distribution of resources. Second, the exploration of alternative opportunities points to the investigation of the emerging exchange structures, the competitive processes in them, the going rates of exchange, and the normative standards that tend to develop. Third, the study of coercive power raises questions concerning the establishment of coalitions and organizations to mobilize power, the differentiation of power in social structures, and the processes that govern the struggle over political power in a society.[6] Fourth, the ability to get along without something originally needed calls attention to the modifications of social values that occur under various conditions, the formation of new ideologies, and conflicts between ideologies.

The main points of the entire discussion presented are summarized in the schema on page 107.

Dependence on the benefits a person can supply does not make others subject to his power but gives him only potential power over them. Realization of this power requires that he actually supply the benefits or commit himself to do so. In a technical sense, we are dependent on all employers who are in a position to offer us better jobs than those we have, but these employers have no power over us, while our employer has the power to command our compliance with his directives, because the salary and other benefits he furnishes obligate us to comply lest we cease to continue to receive them. He alone can withdraw from us benefits to which we have become accustomed, whereas other employers can only tempt us with greater rewards.

The ability to provide superior benefits than are available elsewhere, in a situation where these benefits are needed and cannot be extracted by force, constitutes a very strong claim to power, although not a completely inescapable one. If the power demands are too severe, relinquishing these benefits may be preferable to yielding to the demands. Moreover, a person's or group's resources may not be adequate to obligate others to comply. For these reasons coercive force, which can hardly be resisted, is important as a last resort for exercising power over individuals who cannot otherwise be made to yield. Whereas physical force is a perfect protection against power—killing a man or incarcerating him disposes of his threat—it is an

---

[6] These could also be considered to be implications of the fifth alternative. The third and fifth alternatives are complementary, as they are concerned with power from the perspectives of the two different parties.

Alternatives to Compliance	Conditions of Independence	Requirements of Power	Structural Implications
1. Supply inducements	Strategic resources	Indifference to what others offer	Exchange and distribution of resources
2. Obtain elsewhere	Available alternatives	Monopoly over what others need	Competition and exchange rates
3. Take by force	Coercive force	Law and order	Organization and differentiation
4. Do without	Ideals lessening needs	Materialistic and other relevant values	Ideology formation

imperfect tool for exercising power, since people can choose even death over compliance. Hence, coercive force differs only in degree from the power that rests on the supply of needed benefits, albeit an important degree.

* * *

Legitimation and Organization

Organization involves the coordination of collective effort. Some form of social organization emerges implicitly in collectivities as the result of the processes of exchange and competition, in which the patterns of conduct of individuals and groups and the relations between them become adjusted. These processes have already been discussed. But other organizations are explicitly established for the purpose of achieving specified objectives, whether they are manufacturing goods that can be sold for a profit, participating in bowling tournaments, collective bargaining, or winning political victory. In these formal organizations, special mechanisms exist to effect the coordination of tasks of various members in the pursuit of given objectives. Such coordination of efforts, particularly on a large scale, requires some centralized direction. Power is the resource that makes it possible to direct and coordinate the activities of men.

Stable organizing power requires legitimation. To be sure, men can be made to work and to obey commands through coercion, but the coercive use of power engenders resistance and sometimes active opposition. Power conflicts in and between societies are characterized by resistance and opposition, and while the latter also occur within organizations, effective operations necessitate that they be kept at a minimum there and, especially, that members do not exhibit resistance in discharg-

ing their daily duties but perform them and comply with directives from superiors *willingly*. Only legitimate power commands willing compliance.

Legitimate power is authority, which Weber defines as "the probability that certain commands (or all commands) from a given source will be obeyed by a given group of persons." He adds that a basic criterion of authority "is a certain minimum of voluntary submission," although the specific motives for the obedience to commands may vary.[7] His analysis of three types of authority centers on the value orientations that cause people voluntarily to submit to orders from an authority they accept as legitimate.[8] What is left implicit in this analysis is the specific criterion in terms of which authority can be distinguished from other forms of influence to which individuals voluntarily submit. Indeed, the emphasis on voluntarism is misleading without further specification, since an authoritative command is one a subordinate cannot dismiss at will.

It may be suggested that the distinctive feature of authority is that social norms accepted and enforced by the collectivity of subordinates constrain its individual members to comply with directives of a superior. Compliance is voluntary for the collectivity, but social constraints make it compelling for the individual. In contrast to other forms of influence and power, the pressure to follow suggestions and orders does not come from

[7] Max Weber, *The Theory of Social and Economic Organization.* New York: Oxford University Press, 1947, p. 324.
[8] *Ibid.*, pp. 329–363.

the superior who gives them but from the collectivity of subordinates. These normative constraints may be institutionalized and pervade the entire society, or they may emerge in a group in social interaction. The latter emergent norms define leadership, which, therefore, is considered a type of authority. The authority in formal organizations entails a combination of institutionalized and leadership elements.

Leadership

Furnishing needed contributions in a group empowers a man to effect compliance with his demands. The exercise of power exerts restraints, which are, in effect, inescapable if the need for the contributions is great and no alternative sources for them are available. Compliance is a cost that is judged on the basis of social norms of fairness. Excessive demands in terms of these social standards, though those subject to the power may not be able to refuse them, engender disapproval. A person whose demands on others are fair and modest relative to the great contribution he makes to their welfare, however, earns their approval. For example, a laboratory study of small groups found that the emergent leader was more apt to be liked by the rest if the initiative he took in social interaction was accompanied by a high rate of response from others, that is, by their frequently agreeing with him and turning to him with comments and questions, than if the rate of such feedback was low.[9] This may be interpreted to imply that excessive demands by a leader, as indicated by a low rate of feedback, create disapproval that make him less liked.

Compliance can be enforced with sufficient power, but approval cannot be forced regardless of how great the power. Yet the effectiveness and stability of leadership depend on the social approval of subordinates, as several studies have shown. Thus, the results of two experiments demonstrated that leaders who were accepted and approved by subordinates were more effective in exerting influence on them than superiors who were not.[10] A study of army leadership found that trainees who approved of their officers and noncommissioned officers were less likely to express various forms of aggression, such as going "AWOL" (absent without leave), "blowing their top," drunkenness, and gripe sessions, than those

who described their superiors as arbitrary or weak.[11] The findings of another experiment indicated that group leaders whose suggestions and directives engendered a disproportionate amount of resistance and disagreement were relatively unstable, that is, they were more likely than others to be displaced as leaders in subsequent experimental periods.[12] The disapproval some leadership practices evoke among followers impede a leader's effectiveness because they create resistance, aggression, and possibly opposition that may lead to the downfall of an informal leader.

Collective approval, in contrast, legitimates leadership. The abilities that enable a person to make major contributions to the achievement of a group's goals command respect. The respect of others for him prompts them to follow his suggestion, since they expect to benefit from doing so more than from following the suggestion of someone whose abilities are less respected. The actual contributions to their welfare resulting from following his guidance not only validate the others' respect for such a person but also obligate them to comply with his directives regardless of whether doing so is in their personal self-interest. It is their obligation to comply with his directives, not simply their respect, that bestows leadership upon a person and empowers him to coordinate the activities of the members of a group, which involves directing individuals to do things that are not to their own immediate advantage. The effective coordination of effort produces rewards, and the leader's power enables him to exert a predominant influence on their distribution—how much of the honor and glory of the winning team will reflect on the rest rather than on himself, or how large a share of the material benefits goes to others and how much remains in his hands. It is this distribution of rewards that most directly effects the legitimation of leadership.

If the benefits followers derive from a leader's guidance exceed their expectations of a fair return for the costs they have incurred, both by performing services and by complying with directives, their collective approval of his leadership legitimates it. Their joint obligations for his contributions to their welfare and their common approval of his fairness, reinforced by their consensus concerning the respect his abilities deserve, generate group pressures that enforce compliance with his directives. These social pressures constrain individual group members who for personal reasons are in-

[9] Robert F. Bales, "Task Status and Likability as a Function of Talking and Listening in Decision-making Groups," in Leonard D. White, *The State of the Social Sciences*, University of Chicago Press, 1956, pp. 148–161.

[10] John R. P. French, Jr. and Richard Snyder, "Leadership and Interpersonal Power," in Dorwin Cartwright, *Studies in Social Power*, Ann Arbor: Institute for Social Research, University of Michigan, 1959, pp. 118–149.

[11] Hannan C. Selvin, *The Effects of Leadership*, Glencoe: Free Press, 1960, chapter v.

[12] Elihu Katz, Peter M. Blau, Morton L. Brown, and Fred L. Strodtbeck, "Leadership Stability and Social Change," *Sociometry* 20 (1957), 36–50, esp. pp. 44–46.

clined to resist the leader's guidance to submit to it lest they draw on themselves the social disapproval of their peers. Legitimate leaders command willing compliance, which obviates the need for sanctions to compel or induce others to comply with directives, because the group of subordinates exerts pressures on its members to follow the leader's orders and suggestions.

The social approval of followers that legitimates leadership is distinct from the respect they may have for the leader's abilities. Although the two go often together, a person in power may have abilities that command the respect of subordinates yet make oppressive demands on them to which they react with disapproval. Respect probably does, however, act as a catalyst of legitimate leadership, since it seems to make compliance with a person's directives less burdensome. Indirect support for this statement is provided by some findings from a study of sixty caseworkers in a welfare agency. [13] Generally, the factors that distinguished workers who were often consulted from those who were rarely consulted also distinguished those who were highly respected from those who were not. But some kinds of workers, such as oldtimers, were often consulted without being highly respected. The obligation incurred to consultants inhibited informal sociability with them if the consultants were not particularly respected, but it did not inhibit sociability if they were. This finding suggests that respect for a person legitimates the obligation to comply with his wishes and thus makes this obligation less of an impediment to informal intercourse with him.

Stable leadership rests on power over others and their legitimating approval of that power. The dilemma of leadership is that the attainment of power and the attainment of social approval make somewhat incompatible demands on a person. To achieve power over others requires not only furnishing services that make them dependent but also remaining independent of any services they might offer in return. To legitimate a position of power and leadership, however, requires that a leader be concerned with earning the social approval of his followers, which means that he does not maintain complete independence of them. An individual's refusal to accept offers of favors from others who are in his debt and his insistence on remaining entirely independent of them are usually experienced as rejections and evoke their disapproval. By asserting his dominance over the rest of the group in the process of becoming their leader and exercising his leadership, a person can

hardly help antagonizing at least some of them, thereby endangering his chances of having his leadership legitimated by social approval. Conversely, preoccupation with the approval of followers interferes with a leader's ability to command their respect and compliance by making the greatest contribution to their welfare he can, because concern with being liked prevents him from basing his decisions consistently on criteria of effectiveness alone. Such preoccupation, in other words, induces a leader sometimes to refrain from making what is the best decision in his judgment for fear of antagonizing subordinates.

The dilemma of leadership can be epitomized by saying that its legitimation requires that a leader be magnanimous in the exercise of his power and in the distribution of the rewards that accrue from his leadership, but such magnanimity necessitates that he first mobilize his power and husband the group's resources, that is, act in ways that are the opposite of magnanimous. Once a man has attained much power, however, he can easily make demands that appear only moderate in view of his strength and capacity to supply benefits. In other words, extensive power facilitates obtaining legitimating approval for it.

Two different sets of expectations govern the process of legitimation, since the leader's general expectations define what is extensive or insufficient power, while those of the followers define what are moderate or unfair power demands. The less the leader expects to achieve with his power, the less power will be sufficient to meet his needs and the less demands he will make on those subject to his power. The reactions of the follower's to the leader's demands, in turn, are contingent on their normative expectations of how much a leader can fairly demand in return for his contributions. Small needs for power as well as great power make it easy for a man to exercise his power in ways that elicit legitimating approval from subordinates. The line between exploitative oppression and legitimate leadership is defined by the interplay between the expectations of the man in power that define his needs and the expectations of those subject to his power that define their needs and his complementary rights.

Power must be mobilized before it can be legitimated, because the processes involved in mobilizing it are not compatible with those involved in legitimating it. The dilemma of leadership is resolved by devoting different time periods to coping with its two horns, so to speak. This parallels the conclusion of Bales and Strodtbeck that the dilemma of group problem solving posed by the need for a cognitive orientation to the task and the need for a supportive orientation that

[13] Blau, "Patterns of Choice in Interpersonal Relations," *American Sociological Review* 27 (1962), 41–55, esp. pp. 50–51, 55.

reduces tensions, which are incompatible, is resolved by devoting different time phases to meeting these two needs.[14] The potential leader of a gang uses his physical strength first against the other members to assert his dominance over them. Only then can he organize their activities and lead them in gang warfare, now using his strength and other resources in behalf of his followers against outsiders. If he is successful, his contributions to their welfare evoke legitimating approval of his leadership, which makes his continuing dominance independent of his use of physical sanctions against followers.

The situation of formal leaders in organizations is different from that of informal leaders who emerge in a group. Resources and institutionalized mechanisms place managers in organizations a priori in a dominant position over subordinates, thereby obviating the need for initially asserting their dominance and facilitating the development of legitimate authority.

[14] Bales and Strodtbeck, "Phases in Group Problem Solving," *The Journal of Abnormal and Social Psychology,* 46 (1951), 485–495. Another method for resolving the leadership dilemma is a division of labor within the leadership group, that is, having those leaders who exercise power and restraints supported by other leaders who do not and who command the approval and loyalty of followers; see Philip E. Slater, "Role Differentiation in Small Groups," *American Sociological Review* 20 (1955), pp. 300–310.

Leadership: Affective and Instrumental
Sidney Verba

The purpose of this chapter is to explore one aspect of the leader-follower relationship as it is found in both small experimental groups and on-going social systems. This aspect is the dual function that the leadership structure of a group must perform if the group is successfully to reach the goal that brought it together. In attempting to achieve its goal, a group must ... direct activities both toward the instrumental task it faces and toward the maintenance of the internal structure of the group. The group's internal maintenance function must be performed in such a way that the individual members find their participation in the group at least satisfactory enough to keep them from leaving the group. And ... it is the function of the group leadership to operate in both these areas—the instrumental and the internal group maintenance.

The importance of the affective tone and emotional aspects of the leader-follower relationship in political and other social situations has long been recognized. Individuals do not give their allegiance to a state or their support to a political leader solely because of the material benefits they receive in return. The decision on the part of a follower to accept the directive of a leader is based on more than a rational calculus of the advantages to be gained from that acceptance. Loyalty to a state, for instance, usually has an emotional component, reinforced by more or less elaborate systems of symbols and rituals. Though there has been much analysis of these non-rational aspects of politics insofar as they affect the individual political participant, there has been little systematic consideration of the dynamic interaction between emotional attachment and material outputs within the leader-follower relationship.

* * *

The difficulties of the leadership position derive not merely from the fact that the leader must be active in both the instrumental and affective group tasks, but from the fact that these two tasks are closely related. The way in which the group functions in one area will influence functioning in the other. If group members have a satisfactory affective relationship with the leader, they will be more likely to accept his instrumental directives. On the other hand, if the level of member satisfaction with group leadership is low, members may withdraw from the group, reject the group leader, or reject the group leader's instrumental directives. All these activities lower the instrumental effect-iveness of the group. Conversely, the success or failure of the instrumental activity of the group will influence the affective rewards to the members. Group members may derive satisfaction directly from the successful completion of the instrumental task of the group or from certain other rewards that are the bi-product of that task completion. Insofar as the group cannot achieve its instrumental goal, satisfactions will be lowered. Maintaining a balance between the satisfactions of the group members and the task achievement of the group may well be the most important task of the group leader.

Equilibrium Problem: Maintaining the balance between affective satisfactions and instrumental performance is, however, a difficult and delicate task. Several studies of group process have suggested that attempts to direct the group toward the accomplishment of its instrumental task may be greeted by negative affective reactions on the part of group members. The theoretical and experimental work of Kurt Lewin and his associates first pinpointed the problem within small groups. In Lewin's theoretical formulation, attempts to direct the group toward the group goal disturb the equilibrium of the group by restricting the freedom of the members. This in turn causes a negative reaction that can take two forms: it may take the form of a rejection of the instrumental directive, in which case equilibrium is restored by negating the directive's effect; or the reaction may be an acceptance of the directive accompanied by increased hostility toward the leader. In the latter case, equilibrium is restored but at a higher level of tension between leader and follower.

Examples of this process of negative reaction to directive leadership can be found in the classic experimental work of Lippitt and White carried out under Lewin's direction. In these experiments with democratic and authoritarian group climates, it was noted that directives from an authoritarian leader, though followed, were accompanied by negative affective reactions on the part of the group members, expressed in hostility toward the leader, a scapegoat, or other groups. Furthermore, the acceptance of the leader's directives in the authoritarian situation was external rather than internal. When the leader left the room and the

This reading is reprinted from Sidney Verba, *Small Groups and Political Behavior: A Study of Leadership* (© 1961 by Princeton University Press), pp. 142, 145–150, 159–165, 168, 172–174, and 176–179. Omission of footnotes. Reprinted by permission of Princeton University Press. Verba is a political scientist at the University of Chicago.

external pressure was removed, the group members ceased complying with the instrumental directive. Experimental work in field situations produced similar results; attempts to direct change in a group led to negative affective reactions on the part of the group members that in turn limited the effectiveness of the instrumental directive. Coch and French, for instance, found that an attempt by management to direct certain changes in the work process ". . . had the effect for the members of setting up management as a hostile power field. They rejected the forces induced by this hostile power field, and group standards to restrict production developed within the group in opposition to management." The problem of leadership is clearly presented by these examples. The achievement of the group's instrumental goal must proceed along with the continuing satisfaction of the individual needs of the group members, but frequently the attempts themselves to achieve the instrumental goal lower the level of affective satisfaction of the group members. This lowering will in turn feed back upon the instrumental achievement and hamper it. Thus the several tasks of the leader may not all be consistent with one another.

The treatment of the problem of control and instrumental achievement in the work of Lewin and his associates bears a significant resemblance to the treatment of the problem in the work of Robert F. Bales and his associates at the Harvard Laboratory of Social Relations. In the small experimental groups used by Bales in the formulation of his theoretical system, the formation of the group takes place around the instrumental task presented to the group by the experimenter. The initial differentiation among the group members evolves in response to the demands of this task. Certain members tend to become more active in directing the group toward the completion of its instrumental task. But attempts to control the group in relation to the instrumental task disturb the equilibrium of the group and cause tensions in the expressive-integrative area of the group's activities. These negative reactions to control attempts may, like the negative reactions found in the work of Lewin and his associates, be directed at the leader or at a group scapegoat.

Evidence for the negative reaction received by the group member who attempts to lead the group in the direction of instrumental task achievement is derived from six measures taken by Bales during the group experiments. Two measures are based on interaction counts using the Bales scheme; these are simply measures of the amount of interactions initiated and the amount received. After each group session the members are asked to rate all members on a sociometric test using three criteria:

the member who contributed the best ideas to the group, the member who contributed the best guidance, and the member who was best liked. And after all four group sessions the members are asked to select the one who contributed the best leadership. The percentage of times the same group member occupies the highest position by more than one measure is calculated. Thus on one batch of experimental groups, Slater calculated the percentage of times that the individual selected as the best leader was highest by another criterion. The results follow:

The "best leader" was also ranked highest on guidance 80 per cent of the time; on receiving, 65 per cent; on ideas, 59 per cent; on talking, 55 per cent; and on liking, 25 per cent. Clearly, the member who is best liked is rarely associated in the minds of the group members with the individual who is the best leader. Furthermore, Slater found that "liking" was not associated with any of the other measurements of leadership. The individual chosen highest by the socio-emotional criterion of best-liked was three times as likely to hold the highest position by that measure alone than were those who were most highly chosen by any other measure. Thus, those group members who are active in directing the group, or who are selected by the group members as having contributed to the instrumental task of the group, are not likely to receive choices on a sociometric test using an expressive criterion. The results clearly indicate that the individual who attempts to control the instrumental activities of the group lowers his chances to be highly thought of by the group according to an affective criterion.

External Relations of the Leader: The conflict between directing the group and maintaining one's acceptance by the group would seem to be the unique problem of the group leader. This conflict is heightened in the groups discussed above by the fact that the task toward which the instrumental leader directs the group is set for the group externally by the experimenter. Insofar as the task is set for the group externally rather than chosen by the group, attempts at instrumental control are more likely to engender negative reactions. This proposition is supported in an experimental study by Katz *et al.* of a number of four-man groups. After the performance of one task, the groups were asked to select a leader for a second task. In some cases, the task was one that the group had chosen; in others, it was imposed by the experimenter. The results support the proposition that when the task is imposed upon the group externally, the negative reaction against the leader who attempts to direct the task activity will be greater. In those cases where the group performed a second task that it had selected for itself, all those who had been chosen as leaders after the first task were again so chosen at the end of the second. On the other hand, when the group was assigned a task that it had not selected, only one-third of those who had been chosen as leaders after the first task retained that position after the second.

* * *

A stable leadership structure is important if the group is to accomplish its instrumental task. But such stability is difficult to achieve because of the conflicting demands for task accomplishment and affective satisfactions. Insofar as the group can achieve some satisfactory balance between the instrumental and the affective aspects of its interaction and a stable leadership structure is developed, the group will be effective and contribute to the satisfaction of its members. Insofar as such a balance cannot be reached and such a structure is not developed, groups will either fall apart or continue operating at high levels of tension. This problem, we can assume, is faced not only by small groups, but by larger organizations and political systems as well. Unless the unlikely prospect of a state totally run by coercion is to be considered, some minimum of acceptance of the system by the participants must be maintained at the same time that the organization or political system carries on instrumental activities that inhibit freedom and, presumably, lower the satisfactions of the members. The importance of affective relations in political systems and of the acceptance by the followers of the leader's directives has long been recognized in political science. As Merriam has written: "No power could stand if it relied upon violence alone, for force is not strong enough to maintain itself against the accidents of rivalry and discontent. The might that makes right must be a different might from that of the right arm. It must be a right deep-rooted in emotion, embedded in feelings and aspirations. . . ." The question must then be asked: how do social systems—whether small experimental groups, on-going groups, organizations or political systems—maintain a satisfactory level of affective integration at the same time that they carry on instrumental activities whose tendency may be to lower the degree of affective satisfaction of the participants?

The Two Leaders: To shed some light upon the way in which the conflict between instrumental and affective leadership is resolved, we turn first to the small group experimental literature. The resolution of the conflict in these small groups will then be compared with the resolution in larger, on-going social systems. In the small groups

studied by Bales and his associates, the conflict between instrumental and affective leadership is resolved by a differentiation within the leadership role. In these groups different individuals tend to specialize in the instrumental leadership role and in the socio-emotional leadership role. The evidence for this role differentiation is found in the material cited above: those members highly selected by the group by an affective criterion were not likely to be selected by the group as having contributed to the instrumental task, nor were they likely to be active in giving the group direction toward the accomplishment of that task. On the other hand, the individual selected by the group as contributing the most to the external task (Best Ideas) was also highly selected as contributing most to the instrumental aspect of the internal group task (Best Guidance). High choice by one criterion was closely correlated with high choice by the other, and the individual rated lowest by one was likely to be lowest by the other. The findings by Bales and his associates that the leadership role tends to be split between a task-oriented instrumental leader and a "sociometric star" is supported by small group studies of other authors.

* * *

Activities of the Two Leaders: The fact that group leadership tends to be split between two individuals is reflected not only in the fact that group members choose different individuals by socio-emotional and instrumental criteria, but also in the fact that the behavior patterns of the individuals thus selected differ. When one looks at the interaction rates of the group members most highly selected on the basis of the socio-emotional and the instrumental (Best Ideas) criteria, one finds significant differences. The socio-emotional leader tends to initiate and receive more interactions in the socio-emotional categories of interaction than does the task specialist. He gives and receives more solidarity and tension-release interactions. The task specialist, on the other hand, is more active in giving opinions and suggestions; and he receives larger amounts of agreement, questions, and negative reactions. The difference between the behavior of the two leaders is best described by Slater: "The most salient general difference between the rates of interaction of the two types of leaders is the tendency for the Idea man to initiate interactions more heavily in Area B (Problem Solving Attempts) and the Best-liked man in Area A (Positive reactions). . . . On the Receiving end, the situation is largely reversed, with the Idea man receiving more agreement, questions and negative reactions, while the Best-liked man receives more problem solving attempts, and more solidarity and tension release. The general picture is thus one of specialization and complementarity, with the Idea man concentrating on the task and playing a more aggressive role, while the Best-liked man concentrates more on social emotional problems, giving rewards, and playing a more passive role." The qualitative ratings given the two leaders by the group members are thus reflected in their quantitative interaction rates.

The difference between the two specialists extends to the attitudes of these two group members. Not only do they specialize in certain areas of the group activity, but they receive their satisfactions from those areas. The instrumental leader, it has already been suggested, is relatively less motivated to receive positive affective responses from the group. His personal satisfactions derive not from the affective responses of the group members, but from the instrumental task directly. For the "sociometric star," on the other hand, "... *primary* satisfaction derives from his success in his role as promoter of solidarity and provider of opportunities for tension release. . . ." The socio-emotional leader also tends to be more accepting of the other group members, while the task specialist differentiates among the other members in the degree to which he accepts them. On the sociometric question in which the group members were asked to rate the other members on the degree to which they liked them, 42 per cent of the socio-emotional leaders did not differentiate among the members (they said, in effect, "I like everybody") while only 20 per cent of the task leaders did not so differentiate.

Relations Between the Two Leaders: The balance between affective tone and instrumental accomplishment is maintained in these groups, then, by the development of two leaders. The disturbance in the expressive area caused by the instrumental directives of the task leader is countered by positive affective reactions from the socio-emotional leader. In understanding this process, it is important to note the relations between the two leaders. Bales and Slater found that the two had close relations, one with the other. The task and socio-emotional leaders tended to interact more frequently with each other than did any other pair of members; and, what is equally significant, tended to agree more frequently with each other. In this way, it may be suggested, the task leader receives indirectly through the socio-emotional leader the expressive support that he could not directly obtain because of his instrumental role. That such a coalition between the two group leaders is important for the effective functioning of

the group is suggested by a comparison made by Bales and Slater between High Status Consensus groups and Low Status Consensus groups. In the former type of group—in which, as was pointed out earlier, task accomplishment and member satisfaction are both higher—the relationships between the two leaders are statistically significant. In the Low Consensus groups, though there is a tendency for the two leaders to interact with each other, the pattern is neither as consistent nor as strong.

Conflicting Expectations: Their Resolution in On-going Systems

The conflict in expectations placed upon leaders has now been spelled out. In small experimental groups we have found that this conflict is resolved by the development of two leaders—an affective and a task leader—accompanied by an implicit coalition between the two men. On-going social systems, including political systems, must also deal with instrumental and affective relationships. Political systems, as well as small groups, depend upon inputs from their members of both instrumental activities (contributions of resources, services, etc.) and affect (loyalty, respect, etc.). And these systems maintain the adherence of their members by outputs in both these areas: specific services as well as affective rewards for participation in the system. The model suggested by the studies of experimental groups suggests that the conflict between the affective and the instrumental aspects might best be resolved by a bifurcation of the leadership function. Faced with this conflict, does the on-going social system develop such a differentiated leadership structure, or are other mechanisms available to it to resolve this conflict?

* * *

Experimental groups with no previous experience together differ in a systematic way from [ongoing groups with a history of interaction]. Insofar as members are similar in age, insofar as they are similar in status in the external culture of the group, and insofar as the experimenter supplies no sanction for any particular leadership structure, any directive attempt by a group member will be looked upon as a challenge to the other members. With no status consensus among the group members at the beginning of interaction and no status guides, would-be leaders in the new experimental groups are placed in a clear power struggle. The increased vigor necessary to control the group increases the negative reaction to the leader and heightens the conflict between acceptance and instrumental control.

* * *

Role of Norms in Follower Compliance: One of the most effective ways in which the instrumental directives of a group leader acquire legitimacy and avoid being received as personal, arbitrary challenges to the group members is for the leader to be perceived as acting not as an individual but as the agent of some impersonal force, such as the "demands of the situation" or the group traditions and norms. The invocation of some external authority by the group leader relieves the follower of the burden of accepting the control of another individual. Thibault and Kelley, in a study of power relations in the dyad, conclude that group norms have the effect of reducing the tension between the more powerful and the less powerful member of the group. The impersonalization of expectations of behavior through the adoption of norms makes the influence relationship between the more and the less powerful group member more stable and palatable for both of them. For the less powerful member, the use of controls without a normative base would make those controls arbitrary and unpredictable, and lead to resistance on his part. For the more powerful member of a dyad, the use of purely personal power would also be unpleasant. He must either reduce his attempted control (and thereby perhaps endanger the accomplishment of the group goal) or risk the negative reactions of the other member. Thus the exercise of control in the name of a set of norms that legitimizes the control is to the advantage of both leader and follower. Alvin Gouldner makes a similar point in relation to bureaucratic organizations. The advantage of impersonal rules in a bureaucratic situation is not that these rules completely replace interpersonal influence, but that they make that influence less visible. In a society that stresses equalitarian norms, this reduction in the visibility of control increases legitimacy and reduces tensions.

Impersonalization of control has been noted to be an effective means of social control in a number of contexts. Mannheim maintains that a key transition point in the development of human societies occurs when regulation of conduct ceases to be carried on in the name of an individual and begins to be exercised in the name of the needs of the group. Primitive groups, he points out, develop social functions that must be performed if the group is to survive. "Provision for such necessary functions is the external source and motivation of regulation in contrast to mere person-to-person relationships. The collective responsibility calls for recurrent and lasting functions, including that of leadership. The leader may give orders to the subordinate members of his team and on occasion use physical or psychological pressures. In so doing, he links his personal, physical and mental strength to an objective function.... In this situation a strange metamorphosis occurs: the 'archaic' experience of purely personal power is linked to and, so to speak, transfused into the social function.... The metamorphosis is also significant because it demarcates the beginning of the process that substitutes the control of man by institutions and organizations for that of man by man...."

* * *

The Process of Legitimation: The development of the type of leadership found in experimental groups (leadership perceived by followers to be arbitrary and personal) into the type found in most on-going systems (leadership perceived to be impersonal and proper)—i.e., the process of legitimation of leadership—is probably one of the most important processes in political affairs. How does leadership that is seized by an individual with no sanction from the group become leadership that is accepted and expected by the group? Laboratory studies of groups with no expectations of leadership might be an excellent place to study this question. Do the laboratory studies thus far shed light upon this process of the legitimization of leadership? Unfortunately, at this time the answer is probably no.

The development of a legitimate leadership structure out of the leaderless group structure found at the beginning of the experimental studies would have to move through three stages. In the first place, certain members of the group must, in response to the group task, begin to differentiate their activities from those of the other group members. Secondly, the other group members must perceive the difference in the behavior of the group member or members who devote themselves more directly to the group task. And, lastly, the group members must come to regard this differentiated activity as right and proper. The first stage is reached in almost all experimental groups studied. Behavior counts show that significant differences in the behavior of the various members can be found in the first meetings of the new groups. The second stage, the recognition of the differing activity patterns, is also reached in many small group studies. But it is difficult to say if the third and crucial stage is reached—the stage at which the group members come to consider the differentiated activity of the group leader or leaders right and proper. The problem is that the small groups cited above do not deal with expectations of leadership. This can be seen in the conception of role used in these studies. Role as defined by Slater is ". . . a more or less coherent and unified system of items of interpersonal behavior." A group role is thus defined by the particular behaviors (as measured by interaction counts) in which a member engages. This definition does not take into account the expectations others may hold about the role performer. The existence of expectations as to the leader's behavior is not observed directly in these studies, but is ". . . inferred from consistencies in overt behavior, consensus on ratings, and congruence between behavior and received ratings." This inference is not necessarily valid. That a group member behaves in a certain consistent way and that the other group members agree that he is so behaving do not necessarily imply that the other group members sanction this behavior. The assumption that they do not sanction the leader's behavior is supported by the evidence that he receives negative affect for his instrumental control. In view of the absence of direct measures of expectation, we must agree with the cautious comment of Bales and Slater that "The degree to which differentiated roles in the fully structural sense appear in these small decision-making groups is perhaps a moot point."

Since expectations of behavior are so significant for on-going groups, it is to be hoped that small group researchers will begin to deal with them directly. One problem is that even those studies that do deal with legitimacy deal with it as an independent variable—i.e., legitimacy is introduced by the experimenter to see how it affects some dependent variable such as productivity or acceptance. But if we wish to study the development of legitimate leadership, we must hope for studies of legitimacy as a dependent variable. What group structures, for instance, are conducive to the development of leadership that is accepted by the group? What sort of behavior on the part of an emergent leader indicates to group members that they ought to accord legitimacy to this individual? What type of task encourages the growth of legitimate leadership? These are some of the questions the answers to which would greatly increase our knowledge of political behavior. The small leaderless experimental groups may differ from on-going groups in that they have no pattern of expectations of differentiated leadership behavior. In some ways this limits the usefulness of these small groups for analysis of on-going social systems. But it also presents the possibility of studying in these small groups the process by which such expectations develop.

References
Bales, Robert Freed. *Interaction Process Analysis.* Cambridge, Mass.: Harvard University Press, 1950.
Bales, Robert Freed, and Slater, Phillip E. "Notes on 'Role Differentiation in Small Decision-Making Groups': Reply to Dr. Wheeler." *Sociometry* 20: 152–55.
Coch, Lester, and French, John R. P., Jr. "Overcoming Resistance to Change." In *Basic Studies in Social Psychology,* eds. Harold Proshansky and Bernard Seidenberg. New York: Holt, Rinehart, and Winston, 1965.
Gouldner, Alvin W. *Studies in Leadership: Leadership and Democratic Action.* New York: Harper, 1950.
Katz, Elihu et al. "Leadership Stability and Social Change: An Experiment with Small Groups." *Sociometry* 20: 36–50.
Lewin, Kurt. *Field Theory in the Social Sciences.* New York: Harper, 1951.
Lippitt, Ronald, and White, Ralph K. "An Experimental Study of Leadership and Group Life." In *Basic Studies in Social Psychology,* eds. Harold Proshansky and Bernard Seidenberg. New York: Holt, Rinehart, and Winston, 1965.
Mannheim, Karl. *Freedom, Power, and Democratic Planning.* London: Routledge and Kegan Paul, 1951.
Merriam, Charles E. *Political Power.* New York: McGraw-Hill, 1934.
Parsons, Talcott, and Bales, Robert Freed. *Family, Socialization, and Interaction Process Analysis.* New York: The Free Press, 1955.
Slater, Philip E. "Role Differentiation in Small Groups." *American Sociological Review* 20: 300–310.
Thibault, John W. and Kelley, Harold H. *The Social Psychology of Groups.* New York: John Wiley & Sons, 1959.

Toward a Theory of Interpersonal Tactics

Eugene A. Weinstein

"How are lines of action organized in pursuing interpersonal tasks? How do people go about the business of getting others to do, think or feel what they want them to?"

Interpersonal tasks are pursued (and sometimes even formulated) in encounters. Thus the functional requirements of encounters act as interactional constraints upon goal-oriented behavior and the nature of these constraints must be understood. Perhaps the most basic of these requirements is what Goffman calls the "working consensus." In Goffman's terms, the working consensus is a tacit agreement as to whose claims to what issues will be temporarily honored. It is an agreement as to what the nature of reality is to be, the definition of the situation jointly subscribed to (although not necessarily believed in) by participants in the encounter.

The concept of working consensus has broader definitional implications. For our purpose, these implications may be extended to relate more explicitly to the personal goals of the actors involved. Encounters are embedded in situations, the symbolic content of which changes with each line of action. As situations change so may their definitions by the several participants. Yet situations tend not to be in complete flux. There appear to be boundaries to the moment-to-moment changes in definitions of the situation as well as boundaries to the kinds of tasks which are pursuable and the kinds of lines of action used to pursue them in any encounter. These boundaries are provided by the working consensus and give some stability and structure to the encounter. Four conditions, each dependent on the others preceding, must be satisfied for a working consensus to develop.

1. Each of the participants must indicate willingness to receive communication from the others.

2. At least some of the participants must communicate a claim to pursue certain types of interpersonal tasks and the right to employ particular lines of action.

3. The particular kind of communication within its situational context must imply that a delimited set of tasks will be pursued using a delimited set of lines of action.

4. These implications cannot be overtly denied. If a working consensus is to be established and maintained, no participant can deny another's right to pursue certain types of tasks or his right to employ particular lines of action in doing so.

Since these rights are normatively allocated to roles, or, more precisely, social identities, the working consensus necessarily involves agreement upon the social identities of the participants. Not only the identity claimed by the actor for himself, but those he may actively assign to others in the situation by what has been called "altercasting" must be mutually acceptable. If not, the working consensus, and the interaction it serves to structure cannot be maintained. The alternatives are breakdown in the episode of interaction or renegotiation of the terms of the working consensus.

Any actor has a double problem in interaction. He has his interpersonal tasks. But he is involved with other actors, each with their own purposes and associated preference orderings which, in all likelihood, are somewhat different from his. As Goode emphasizes, the actor, in seeking to achieve his own goals in the encounter, must also keep the others bound in the relationship. The working consensus must be maintained. Of particular importance in this, as Goffman notes, is maintaining the acceptability of the identities of the participants, his own included. Thus, we should expect to find that many lines of action are designed to serve this double function, pursuing goals and promoting or maintaining identities congruent with those goals. We turn now to examining some commonly used interpersonal tactics in the light of their double imperative. The neologisms coined in the process are not, as will become apparent, to be taken too seriously.

Insuring Appropriate Interpretation

One of the prime requisites of a successful line of action is that it have the meaning for the other intended by the actor. Goffman describes how important content is dramatized, unimportant or contradictory content is suppressed as a means of guiding inferences. We shall be concerned with further amplifying his analysis, focussing on lines of action which insure that inappropriate *evaluative* implications regarding one's own identity or the identity of the other are not made. Such lines of action form an important segment of that vast class of acts which might be called communication about communication.

This reading is reprinted from Eugene A. Weinstein, "Toward a Theory of Interpersonal Tactics," pp. 395–398 in Carl W. Backman and Paul F. Secord (eds.) *Problems in Social Psychology*. New York: McGraw-Hill, 1966. Reprinted by permission. Weinstein is a sociologist at the State University of New York at Stony Brook.

When an act can have several meanings to another, which carry different evaluative implications regarding the actor, one way of trying to insure favorable evaluation is to offer an interpretation prior to action (pre-interpretation or printerp). "Now, be sure not to take this the wrong way. I don't want you to think...." Printerps may also function to protect or enhance the identity of the other. Not uncommon is the printerp which, by first asserting that nothing detrimental about the other is intended, allows us to insult them at will.

However, not all communication about communication takes place prior to action. The other's response may provide us with information that he has drawn inferences from our acts which are undesired. Posterps are used as corrective devices. "Oh no, that's not what I meant..." followed by some statement taking the apparent evaluative sting out of some prior acts is a ubiquitous post-interpretation.

Printerps and posterps can serve a number of functions in the attempt to direct the evaluative implications of lines of actions. Sometimes, we find ourselves in circumstances in which we feel impelled to maintain interaction but in which we fear our acts or communications will not meet the evaluative standards appropriate for the situation. One common line of action is to apologize in advance for what is to come (pre-apology which is readily abbreviated to prepalog). "I'm not quite sure of this ... but ... ," or "Off the top of my head, I'd say ..." are examples of prepalogs which request the others not to negatively evaluate the actor. Akin to these are prepalogs of the form, "I'm really not a very good ... (tennis player, bridge player, cook, etc.)" which request others to apply less stringent evaluative criteria in judging the actor's performance in the encounter. Both forms serve a common function; they are attempts to divorce evaluation of the actor (and hence, the acceptability of his identity) from evaluation of his actions.

The prepalog may also be a useful tool in securing overt assurances concerning the acceptability of one's identity. Statements making overt negative references to self are so frequently met with responses of denial or assurance that they have acquired a label in the common parlance, "fishing."

An important type of communication about communication, subsumable under the more generic categories of pre- and post-interpretation, are statements about the causes of or which reveal the motives for one's actions (motive revelations or motrels). Motrels are invaluable tools for either associating or dissociating identities and actions. Personalized motrels are those in which the actor refers to causes of his behavior which are within his rational control implying that particularistic value choices are open to him. The actor thus assumes responsibility for the evaluative implications of his acts. In depersonalized motrels, the actor refers to causes of behavior beyond his control, his biology, random happenstance, universalistic normative prescriptions and the like—in short, alibis. The differences between them can be best seen in differential responses to requests.

When one makes a request, he implicitly indicates that both he and it are worthy of consideration. The rejection of a request entails risks for both parties. In consequence, there is an elaborate set of lines of action regarding the making, accepting, and denying of requests.

One defensive device for the minimization of risk by the actor (especially the risk of being seen as presuming beyond his rights) is to make the request without actually asking. This often takes the form of communicating a need without asking the other to fill it. Assent in such cases tends to take the form of a personalized motrel, e.g. "I'd be glad to...." In extended sequences this can be countered with, "I really don't want to impose," a very useful gambit. It serves as a prepalog and, at the same time, casts the other into the role of defending the reasonableness of the request.

Depersonalized motrels predominate when denying others' requests. They serve to deny not only the request, but, because one's response is beyond one's control, they also implicitly deny any negative implications concerning the requestor. Thus one divorces the *other's* identity from one's acts.

Another tactic which serves the same function is the altruistic motrel, a statement that one's acts are being made for the benefit of the other. Children rapidly become expert at discounting such claims when they preface parental action. Such statements attempt to establish a working consensus in which acts potentially threatening to certain aspects of the other's identity can be made. The motrel both assures the other of overall acceptance, and claims for the actor a relationship of intimacy with him.

In this latter respect, altruistic motrels are one (of a large number) of tactics used to enhance the credibility of what one says. Presumably, those who have our best interests at heart will provide us with valid information so we can maximize the effectiveness of our own actions. The altruistic motrel thus shifts the question of credibility of the act to its preface. It attaches the actor's identity to what follows, meaning that the other has a good deal more to disbelieve. Overt disbelief by the other runs the risk of being construed as a rejection of the actor.

A similar pattern is seen in another credibility enhancing tactic, the display of involvement. Involvement is indexed by the intensity of the action expressed in decibel level, qualifying adjectives, inflections, bodily gestures, etc. When great involvement in one's actions is displayed by such means, especially in communication about such intrapersonal "facts" as feelings, disbelief of the communication has greater implications for discrediting the actor's identity. Others may be hesitant to display doubt under such conditions because it runs a greater risk of disrupting the working consensus. That the display of involvement itself must be credible is well attested to in the Shakespearean admonition, "The lady doth protest too much, methinks."

A final tactic in the same vein is the icon (short for identity confirmation). Here we are concerned with the actor's droppings—name dropping, place dropping, experience dropping, and the like: "After 25 years of experience in this business . . ." or, "Back at Harvard. . . ." One function of such acts is to legitimize information given. Again, the question of credibility shifts to the preface, with the actor in essence saying "Believe what I say because of what I am." Icons may be directed at other types of tasks as well. They are handy tools for establishing relative evaluative superiority in an encounter, especially when the characteristics referred to are gratuitously offered, have high social evaluation, and are unequally distributed among the other participants—in essence, the ploy.

In addition to their tongue-in-cheek terminology, the small sample of lines of action reviewed have a common theme. They illustrate ways the problem of managing evaluative implications is dealt with in everyday social intercourse. Many are techniques for either associating or dissociating one's face (or the face of the other) from one's acts. Facework would be an excellent name for the process had Goffman not preempted the term for a somewhat different idea. Its ubiquity attests to the importance of maintaining the acceptability of the identities of the participants in an encounter. But why this importance? Or is it important? Perhaps what we have been describing are merely instances of middle-class politeness with its show of concern for the feelings of others.

An answer to this question may come from re-asking one raised earlier in this paper: How are lines of action selected in relation to interpersonal tasks? We can offer the hypothesis that those lines of action will tend to be used which maximize the likelihood of task success (even allowing for wide individual differences in interpersonal competence). One might hold that maximization is due to conscious rationality in the selection of interpersonal tactics. And certainly we have intro-

spective evidence in support of this. Who cannot recall thinking ahead to an upcoming encounter, focussing on just what might be the best impression to convey, the best tone to strike, the best tack to take to achieve our purposes? But a good deal of our tactics are not consciously selected. Many lines of action, well designed to elicit task responses from others, are used not because we are aware of their tactical advantages but because we have learned they are situationally appropriate. We may use prepalogs or motrels in order to satisfy, in our own eyes, standards of tactfulness we have internalized and not particularly because we recognize that they help to keep the other bound in the relationship so we can get him to do what we want.

Yet it is precisely this capacity to facilitate goal directed interaction that accounts for the importance of the rules of polite intercourse and their centrality in socialization. That they predominate in middle-class socialization is not surprising since middle-class goals are pursued more frequently in interpersonal relations; much more of lower-class life is concerned with action toward inanimate objects. Moreover, even among the middle class, the rules of polite intercourse are most likely to be violated in relationships to which commitment is the strongest. Contrast the treatment sometimes received by wives and children with that received by clients or by well dressed strangers for that matter.

A strong argument can be made for the functional necessity of tactics which serve to preserve the acceptability of the identities of participants in interaction. They do more than save feelings, they help to preserve the working consensus providing the structure within which encounters can be maintained and interpersonal tasks pursued. If the sociologist's principal abstraction, social structure, has any concrete expression it is to be found in countless myriad everyday social encounters. The operation of this larger structure is dependent upon the successful functioning of the microscopic and episodic action systems generated in these encounters. And these, in turn, are dependent upon conditions which will allow interpersonal tasks to be effectively pursued. If social structure is to be stable, in the long run individuals must be successful in achieving personal purposes.

References

Goffman, Erving. "On Facework." *Psychiatry* 18: 213–255.

Goffman, Erving. *The Presentation of Self in Everyday Life*. Garden City, N.Y.: Doubleday, 1959.

Goode, William J. "A Theory of Role Strain." *American Sociological Review* 25: 483–96.

Goode, William J. "Norm Commitment and Conformity to Role-Status Obligations." *American Journal of Sociology* 66: 246–58.

Part 6

The Quest for Community

Members of SIMSOC confront problems of scarcity, problems of social protest, power struggles, and the like. In most cases, they are able to handle such issues only to discover that, even when these problems are well in hand, important ones remain. Members begin to question the goals of the society and to raise questions about the quality of life and the usefulness of social institutions for satisfying a wider range of human needs. Frequently, SIMSOC members are no longer content with merely solving the problems of survival. Rather, they seek to create in their simulated society a deeper sense of community which they see lacking in the real society.

The readings in this section focus on this quest. Their concern is more with culture than with social structure and more on the intrinsic and immediate quality of social relationships than on their relevance to solving societal problems. The question becomes not what one must do to make the society survive but whether or not it deserves to survive. The central issue is that of commitment—to other individuals and to the community as a whole. The selection by Kanter discusses this quest as it is found in the many communes that are springing up around America today. She compares these communes with successful and unsuccessful nineteenth-century utopian communities and speculates about the prospects of contemporary communes for long term success. Slater examines the challenge which the new culture with its communal values presents to the dominant culture with its emphasis on individual success. He is strongly critical of the old culture and sympathetic to the new. But his sympathy does not prevent him from recognizing and anticipating many of the emerging problems and tensions which the new culture has yet to confront.

Communes

Rosabeth Moss Kanter

"Life together" is the experience of communal living expressed by one founder of a new 30-member commune in Vermont. Like others, she is participating in a renewed search for utopia and community, brotherhood and sharing, warmth and intimacy, participation and involvement, purpose and meaning. Today's utopians want to return to fundamentals. They want to put people back in touch with each other, nature and themselves.

This quest for togetherness is behind the proliferation of communal-living experiments. The ventures vary widely. There are small urban groups that share living quarters and raise their families together but hold outside jobs, and there are rural farming communes that combine work and living. Some are formal organizations with their own business enterprises, such as the Bruderhof communities, which manufacture Community Playthings. Others are loose aggregates without chosen names.

They have been started by political radicals, return-to-the-land homesteaders, intellectuals, pacifists, hippies and drop-outs, ex-drug addicts, be-

This reading is reprinted from Rosabeth Moss Kanter, "Communes." In *Psychology Today* (July, 1970), pp. 53–57 and 78. Kanter is a sociologist at Brandeis University.

havioral psychologists following B. F. Skinner's *Walden Two*, humanistic psychologists interested in environments for self-actualization, Quakers in South America, ex-monks in New Hampshire, and Hasidic Jews in Boston. Estimates of the number of communal experiments today run to the hundreds. There are inter-community magazines, newsletters, information clearinghouses and conferences to share experiences, help build new utopias and bring potential communards together.

Now. Today's communal movement is a reawakening of the search for utopia in America that started as early as 1680, when religious sects first retreated to the wilderness to live in community. While experiments in communal living have always been part of the American landscape, only a few dozen survived for more than a few years. Building community has been difficult, and today's communes are heirs to the problems.

I have studied 19th-Century American communities, comparing 21 that lasted with nine that didn't, and have gathered information from 20 contemporary communes and from growth-and-learning communities. I then compared successful 19th-Century utopias with today's anarchist communes and growth-center communities and found that while the growth centers tend to incorporate important features of the 19th-Century groups that were successful, many of the anarchist communes do not.

Family. Today's communes seek a family warmth and intimacy, to become extended families. A 50-person hippie commune in California, for example, called itself "the Lynch family"; a New Mexico commune "The Chosen Family"; a New York City group simply "The Family."

For some communes becoming a family means collective child-rearing, shared responsibility for raising children. Children and adults in a Vermont commune have their own separate rooms, and the children consider all the adults in the community their "parents." Other communes experiment sexually to change the man-woman relationship from monogamy to group marriage.

The desire is to create intense involvement in the group—feelings of connectedness, belonging and the warmth of many attachments. How did the successful utopias of the past achieve this? [See Table.]

Intimacy was a daily fact of life for successful 19th-Century communities. The group was an ever-present part of the member's day, for his fellows were his work-mates as well as his neighbors, and people ate and slept together in central buildings. Many successful communities saw themselves as families and addressed leaders in parental

terms—Father Noyes in Oneida, Father Rapp in Harmony.

Exclusive couples and biological families were discouraged through celibacy, free love or group marriage. In Oneida's system of complex marriage, for example, each member had sexual access to every other member, with his or her consent and under the general supervision of community leaders. A man interested in a liaison would approach a woman through a third party; she had the right to refuse his attentions. Couples showing an excess of special love would be broken up or forced into relationships with others.

Successful 19th-Century communities tended to separate biological families and place children in dwelling units apart from their parents, creating instead a "family of the whole." In Oneida children were raised communally from soon after weaning. The heads of the children's department raised the children; they were called "papa" and "mother." Children visited their own parents individually once or twice a week but accepted the community's family life as the focus of their existence.

They also celebrated their togetherness joyfully in group rituals such as singing, religious services and observance of anniversaries, holidays and other festive occasions.

Group. Many members look to today's communities for personal growth through small-group processes in which members honestly and openly criticize and support one another. T-group interaction or mutual criticism in its various forms can be a primary and essential part of a community's goals. In the Synanon groups, community was first embodied in self-help group sessions for drug addicts and only later grew into the desire to establish a total way of life.

Other communes use group process to work out disagreements, to regenerate commitment, and to create a sense of intimate involvement. A Vermont commune reached a crisis when so many problems accumulated that people asked: *Just what are we doing here anyway?* An extended encounter group was held and the sense of common purpose reaffirmed.

Successful 19th-Century communities used a variety of group techniques, including confession, self-criticism, and mutual-criticism sessions, to solidify the group and deal with deviance and discontent before they became disruptive. The individual could bare his soul to the group, express his weaknesses, failings, doubts, problems, inner secrets. Disagreements between members could be discussed openly. These T-group-like sessions also showed that the content of each person's inner

Comparison of Nine Successful and 21 Unsuccessful Communities		
	Successful:	Unsuccessful:
GROUP RELATIONS	Percentage that adhered to the practice	
Communal family structure:		
Free love or celibacy	100%	29%
Parent-child separation	48%	15%
Biological families not living together	33%	5%
Ritual:		
Songs about the community	63%	14%
Group singing	100%	73%
Special community occasions celebrated	83%	50%
Mutual criticism:		
Regular confession	44%	—
Mutual-criticism sessions	44%	26%
Daily group meetings	56%	6%
PROPERTY & WORK		
Communistic sharing:		
Property signed over to community at admission	100%	45%
Community-as-whole owned land	89%	76%
Community-owned buildings	89%	71%
Community-owned furniture, tools	100%	79%
Community-owned clothing, personal effects	67%	28%
Communal labor:		
No compensation for labor	100%	41%
No charge for community services	100%	47%
Job rotation	50%	44%
Communal work efforts	100%	50%
Fixed daily routine	100%	54%
Detailed specification of routine	67%	13%

world was important to the community. Oneidans periodically submitted themselves for criticism by a committee of six to 12 judges and were expected to receive the criticism in silence and acquiesce to it in writing. Excessive introspection was considered a sin, and no matter was too private for mutual criticism.

The Llano Colony, a 20th-Century, socialist utopia, had a weekly "psychology" meeting that one observer described as a combination of "revival, pep meeting, and confessional."

Possibly because they developed such strong group ties, successful 19th-Century groups stayed together in the face of outside persecution, financial shakiness, and natural disasters. Unsuccessful utopias of the past, on the other hand, did not tend to build these kinds of group relations.

Property. The desire for sharing, participation and cooperation in today's communes extends to property and work. One ideal is to create econom-

ically self-sufficient communities, with all property owned in common. The desire for self-sufficiency and control over their own financial destinies leads many communes to form around farms, to attempt to provide for their maintenance needs themselves, to live in simple dwellings and to work the land.

Many of today's communards believe that money and private property create barriers between people. Money should be thrown into a common pot and property should belong to anyone who uses it. This acceptance of common ownership is reflected in the answer of a small child in a Cambridge commune, questioned about who owned a cat. He said, *"The cat is everyone's."*

Many urban communes where members work at outside jobs try to operate with common exchequers. The commune has the responsibility to provide for everyone economically. In Synanon's new Tomales Bay city, as in all Synanon houses, goods and facilities are community-owned. Members receive small amounts of "walking-around money."

A common-work community is another important goal of today's groups. Some have their own businesses—agriculture, crafts, toy manufacturing (the Bruderhof), advertising specialties and gas stations (Synanon), schools, film and other media. In the Bruderhof groups, members work at assigned jobs in the household or school or factory, sharing kitchen and dining-room chores. Other communes without money-making enterprises may still expect strong participation in community upkeep.

In most successful 19th-Century utopias, property was jointly owned and shared, goods equally distributed to all members, and private property abolished. The successful groups all required members to sign over their property and financial holdings to the community on admission. At one point in Harmony's history the leader, George Rapp, even burned the contribution record book.

The successful groups tended to have their own means of support. Generally all members worked within the community. Oneidans, for example, first supported themselves by farming. Because of financial difficulties, they later engaged in manufacturing enterprises ranging from steel traps to silverware. A business board of individual department heads and other interested members regulated the industries. Work was a community-wide affair where possible, and jobs were rotated among members.

Such work arrangements required central coordination; how a member spent his time was a matter of community policy. In unsuccessful communities like Brook Farm, individual members made their own decisions about when and how long to work. The Shakers, on the other hand, instituted a minute-by-minute routine with bells ringing to mark the time.

These property and work arrangements were conducive to a strong community commitment and help account for the successful groups' longevity.

Believers. Often today's communities are founded to implement elaborate philosophies or world views communicated through charismatic leaders. Synanon coalesced 11 years ago around the visions of Chuck Dederich, who formed the community (now numbering in the thousands) on a $33 unemployment check. His personal example and teachings continue to guide the community. Mel Lyman is the central presence for Fort Hill. A number of communes consider their leaders manifestations of Christ, great prophets, or seers.

Many successful 19th-Century communities had charismatic figures; they were considered god-like, if not actually manifestations of God, and were viewed with awe by members, treated with deference and respect, and accorded special privileges and immunities. In successful communities when the charismatic died his teachings lived on. The Shakers continued to coalesce around Mother Ann Lee after her death, and today the Bruderhof still are translating the teachings of their founder from the German.

The emphasis on a value-based and value-oriented life required an ideological commitment or a set of vows for admission, a striking contrast with some of the unsuccessful communities. New Harmony, for example, merely advertised for anyone interested in joining a communal experiment.

Two Kinds. Today's communities differ as widely in structure, values and ideology among themselves as the 19th-Century ones did. One set of present-day utopias, religious communities such as the Bruderhof and the Hutterian Brethren, have their roots in the traditional communities of the past. But two distinct kinds of groups are emerging as the *now* forms: small anarchistic communes and communities formed around growth centers, of which Esalen, Kairos, Cumbres are examples.

Some of today's communes are small and anarchistic, consisting of 12, 20, to 30 persons. They seek intimacy and involvement, but refuse to structure community life. Everyone does his own thing at his own time. They are concerned with flexibility and mobility, not with permanence. They reject the control of other groups. Many tend to share living arrangements in which members continue to work outside instead of developing self-sufficient communities. Their lack of solid financial bases is a great problem. In addition they report that many jobs within the commune remain undone, many conflicts never get ironed out, and "family feeling" develops only with difficulty.

I find little definable pattern, rule, or group structure in many of today's anarchist communes. In a Maryland commune of 12, one pays nothing to join. Private property remains private, although members report that it is shared freely. Most members have outside jobs and contribute $30 a month each for food and utilities. All work within the community is voluntary. There are no leadership positions. Decisions are made individually.

Some of these communes do try to develop the intimate, T-group-like sessions of the 19th-Century utopias. But the anarchist groups have a tendency not to do this on a regular or formal basis.

Today's anarchist communes tend to lack integrating philosophies. Many begin with only a vague desire for closer personal relationships and group living in the most general sense.

A member of one short-lived commune talked about its failure: "We weren't ready to define who we were; we certainly weren't prepared to define who we weren't—it was still just a matter of intuition. We had come together for various reasons—not overtly for a common idea or ideal. . . . The different people managed to work together side by side for a while, but there really was no shared vision."

Anarchist communes tend to be open to all comers at the start. In strong contrast with the successful 19th-Century communities, some anarchist communes do not make a member/non-member distinction. A member of a rural California commune that dissolved after a year saw this as one of their problems: "We were entirely open. We did not say no—we felt that this would make a more dynamic group. But we got a lot of sick people. . . . Most people came here just to get out of the city. . . . they had no commitment."

The prospects for most of today's anarchistic communes are dim: they lack the commitment-building practices of the successful communities of the 19th Century.

Today's growth-and-learning centers, on the other hand, offer greater prospects for success in longevity, economic viability and personal fulfillment. These groups tend to be highly organized by comparison with their anarchistic cousins. In their own ways they implement many of the practices of successful 19th-Century groups.

These 100 or so growth centers—many of them outgrowths of the encounter-group movement—provide temporary communities in which their guests find intimacy and expressive involvement. For their staffs they are permanent communities of total involvement.

Growth-and-learning communities are centered around small-group interaction that generates strong group ties and family feeling. Encounter groups are part of the community life. Lama, in New Mexico, has a group meeting every evening for personal growth and the release of interpersonal tensions. The Synanon game is in many ways the Synanon community's most central activity.

At some communities, family feeling is extended; the community encourages sexual experimentation and acting on physical feelings. While some members may be married, they are not bound by monogamy. Finally, in these communities there is often an abundance of group rituals—from Tai Chi exercises (a Chinese moving meditation that resembles dance) to mixed-media celebrations of important events.

The growth-and-learning communities also tend to have explicit sets of values, integrating philosophies that members must share—from the principles of zazen to humanistic psychology. Members are expected to grow in the community spirit and, as at Synanon, character is the only status.

Some communities have communal living arrangements with minimum privacy. They tend to have stringent entrance requirements: potential members must meet community standards and often must serve long apprenticeships to be accepted.

In the growth-and-learning communities work tends to be communal; a member may lead a workshop, then clean the kitchen, sharing responsibility as a growth experience. Discipline through work is a theme at Zen learning centers; a new Synanon member's first job often is to scrub toilets.

These communities also tend to have fixed daily routines and schedules, with tasks assigned in advance.

Like the successful utopias of the past, the growth communities have their charismatic figures, from the late Fritz Perls and William Schutz at Esalen to Cesareo Pelaez at Cumbres in New Hampshire.

Growth-and-learning communities, in short, tend to create family-like feeling, to use mutual criticism, to provide a strong sense of participation and responsibility, to affirm their bonds through ritual, to organize work communally, to have stringent entrance requirements, and to develop strong values symbolized by charismatic leaders.

In the light of history, the small anarchistic commune does not seem to be stable or enduring, while the growth-and-learning community appears to have much greater prospects. Yet in today's world—a mobile, change-oriented society that is increasingly wary of long-range commitments—there may be room for both kinds of groups. The small, dissolvable, unstructured commune may meet its members' needs for a temporary home and family. The more permanent growth-and-learning center is a place for enduring commitment for those who want a rooted way of life in community.

The Pursuit of Loneliness
Philip E. Slater

I would like to suggest three human desires that are deeply and uniquely frustrated by American culture:

(1) The desire for *community*—the wish to live in trust and fraternal cooperation with one's fellows in a total and visible collective entity.

(2) The desire for *engagement*—the wish to come directly to grips with social and interpersonal problems and to confront on equal terms an environment which is not composed of ego-extensions.

(3) The desire for *dependence*—the wish to share responsibility for the control of one's impulses and the direction of one's life.

When I say that these three desires are frustrated by American culture, this need not conjure up romantic images of the individual struggling against society. In every case it is fair to say that we participate eagerly in producing the frustration we endure—it is not something merely done to us. For these desires are in each case subordinate to their opposites in that vague entity called the American Character. The thesis of this chapter is that Americans have voluntarily created and voluntarily maintain a society which increasingly frustrates and aggravates these secondary yearnings, to the point where they threaten to become primary. Groups that in any way personify this threat are therefore feared in an exaggerated way, and will be until Americans as a group are able to recognize and accept those needs within themselves.

I. Community and Competition

We are so accustomed to living in a society that stresses individualism that we need to be reminded that "collectivism" in a broad sense has always been the more usual lot of mankind, as well as of most other species. Most people in most societies have been born into and died in stable communities in which the subordination of the individual to the welfare of the group was taken for granted, while the aggrandizement of the individual at the expense of his fellows was simply a crime.

This is not to say that competition is an American invention—all societies involve some sort of admixture of cooperative and competitive institutions. But our society lies near or on the competitive extreme, and although it contains cooperative institutions I think it is fair to say that Americans suffer from their relative weakness and peripheral-

ity. Studies of business executives have revealed, for example, a deep hunger for an atmosphere of trust and fraternity with their colleagues (with whom they must, in the short run, engage in what Riesman calls "antagonistic cooperation"). The competitive life is a lonely one, and its satisfactions are very short-lived indeed, for each race leads only to a new one.

In the past, as so many have pointed out, there were in our society many oases in which one could take refuge from the frenzied invidiousness of our economic system—institutions such as the extended family and the stable local neighborhood in which one could take pleasure from something other than winning a symbolic victory over one of his fellows. But these have disappeared one by one, leaving the individual more and more in a situation in which he must try to satisfy his affiliative and invidious needs in the same place. This has made the balance a more brittle one—the appeal of cooperative living more seductive, and the need to suppress our longing for it more acute.

In recent decades the principal vehicle for the tolerated expression of this longing has been the mass media. Popular songs and film comedies have continually engaged in a sentimental rejection of the dominant mores, maintaining that the best things in life are free, that love is more important than success, that keeping up with the Joneses is absurd, that personal integrity should take precedence over winning, and so on. But these protestations must be understood for what they are: a safety valve for the dissatisfactions that the modal American experiences when he behaves as he thinks he should. The same man who chuckles and sentimentalizes over a happy-go-lucky hero in a film would view his real-life counterpart as frivolous and irresponsible, and suburbanites who philosophize over their back fence with complete sincerity about their "dog-eat-dog-world," and what-is-it-all-for, and you-can't-take-it-with-you, and success-doesn't-make-you-happy-it-just-gives-you-ulcers-and-a-heart-condition—would be enraged should their children pay serious attention to such a viewpoint. Indeed, the degree of rage is, up to a point, a function of the degree of sincer-

This reading is reprinted from Philip E. Slater, *The Pursuit of Loneliness: American Culture at the Breaking Point.* Boston: Beacon Press, 1970, pp. 5–7, 97, 103–104, 106–110, 113–115, 117–118, 145–146, and 148–150. © 1970 by Philip E. Slater. Reprinted by permission of The Beacon Press and Penguin Books Ltd. Slater is a sociologist at Brandeis University.

ity: if the individual did not feel these things he would not have to fight them so vigorously. The peculiarly exaggerated hostility that hippies tend to arouse suggests that the life they strive for is highly seductive to middle-aged Americans.

The intensity of this reaction can in part be attributed to a kind of circularity that characterizes American individualism. When a value is as strongly held as is individualism in America the illnesses it produces tend to be treated by increasing the dosage, in the same way an alcoholic treats a hangover or a drug addict his withdrawal symptoms. Technological change, mobility, and the individualistic ethos combine to rupture the bonds that tie each individual to a family, a community, a kinship network, a geographical location—bonds that give him a comfortable sense of himself. As this sense of himself erodes, he seeks ways of affirming it. But his efforts at self-enhancement automatically accelerate the very erosion he seeks to halt.

It is easy to produce examples of the many ways in which Americans attempt to minimize, circumvent, or deny the interdependence upon which all human societies are based. We seek a private house, a private means of transportation, a private garden, a private laundry, self-service stores, and do-it-yourself skills of every kind. An enormous technology seems to have set itself the task of making it unnecessary for one human being ever to ask anything of another in the course of going about his daily business. Even within the family Americans are unique in their feeling that each member should have a separate room, and even a separate telephone, television, and car, when economically possible. We seek more and more privacy, and feel more and more alienated and lonely when we get it. What accidental contacts we do have, furthermore, seem more intrusive, not only because they are unsought but because they are unconnected with any familiar pattern of interdependence.

*   *   *

When I talk of two separate cultures in America I do not mean rich and poor, or black and white (or science and humanism), but rather the opposition between the old scarcity-oriented technological culture that still predominates and the somewhat amorphous counterculture that is growing up to challenge it. At times this distinction may seem synonymous with old-versus-young, or radical-versus-conservative, but the overlap is only approximate. There are many young people who are dedicated to the old culture and a few old people attracted to the new; while as to politics,

nothing could be more old-culture than a traditional Marxist.

I speak of two cultures, first because each is in fact a total system with an internal logic and consistency: each is built upon a set of assumptions which hangs together and is viable under some conditions. Second, I wish to emphasize a fact which has escaped the liberal-centrist group that plays so dominant a role in America: that they are no longer being wooed so fervently by those to the left and right of them. The seduction of the center is a phenomenon that occurs only in societies fundamentally united. This has in the past been true of the United States and most parliamentary democracies, but it is true no longer. I speak of two cultures because we no longer have one. Mixing the two that exist does not add up to the American way of life. They cannot be mixed. From two opposing systems—each tightly defined—can only come a collision and a confusion. No meaningful compromise can be found if the culture as a whole is not articulated in a coherent way. American centrists—liberal university presidents are the best example—are still operating under the illusion that all Americans are playing by the same rules, an assumption which puts the centrists into the advantageous position of mediators. But this is not the case. Indeed, the moderates are increasingly despised by both radicals and conservatives as hypocritical, amoral, and opportunistic—people who will take no stand and are only interested in their own careers.

*   *   *

The core of the old culture is scarcity. Everything in it rests upon the assumption that the world does not contain the wherewithal to satisfy the needs of its human inhabitants. From this it follows that people must compete with one another for these scarce resources—lie, swindle, steal, and kill, if necessary. These basic assumptions create the danger of a "war of all against all" and must be buttressed by a series of counternorms which attempt to qualify and restrain the intensity of the struggle. Those who can take the largest share of the scarce resources are said to be "successful," and if they can do it without violating the counternorms they are said to have character and moral fibre.

The key flaw in the old culture is, of course, the fact that the scarcity is spurious—man-made in the case of bodily gratifications and man-allowed or man-maintained in the case of material goods. It now exists only for the purpose of maintaining the system that depends upon it, and its artificiality becomes more palpable each day. Americans continually find themselves in the position of having killed someone to avoid sharing a meal which turns out to be too large to eat alone.

The new culture is based on the assumption that important human needs are easily satisfied and that the resources for doing so are plentiful. Competition is unnecessary and the only danger to humans is human aggression. There is no reason outside of human perversity for peace not to reign and for life not to be spent in the cultivation of joy and beauty. Those who can do this in the face of the old culture's ubiquity are considered "beautiful."

The flaw in the new culture is the fact that the old culture has succeeded in hiding the cornucopia of satisfactions that the new assumes—that a certain amount of work is required to release the bounty that exists from the restraints under which it is now placed. Whereas the flaw in the old culture has caused it to begin to decompose, the flaw in the new culture has produced a profound schism in its ranks—a schism between activist and dropout approaches to the culture as it now exists. We will return to this problem a little later.

It is important to recognize the internal logic of the old culture, however absurd its premise. If one assumes scarcity, then the knowledge that others want the same things that we have leads with some logic to preparations for defense, and, ultimately (since the best defense is offense), for attack. The same assumption leads to a high value being placed on the ability to postpone gratification (since there is not enough to go around). The expression of feelings is a luxury, since it might alert the scarce resources to the fact that the hunter is near.

* * *

Another logical consequence of scarcity assumptions is structured inequality. If there is not enough to go around, then those who have more will find ways to prolong their advantage, and even legitimate it through various devices. The law itself, although philosophically committed to equality, is fundamentally a social device for maintaining structured systems of inequality (defining as crimes, for example, only those forms of theft and violence in which lower class persons engage). One of the major thrusts of the new culture, on the other hand, is equality: since the good things of life are plentiful, everyone should share them: rich and poor, black and white, female and male.

It is a central characteristic of the old culture that means habitually become ends, and ends means. Instead of people working in order to obtain goods in order to be happy, for example, we find that people should be made happy in

order to work better in order to obtain more goods, and so on. Inequality, originally a consequence of scarcity, is now a means of creating artificial scarcities. For in the old culture, as we have seen, the manufacture of scarcity is the principal activity. Hostile comments of old-culture adherents toward new-culture forms ("people won't want to work if they can get things for nothing," "people won't want to get married if they can get it free") often reveal this preoccupation. Scarcity, the presumably undesired but unavoidable foundation for the whole old-culture edifice, has now become its most treasured and sacred value, and to maintain this value in the midst of plenty it has been necessary to establish invidiousness as the foremost criterion of worth. Old-culture Americans are peculiarly drawn to anything that seems to be the exclusive possession of some group or other, and find it difficult to enjoy anything they themselves have unless they can be sure that there are people to whom this pleasure is denied. For those in power even life itself derives its value invidiously: amid the emptiness and anesthesia of a power-oriented career many officials derive reassurance of their vitality from their proximity to the possibility of blowing up the world.

The centrality of invidiousness offers a strong barrier to the diffusion of social justice and equality. But it provides a *raison d'être* for the advertising industry, whose primary function is to manufacture illusions of scarcity. In a society engorged to the point of strangulation with useless and joyless products, advertisements show people calamitously running out of their food or beer, avidly hoarding potato chips, stealing each other's cigarettes, guiltily borrowing each other's deodorants, and so on. In a land of plenty there is little to fight over, but in the world of advertising images men and women will fight before changing their brand, in a kind of parody of the Vietnam war.

The fact that property takes precedence over human life in the old culture also follows logically from scarcity assumptions. If possessions are scarce relative to people they come to have more value than people. This is especially true of people with few possessions, who come to be considered so worthless as to be subhuman and hence eligible for extermination. Many possessions, on the other hand, entitle the owner to a status somewhat more than human. But as a society becomes more affluent these priorities begin to change—human life increases in value and property decreases. New-culture adherents challenge the high relative value placed on property, although the old priority still permeates the society's normative structure. It is still considered permissible, for example, to kill someone who is stealing your property under certain conditions. This is especially true if that person is without property himself—a wealthy kleptomaniac (in contrast to a poor black looter) would probably be worth a murder trial if killed while stealing.

A recent sign of the shift in values was the *Pueblo* courtmartial. While the Navy, standing firmly behind old-culture priorities, argued that the Commander of the spy ship should have sacrificed the lives of ninety men to prevent the loss of "expensive equipment" to the enemy, the public at large supported his having put human life first. Much of the intense legal upheaval visible today—expressed most noticeably in the glare of publicity that now attaches to the activities of the U.S. Supreme Court—derives from the attempt to adapt an old-culture legal system to the changing priorities that render it obsolete.

It would not be difficult to show how the other characteristics of the old culture are based on the same scarcity assumptions, or to trace out in detail the derivation of the new culture from the premise that life's satisfactions exist in abundance and sufficiency for all. Let us instead look more closely at the relationship that the new culture bears to the old—the continuities and discontinuities that it offers—and explore some of the contradictions it holds within itself.

First of all it should be stressed that affluence and economic security are not in themselves responsible for the new culture. The rich, like the poor, have always been with us to some degree, but the new culture has not. What is significant in the new culture is not a celebration of economic affluence but a rejection of its foundation. The new culture is concerned with rejecting the artificial scarcities upon which material abundance is based. It argues that instead of throwing away one's body so that one can accumulate material artifacts, one should throw away the artifacts and enjoy one's body. The new culture is not merely blindly reactive, however, but embodies a sociological consciousness. In this consciousness lies the key insight that possessions actually generate scarcity. The more emotion one invests in them the more chances for significant gratification are lost—the more committed to them one becomes the more deprived one feels, like a thirsty man drinking salt water. To accumulate possessions is to deliver pieces of oneself to dead things. Possessions can absorb an emotional cathexis, but unlike personal relationships they feed nothing back. Americans have combined the proliferation of possessions with the disruption, circumscription, and trivialization of most personal relationships. An alcoholic becomes malnourished because drinking obliterates his hunger. Americans become unhappy

and vicious because their preoccupation with amassing possessions obliterates their loneliness. That is why production in America seems to be on such an endless upward spiral: every time we buy something we deepen our emotional deprivation and hence our need to buy something. This is good for business, of course, but those who profit most from this process are just as trapped in the general deprivation as everyone else. The new-culture adherents are thus not merely affluent—they are trying to substitute an adequate emotional diet for a crippling addiction.

The new culture is nevertheless a product of the old, not merely a rejection of it. It picks up themes latent or dormant or subordinate in the old and magnifies them. The hippie movement, for example, is brimming with nostalgia—a nostalgia peculiarly American and shared by old-culture adherents. This nostalgia embraces the Old West, Amerindian culture, the wilderness, the simple life, the utopian community—all venerable American traditions. But for the old culture they represent a subordinate, ancillary aspect of the culture, appropriate for recreational occasions or fantasy representation—a kind of pastoral relief from everyday striving—whereas for the new culture they are dominant themes. The new culture's passion for memorabilia, paradoxically, causes uneasiness in old-culture adherents, whose future-oriented invidiousness leads to a desire to sever themselves from the past. Yet for the most part it is a question of the new culture making the old culture's secondary themes primary, rather than simply seeking to discard the old culture's primary theme. Even the notion of "dropping out" is an important American tradition—neither the United States itself nor its populous suburbs would exist were this not so.

Americans have always been deeply ambivalent about the issue of social involvement. On the one hand they are suspicious of it and share deep romantic fantasies of withdrawal to a simple pastoral or even sylvan life. On the other hand they are much given to acting out grandiose fantasies of taking society by storm, through the achievement of wealth, power, or fame. This ambivalence has led to many strange institutions—the suburb and the automobile being the most obvious. But note that both fantasies express the viewpoint of an outsider. Americans have a profound tendency to feel like outsiders—they wonder where the action is and wander about in search of it (this puts an enormous burden on celebrities, who are supposed to know, but in fact feel just as doubtful as everyone else). Americans have created a society in which they are automatically nobodies, since no one has any stable place or enduring connection. The village idiot of earlier times was less a "nobody" in this sense than the mobile junior executive or academic. An American has to "make a place for himself" because he does not have one.

Since the society rests on scarcity assumptions, involvement in it has always meant competitive involvement, and, curiously enough, the theme of bucolic withdrawal has often associated itself with that of cooperative, communal life. So consistently, in fact, have intentional communities established themselves in the wilderness that one can only infer that society as we know it makes cooperative life impossible.

Be that as it may, it is important to remember that the New England colonies grew out of utopian communes, so that the dropout tradition is not only old but extremely important to our history. Like so many of the more successful nineteenth century utopian communities (Oneida and Amana, for example), the puritans became corrupted by involvement in successful economic enterprise and the communal aspect was eroded away—another example of a system being destroyed by what it attempts to ignore. The new culture is thus a kind of reform movement, attempting to revive a decayed tradition once important to our civilization.

* * *

Up to this point we have (rather awkwardly) discussed the new culture as if it were an integrated, monolithic pattern, which is certainly very far from the case. There are many varied and contradictory streams feeding the new culture, and some of these deserve particular attention, since they provide the raw material for future axes of conflict.

The most glaring split in the new culture is that which separates militant activism from the traits we generally associate with the hippie movement. The first strand stresses political confrontation, revolutionary action, radical commitment to the process of changing the basic structure of modern industrial society. The second involves a renunciation of that society in favor of the cultivation of inner experience and pleasing internal feeling-states. Heightening of sensory receptivity, commitment to the immediate present, and tranquil acceptance of the physical environment are sought in contradistinction to old-culture ways, in which the larger part of one's immediate experience is overlooked or grayed out by the preoccupation with utility, future goals, and external mastery. Since, in the old culture, experience is classified before it is felt, conceptualization tends here to be forsworn altogether. There is also much emphasis on aesthetic expression and an overarching belief in the power of love.

This division is a crude one, and there are, of course, many areas of overlap. Both value systems share an antipathy to the old culture, both share beliefs in sexual freedom and personal autonomy. Some groups (the Yippies, in particular) have tried with some success to bridge the gap in a variety of interesting ways. But there is nonetheless an inherent contradiction between them. Militant activism is task-oriented, and hence partakes of certain old-culture traits such as postponement of gratification, preoccupation with power, and so on. To be a competent revolutionary one must possess a certain tolerance for the "Protestant Ethic" virtues, and the activists' moral code is a stern one indeed. The hippie ethic, on the other hand, is a "salvation now" approach. It is thus more radical, since it remains relatively uncontaminated with old-culture values. It is also far less realistic, since it ignores the fact that the existing culture provides a totally antagonistic milieu in which the hippie movement must try to survive in a state of highly vulnerable parasitic dependence. The activists can reasonably say that the flower people are absurd to pretend that the revolution had already occurred, for such pretense leads only to severe victimization by the old culture. The flower people can reasonably retort that a revolution based to so great a degree on old-culture premises is lost before it is begun, for even if the militants are victorious they will have been corrupted by the process of winning.

The dilemma is a very real one and arises whenever radical change is sought. For every social system attempts to exercise the most rigid control over the mechanisms by which it can be altered—defining some as legitimate and others as criminal or disloyal. When we examine the characteristics of legitimate and nonlegitimate techniques, however, we find that the "legitimate" ones involve a course of action requiring a sustained commitment to the core assumptions of the culture. In other words, if the individual follows the "legitimate" pathway there is a very good chance that his initial radical intent will be eroded in the process. If he feels that some fundamental change in the system is required, then, he has a choice between following a path that subverts his goal or one that leads him to be jailed as a criminal or traitor.

* * *

Closely related to the activist-hippie division is the conflict over the proper role of aggression in the new culture. Violence is a major theme in the old culture and most new-culture adherents view human aggression with deep suspicion. Nonviolence has been the dominant trend in both the activist and hippie segments of the new culture until recently. But more and more activists have become impatient with the capacity of the old culture to strike the second cheek with even more enthusiasm than the first, and have endorsed violence under certain conditions as a necessary evil.

For the activists the issue has been practical rather than ideological: most serious and thoughtful activists have only a tactical commitment to violence. For the dropout ideologues, however, aggression poses a difficult problem: if they seek to minimize the artificial constriction of emotional expression, how can they be consistently loving and pacific? This logical dilemma is usually resolved by ignoring it: the love cult typically represses aggressive feelings ruthlessly—the body is paramount only so long as it is a loving body.

At the moment, the old culture is so fanatically absorbed in violence that it does the work for everyone. If the new culture should prevail, however, the problem of human aggression would probably be its principal bone of contention. Faced with the persistence of aggressiveness (even in the absence of the old culture's exaggerated violence-inducing institutions), the love cult will be forced to reexamine its premises, and opt for some combination of expression and restraint that will restore human aggression to its rightful place as a natural, though secondary, human emotion.

A third split in the new culture is the conflict between individualism and collectivism. On this question the new culture talks out of both sides of its mouth, one moment pitting ideals of cooperation and community against old-culture competitiveness, the next moment espousing the old culture in its most extreme form with exhortations to "do your own thing." I am not arguing that individualism need be totally extirpated in order to make community possible, but new-culture enterprises often collapse because of a dogmatic unwillingness to subordinate the whim of the individual to the needs of the group. This problem is rarely faced honestly by new-culture adherents, who seem unaware of the conservatism involved in their attachment to individualistic principles.

It is always disastrous to attempt to eliminate any structural principle altogether; but if the balance between individualistic and collective emphases in America is not altered, everything in the new culture will be perverted and caricatured into simply another bizarre old-culture product. There must be continuities between the old and the new, but these cannot extend to the relative weights assigned to core motivational principles. The new culture seeks to create a tolerable society within the context of persistent American strivings—utopianism, the pursuit of happiness. But nothing will change until individualism is assigned a subordinate place in the American value system—for individualism lies at the core of the old culture, and a prepotent individualism is not a viable foundation for any society in a nuclear age.

* * *

The fundamental political goal of the new culture is the diffusion of power, just as its fundamental economic goal is the diffusion of wealth. Marxist theory seeks to achieve this through a transfer of concentrated power into the hands of revolutionaries, in order first to secure economic diffusion. In the United States, however, economic diffusion is a far more easily attained goal than the diffusion of power, so that it becomes more important to ensure the latter, and to be skeptical of its postponement.

Activists have achieved considerable dispersion of power on a local scale merely through unmasking, exposing, and threatening to expose those at the centers of power. The ability to maintain a permanent concentration of power depends upon the ability to maintain and enforce secrecy, and dispersal tends to follow automatically upon the breakdown of this ability. Old-culture leaders are peculiarly vulnerable on this point because they are not sensitive to certain inherent characteristics of mass media. They think in terms of news management and press releases and public statements—of *controlling* the media in the old-fashioned propagandistic sense. Indeed, traditional Marxists share their views, and devote their energies to worrying about the fact that all news media are controlled by a relatively small number of wealthy and conservative men. New-culture activists, on the other hand, are attuned to the media. They recognize that the media are *inherently* stimulus-hungry, and that by their very nature they seek exposure and drama. They know a crowd is more interesting than a press conference, a march than a speech. Successful use of television today requires an improvisational looseness and informality that old-culture leaders lack. Their carefully managed statements become too obviously hollow with repetition, their pomposity too easily punctured by an awkward incident, their lies too recently stated and well-remembered to be ignored. It seems astonishing to us when statesmen and generals who support the war in Vietnam put themselves in the position of saying, in effect, "Well, I lied to you before, but this time I'm telling the truth." But prior to television it was quite possible to assume that the mass of the population was substantially without memory.

I am suggesting that with increasing numbers, and the expansion of the arena of protest and confrontation, the diffusion of power could occur with little change in the *formal* machinery of government, which, after all, can lend itself to a wide range of political types. Instead of a single traditional revolution, concentrated in time and space (the notion of a crowd descending on the White House with carbines seems hopelessly archaic), one can imagine a prolonged series of revolutionary challenges occurring in one segment of the society after another, forcing dispersion of power in every kind of organizational structure.

* * *

Alone Together

The most serious internal danger to the new culture is the insidious transmission of individualism from the old culture, in part through confusion with the new culture's otherwise healthy emphasis on emotional expression. Ambivalence about the issue of individualism-versus-social-commitment is deep and unresolved. On the one hand there is increasing experimentation with communes and communal arrangements, and a serious awareness of the Nuremberg Trials and their proclamation of man's personal responsibility to all men. On the other hand there is great fascination with the concept of anarchy—with the attempt to eliminate coercion and commitment in any form from human life.

But to generalize the need to free oneself from the emotional barrenness and depersonalized control mechanisms of the old culture to freedom from *all* social conditions is simply to return the new culture to the old one. Anarchy is merely a radical extension of the old culture. It is also a way of retaining the pristine American fantasy of being special—a condition which American society promises, and withholds, more than any society in history. The unstated rider to "do your own thing" is that everybody will watch—that a special superiority will be granted and acknowledged by others. But in a satisfying society this specialness is not needed, and for a satisfying society to exist the recognition that people can and must make demands upon one another must also exist. Any community worthy of the name (one in which the relationships between people are regulated by people, instead of by machines) would seem "totalitarian" to today's youth, not in the sense of having an authoritarian leadership structure, but in the sense of permitting group intrusion into what is for most Americans the private sphere. This will be the most difficult problem new-culture adherents will face, for we are long accustomed to an illusory freedom based on subtle compulsion by technology and bureaucratic mechanisms. But there is no way for large numbers of people to coexist without governing and being governed by each other, unless they establish machines to do it; at which point they risk losing sight and understanding of the interconnectedness itself—a process well advanced in our culture today. There is something wildly comic about cars stopping and starting in response to a traffic light, for example, but most Americans have lost the capacity to experience it. It seems right and natural for machines to tell us how to relate to each other.

The goal of many early Americans was to find or to create or to participate in a utopian community, but they became distracted by the dream of personal aggrandizement and found themselves farther and farther from this goal. When we think today of the kind of social compliance that exists in such communities (as well as in the primitive communities we romanticize so much) we shrink in horror. We tell each other chilling stories of individuals in imagined societies of the future being forced to give up their dreams for the good of the group, of not being allowed to stand out. But this, in some degree, is just the price we must pay for a tolerable life in a tolerable community. We need to understand this price, to consider it, to reflect on its consequences and the consequences of not paying it. Is an occasional group viciousness really worse than the unfocused universal snarl that has replaced it in our mechanically regulated society? It is the structured narcissism of the old culture that brings down upon our heads all of the evils we detest, and we will only escape these evils when we have abandoned the narcissistic dreams that sustain them.

Past efforts to build utopian communities failed because they were founded on scarcity assumptions. But scarcity is now shown to be an unnecessary condition, and the distractions that it generated can now be avoided. We need not raise the youth of new utopias to feel that life's primary gratifications are in such short supply. Hence the only obstacle to utopia is the persistence of the competitive motivational patterns that past scarcity assumptions have spawned. Nothing stands in out way except our invidious dreams of personal glory. Our horror of group coercion reflects our reluctance to relinquish these dreams, although they have brought us nothing but misery, discontent, hatred, and chaos. If we can overcome this horror, however, and mute this vanity, we may again be able to take up our original utopian task.

Forms

Form A Choice Sheet. To specify your preference for a basic group.

Form B Assignment Sheet. For the coordinator to indicate the basic group you are head of (if any), your travel or subsistence agency (if any), and your home region.

Form C Moving Sheet. For moving from your original home region to another home region of your choice.

Form D Private Transportation Certificate. For purchasing private travel privileges.

Form E Permanent Subsistence Certificate. For purchasing subsistence for the duration of the society.

Form F Transfer of Certificates or Agencies. For switching ownership of agencies or of Forms D or E from one member to another.

Form G Job Schedule. For hiring and firing members of basic groups, including removing the head of the group.

Form H Industry Manufacturing Form. For purchasing anagrams from the coordinator and for filing completed words for credit.

Form I Withdrawal of Assets Form. For the withdrawal of BASIN and INNOVIN assets by the head of these groups.

Form J JUDCO Decision Form. For issuing official judgments resolving any ambiguities in the rules of SIMSOC.

Form K Minority Group Member Action Sheet. For removing Minority Group Members from their jobs and ownership of agencies.

Form L Creating a SIMFORCE. For creating a SIMFORCE.

Form M SIMFORCE Action Form. For arresting individuals, releasing those arrested earlier, and removing police forces.

Form N Assessment Sheet. For individuals to assess how well they are achieving their personal goals, group goals, political party performance, and overall societal performance.

CHOICE SHEET

Form A

Name _____ Date _____

Preferred basic group (place a 1 next to your first choice, a 2 next to your second choice, and a 3 next to your third choice).

BASIN _____ POP or SOP _____ MASMED _____

INNOVIN _____ EMPIN _____ JUDCO _____

• •

ASSIGNMENT SHEET

Form B

Name _____ Date _____

(The remainder of this form is to be filled out by the coordinator—please leave it blank.)

1. You are the head of the following basic group: (circle one)

   NONE   BASIN   INNOVIN   POP

        SOP   EMPIN   MASMED   JUDCO

2. You are head of the following agency: (circle one)

   NONE   SUBSISTENCE   TRAVEL

3. You live in the following region: (circle one)

   RED   YELLOW   BLUE   GREEN

4. (Circle one, if appropriate)

   MINORITY GROUP   NON-MINORITY GROUP
   MEMBER   MEMBER

MOVING SHEET   Form C

Session # _____

Please record the fact that _____ is moving from the
                                                    (name)

(circle one)   Red   Yellow   Blue   Green   Region

to the (circle one)   Red   Yellow   Blue   Green   Region.

Note: A fee of $10 must be paid to the bank.

- -

PRIVATE TRANSPORTATION CERTIFICATE   Form D

Session # _____

This is to certify that _____ has purchased a Private
                                            (name)

Transportation Certificate on _____ and henceforth is free to travel at will.
                                          (date)

                                                                    _____
Fee = $25   (signature or initials of coordinator or assistant)

- -

PERMANENT SUBSISTENCE CERTIFICATE   Form E

Session # _____

This is to certify that _____ has purchased a Permanent
                                            (name)

Subsistence Certificate on _____ and henceforth lives in the (circle one)
                                          (date)

Red   Yellow   Blue   Green   Region.

                                                                    _____
Fee = $25   (signature or initials of coordinator or assistant)

TRANSFER OF CERTIFICATES OR AGENCIES

Form F

Session # _____

This is to certify the transfer of: (circle one)

    Subsistence Agency   Permanent Subsistence Certificate

    Travel Agency   Private Transportation Certificate

from:_____
                          (name of old owner)

to: _____
                          (name of new owner)

Date:_____   (signatures of both old and new owners):

                                      _____

                                      _____

To use transferred certificates, present this form with the original certificate of purchase to the coordinator.

JOB SCHEDULE

Form G

This is (check one): an initial organization _____ or a revision _____ of (circle one):

BASIN   INNOVIN   POP   SOP

EMPIN   MASMED   JUDCO

Job Title   Name of Appointee

Head: (president, chairman, director, editor, etc.)   _____

(fill in position)   _____

_____

_____

_____

Red regional representative   _____

Blue regional representative   _____

Yellow regional representative   _____

Green regional representative   _____

Date: _____ Session # _____

Authorizing signature(s) (see instructions below): _____

_____

_____

_____

_____

Instructions: Only the head of the organization needs to sign this form except in one case: if the employees of the organization are removing the head against his will, all employees who are present must sign.

JOB SCHEDULE

Form G

This is (check one): an initial organization _____ or a revision _____ of (circle one):

BASIN   INNOVIN   POP   SOP

EMPIN   MASMED   JUDCO

Job Title

Name of Appointee
_____

Head: (president, chairman,
   director, editor, etc.)

                     _____

_____

_____
(fill in position)

_____

_____

_____

_____

_____

_____

_____

Red regional representative

_____

Blue regional representative

_____

Yellow regional representative

_____

Green regional representative

_____

Date: _____ Session # _____

Authorizing signature(s) (see instructions below): _____

_____

_____

_____

_____

_____

Instructions: Only the head of the organization needs to sign this form except in one case: if the employees of the organization are removing the head against his will, all employees who are present must sign.

JOB SCHEDULE

Form G

This is (check one): an initial organization _____ or a revision _____ of (circle one):

BASIN   INNOVIN   POP   SOP

EMPIN   MASMED   JUDCO

Job Title   Name of Appointee

Head: (president, chairman, director, editor, etc.)

_____

(fill in position)

_____

_____

_____

Red regional representative

Blue regional representative

Yellow regional representative

Green regional representative

Date: _____ Session # _____

Authorizing signature(s) (see instructions below): _____

_____

_____

_____

_____

Instructions: Only the head of the organization needs to sign this form except in one case: if the employees of the organization are removing the head against his will, all employees who are present must sign.

INDUSTRY MANUFACTURING FORM   Form H

Industry (circle one):   BASIN   INNOVIN   Session # _____

Anagrams purchased

(To be filled in by the coordinator)

Words Completed

(To be filled in by the group)

1.____ ____ ____ ____ ____   1.____ ____ ____ ____ ____

2.____ ____ ____ ____ ____   2.____ ____ ____ ____ ____

3.____ ____ ____ ____ ____   3.____ ____ ____ ____ ____

4.____ ____ ____ ____ ____   4.____ ____ ____ ____ ____

5.____ ____ ____ ____ ____   5.____ ____ ____ ____ ____

Authorization (must be signed by head of purchasing group):

_____

....

INDUSTRY MANUFACTURING FORM   Form H

Industry (circle one):   BASIN   INNOVIN   Session # _____

Anagrams purchased

(To be filled in by the coordinator)

Words Completed

(To be filled in by the group)

1.____ ____ ____ ____ ____   1.____ ____ ____ ____ ____

2.____ ____ ____ ____ ____   2.____ ____ ____ ____ ____

3.____ ____ ____ ____ ____   3.____ ____ ____ ____ ____

4.____ ____ ____ ____ ____   4.____ ____ ____ ____ ____

5.____ ____ ____ ____ ____   5.____ ____ ____ ____ ____

Authorization (must be signed by head of purchasing group):

_____

WITHDRAWAL OF ASSETS FORM   Form I

Session # _____

Please give me_____to be charged to the assets of (circle one):
(specify amount)

BASIN   INNOVIN

Date _____   _____
                                              (signature of company president)

. . . .

WITHDRAWAL OF ASSETS FORM   Form I

Session # _____

Please give me_____to be charged to the assets of (circle one):
(specify amount)

BASIN   INNOVIN

Date_____   _____
                                              (signature of company president)

. . . .

WITHDRAWAL OF ASSETS FORM   Form I

Session # _____

Please give me _____to be charged to the assets of (circle one):
(specify amount)

BASIN   INNOVIN

Date: _____   _____
                                              (signature of company president)

JUDCO DECISION FORM

Form J

The following question has arisen:

It is the opinion of JUDCO that:

Date: _____

Session # _____

Concurring in this opinion:

_____

_____

_____

_____

_____

The following question has arisen:

It is the opinion of JUDCO that:

Date: _____

Session # _____

Concurring in this opinion:

_____

_____

_____

_____

_____

MINORITY GROUP MEMBER ACTION SHEET

Form K

Session # _____

Please remove the following Minority Group Members from all positions they hold with any basic groups—including head—and from all subsistence and travel agencies they may hold:

(list names)

_____   _____

_____   _____

_____   _____

Authorization (must be signed by any two non-Minority Group Members):

_____.   _____

· ·

MINORITY GROUP MEMBER ACTION SHEET

Form K

Session # _____

Please remove the following Minority Group Members from all positions they hold with any basic groups—including head—and from all subsistence and travel agencies they may hold:

(list names)

_____   _____

_____   _____

_____   _____

Authorization (must be signed by any two non-Minority Group Members):

_____   _____

CREATING A SIMFORCE

Session # _____

The following people wish to create a SIMFORCE (please designate a head):

Head: _____

_____   _____

_____   _____

_____   _____

_____   _____

_____   _____

The size of this force is: _____ (indicate by number of Simbucks)

Orders of this SIMFORCE are official when signed by: (indicate a clear and unambiguous rule which the coordinator can follow—for example, "the head and any two other members," or "a majority of the members," or "all members").

_____

_____

The members listed above are automatically under the protection of the force. In addition, please place the following individuals under its protection:

_____   _____

_____   _____

_____   _____

SIMFORCE ACTION FORM

Form M

1. Place the following individuals under arrest:

_____   _____

_____   _____

_____   _____

_____   _____

_____   _____

2. Release the following individuals from arrest:

_____   _____

_____   _____

_____   _____

_____   _____

3. Remove the police force headed by:

_____

(identify force to be removed by name of head)

(Authorizing signatures)

_____   _____

_____   _____

_____   _____

_____   _____

_____   _____

_____   _____

SIMFORCE ACTION FORM

Form M

1. Place the following individuals under arrest:

_____   _____

_____   _____

_____   _____

_____   _____

_____   _____

2. Release the following individuals from arrest:

_____   _____

_____   _____

_____   _____

_____   _____

3. Remove the police force headed by:

_____

(identify force to be removed by name of head)

(Authorizing signatures)

_____   _____

_____   _____

_____   _____

_____   _____

_____   _____

ASSESSMENT SHEET   Form N

Name_____ Session # _____
                                                        (just completed)

1. My personal goal is (circle the appropriate answer):

   a. Power   b. Center of Attention   c. Style of Life   d. Security

   e. Other (please specify) _____

   _____

2. How well do you feel you are doing in achieving your personal goal? Please explain why you feel this way.

3. Which three people do you think have had the most influence (for better or worse) on the way things have been going in the society?

   _____   _____   _____

4. (Circle groups to which you belong)

   BASIN   INNOVIN   POP   SOP   EMPIN   MASMED   JUDCO

   How well do you feel that your groups are doing in achieving their goals? Please explain why you feel this way.

5. Which political party do you prefer, if any?   POP   SOP   Neither
   Please explain why you feel this way.

6. How well do you feel that the society as a whole is doing? (circle appropriate answer)

      Very well   Fairly well   Not too well

   Why do you feel this way?

(Use other side for answers if more space is necessary)

ASSESSMENT SHEET

Form N

Name _____ Session # _____
                                                           (just completed)

1. My personal goal is (circle the appropriate answer):

    a. Power   b. Center of Attention   c. Style of Life   d. Security

    e. Other (please specify) _____

    _____

2. How well do you feel you are doing in achieving your personal goal? Please explain why you feel this way.

3. Which three people do you think have had the most influence (for better or worse) on the way things have been going in the society?

    _____   _____   _____

4. (Circle groups to which you belong)

    BASIN   INNOVIN   POP   SOP   EMPIN   MASMED   JUDCO

    How well do you feel that your groups are doing in achieving their goals? Please explain why you feel this way.

5. Which political party do you prefer, if any?   POP   SOP   Neither
   Please explain why you feel this way.

6. How well do you feel that the society as a whole is doing? (circle appropriate answer)

    Very well   Fairly well   Not too well

    Why do you feel this way?

(Use other side for answers if more space is necessary)

ASSESSMENT SHEET

Form N

Name_____ Session # _____
(just completed)

1. My personal goal is (circle the appropriate answer):

   a. Power   b. Center of Attention   c. Style of Life   d. Security

   e. Other (please specify) _____

   _____

2. How well do you feel you are doing in achieving your personal goal? Please explain why you feel this way.

3. Which three people do you think have had the most influence (for better or worse) on the way things have been going in the society?

   _____   _____   _____

4. (Circle groups to which you belong)

   BASIN   INNOVIN   POP   SOP   EMPIN   MASMED   JUDCO

   How well do you feel that your groups are doing in achieving their goals? Please explain why you feel this way.

5. Which political party do you prefer, if any?   POP   SOP   Neither
   Please explain why you feel this way.

6. How well do you feel that the society as a whole is doing? (circle appropriate answer)

   Very well   Fairly well   Not too well

   Why do you feel this way?

(Use other side for answers if more space is necessary)